Conversations on Human Nature

Conversations on Human Nature

Agustín Fuentes and Aku Visala

Routledge
Taylor & Francis Group

LONDON AND NEW YORK

First published 2016 by Left Coast Press, Inc.

Published 2016 by Routledge
2 Park Square, Milton Park, Abingdon, Oxon OX14 4RN
711 Third Avenue, New York, NY 10017, USA

Routledge is an imprint of the Taylor & Francis Group, an informa business

Library of Congress Cataloging-in-Publication Data
Names: Fuentes, Agustin, author. | Visala, Aku, author.
Title: Conversations on human nature / Agustin Fuentes and Aku Visala.
Description: Walnut Creek, California : Left Coast Press, Inc., [2015] |
    Includes bibliographical references.
Identifiers: LCCN 2015024039| ISBN 9781629582269 (hardback : alk. paper) |
    ISBN 9781629582276 (pbk.   ) | ISBN 9781629582290 (consumer
    ebook)
Subjects: LCSH: Philosophical anthropology. | Human beings. |
    Scholars--Interviews.
Classification: LCC BD450 .F79455 2015 | DDC 128--dc23
LC record available at http://lccn.loc.gov/2015024039

ISBN 978-1-62958-226-9 hardback
ISBN 978-1-62958-227-6 paperback

CONTENTS

 **PROLOGUE**

Human Nature—
A Contested Concept

Reading the news on a daily basis we've all at one point in time or another lost hope and cursed humanity to the deepest depths of hell: "human beings are just evil!" At the same time, faced with virtuous acts of self-sacrifice or courage, we've also had the opposite experience: perhaps there is still goodness in humanity. Acts of great goodness and unspeakable evil highlight a curious ambivalence—the ambivalence of being human.

We are indeed paradoxes to ourselves. On the one hand, we observe great individual differences. Our friends have different interests, backgrounds, and tastes. One likes heavy metal, whereas another cannot stand it. One is tall and introverted, the other short and extroverted. A colleague from Argentina has a different way of doing things than another colleague from Finland. It seems that we are, as individuals and cultures, truly distinct and different.

On the other hand, there seem to be many things that unite us. A mother playing with her children shows the same kind of love and care in New York and New Delhi. Wherever we go we see weddings and funerals, expressions of love and friendship, fear and hate. Perhaps we are, underneath our respective layers of culture, all the same.

These basic ambivalences of good and evil, similarity and dissimilarity, lead us to ask about human nature. Is there such a thing?

Is there something that is at the root of being human, something that would unite us? Or does human nature consist merely of the basic human capacity to be endlessly molded by our experiences and culture?

The question of human nature has been and is a central topic of philosophy, ethics, religion, and the sciences. It is, however, most often the poet and the religious individual who are able to pose the question of human nature in ways that express our ambivalent experience of being human. Consider Alexander Pope's (1688-1744) *An Essay on Man*:

Know then thyself, presume not God to scan;

The proper study of mankind is Man.
Placed on this isthmus of a middle state,
A being darkly wise, and rudely great:
With too much knowledge for the Skeptic side
With too much weakness for the Stoic's pride,
He hangs between; in doubt to act, or rest.
In doubt to deem himself a god, or beast;
In doubt his mind or body to prefer,
Born to die, and reasoning but to err;
Alike in ignorance, his reason such,
Whether he thinks too little, or too much:
Chaos of thought and passion, all confused;
Still by himself abused, or disabused;
Created half to rise, and half to fall;
Great lord of things, yet a prey to all;
Sole judge of truth, in endless error hurled;
The glory, jest, and riddle of the world![1]

In the current increasingly globalized world, whether or not there is such a thing as human nature can surely make a difference as to the way we live our lives. We are faced with controversies over

---

1 We keep the text as in the original, but point out here that we would replace "Man" with "Human" and suggest that the use of the term "man" as a gloss for humankind is not helpful, and may even be harmful, in the quest to understand human nature.

increasing inequalities in health, wealth, and power, and with the possibility of human enhancement, the ethical challenges of biological technologies, the beginning and end of life, and various expressions of human sexuality. All these debates involve assumptions about what humans are like. Are there natural, psychological tendencies or not? Do patterns of social inequalities reflect "natural" human tendencies? To what extent is our behavior under our control? Where do our lives begin and end? What about the status of animals or sophisticated computer programs? Can we alter our development by changing our biology, and is it moral to do so?

Some have claimed that biological and psychological sciences can and will answer most of these questions, and that evolutionary biology and neuroscience will reveal to us what our nature is like. Others have rejected such attempts as crude scientism and sought answers from various philosophies, political ideologies, religions, and theologies.

It is clear that what human nature is and whether we actually have one depends on a number of empirical issues about our genes, psychological makeup, culture, evolution, and so forth. However, it seems to us that human nature is not simply a scientific, empirical notion but involves various normative, conceptual, and even metaphysical aspects. As such, our inquiries into human nature are closely connected to a number of ultimate questions regarding the nature of the cosmos, human origins, teleology, and the ways in which we obtain knowledge.

This book is for those, who are, like us, convinced that human nature is a meaningful notion, but also acknowledge that it can be understood in many different ways, some more problematic than others. This is why we take a consciously transdisciplinary approach to human nature. We have invited perspectives from many different disciplines[2] and hoped that something new could come out from the dialogue. Most books on human nature focus on one perspective only, usually a scientific one from biology, psychology,

....

2   But not from all disciplines. In this project we focused on Anthropology, Biology, Psychology, Philosophy, and Theology as a core set of areas that deal regularly, and intensively, with foundational concepts surrounding human nature.

or neuroscience. Our aim is not to provide a novel view of human nature but instead point out how human nature cannot be reduced to one single perspective or definition, scientific or otherwise. This is to be expected: our experience of being human does not reduce neatly into predetermined categories. This is why we should not only include the sciences but the social sciences, theology, and philosophy as well.

This book is the outcome of our collaboration on the *Human Nature(s) Project: Assessing and Understanding Transdisciplinary Approaches to Culture, Biology and Human Uniqueness* (2011–2014). This John Templeton Foundation funded project[3] had as its goal a road map of how human nature is approached in different fields spanning from anthropology, philosophy, and theology to biology and psychology. The project involved comparisons of diverse and dense literatures, interviews with leading figures in the investigation of human nature across disciplines. A key aim of the project was to focus on deeper integration between participant disciplines. The volume you hold in your hand is one of the outcomes of these endeavors.

The book consists of six chapters, the first of which is designed to offer some background on debates about human nature in such a way as to make the interviews themselves more understandable. The four chapters that follow contain the interviews of twenty-one eminent representatives of various fields studying human nature, including biology, psychology, anthropology, philosophy, and theology. The goal with the interviews was to move beyond the published literature to get thoughtful and informal perspectives from a group of individuals who have spent their careers circumnavigating and engaging the themes of what it means to be human. The interviews themselves are organized under four broad headings: (1) evolution, brains, and human nature; (2) biocultural human nature; (3) persons, minds, and human nature, (4) religion, theology, and human nature. A brief biographic note, a contextual stage-setting "slogan," and a companion reading list suggested by the interviewee preface each interview. Following the final interview, the sixth chapter is a

3   Along with substantial support from the Dean of the College of Arts and Letters and the Institute for Scholarship in the Liberal Arts at the University of Notre Dame.

brief concluding note by us musing on where we find the quest for human nature here in the second decade of the twenty-first century.

Although the main aim of the book is to introduce contemporary debates and the debaters without taking sides, the introduction and the interviews are undergirded by our own view of human nature. On the one hand, we, as well as most of our interviewees, want to maintain some meaningful use of the concept of human nature. Some radically postmodern authors as well as several scientists and philosophers have claimed that the notion of human nature is both scientifically invalid and ethically problematic. We, at least to some extent, reject such criticisms.

On the other hand, we, like most of our interviewees, want to steer clear of very strong notions of innate and biologically determined views of human nature (or "nativism") exhibited by traditional sociobiological perspectives, such as that of Edward O. Wilson's sociobiology (1975). With our interviewees we seek a meaningful middle-way between strong nativism and no-nature views. We believe that by exploring the interfaces of cultural and biological evolution, human nature and personality, and the flexibility of the human mind, such a middle way can be found.

Agustín Fuentes and Aku Visala

 CHAPTER 1

Defining and Debating Human Nature

There are some that believe human nature to be an outdated, old-fashioned notion. Does not Darwinian evolutionary biology deliver us from essentialism? Is it not crudely deterministic and reductionistic to claim that we humans have some core properties? Such questions and problems have led many to reject the notion of human nature. We do not share these sentiments. There are many reasons why the notion is still useful and relevant.

One reason is that human nature has recently become a hot topic of debate in the sciences. Indeed, the last few decades have seen an unprecedented surge of empirical research into the evolutionary history of *Homo sapiens*, the origins of the mind/brain and human culture. The research and its popular interpretations have sparked heated debates about the nature of human beings and how knowledge about humans from the sciences and humanities should be properly understood.

Compare, for instance, Steven Pinker's *The Blank Slate: The Modern Denial of Human Nature* (2002) and Jesse Prinz's *Beyond Human Nature: How Culture and Experience Shape the Human Mind* (2012), to see how wildly experts disagree on the topic. For some, human nature is an enemy that needs to be abolished or an outdated scientific idea, whereas for others, it is the cornerstone of the scientific study of humanity.

Agustín Fuentes and Aku Visala, *Conversations on Human Nature*, pp. 13-42. © 2016 Left Coast Press, Inc. All rights reserved.

Representatives of evolutionary psychology, for instance, fall into the latter camp. Pinker, among others, has argued that behind the dizzying variety of human cultures, lays a universal psychology that strongly constrains possible expressions of human thinking and behavior. Furthermore, this universal psychology is largely innate in the sense that its various aspects are adaptations to the challenges that humans faced during the last two million years of our evolution. The driving force behind the evolutionary psychologist's program, it seems, is the conviction that biological and psychological sciences can and will answer our questions about human nature.

Critics have maintained that not only are these programs based on questionable philosophical and methodological assumptions, but they also fail to account for all the relevant data. Cultures and behaviors are far too diverse to be accounted for by invoking an innate, universal cognition. Furthermore, recent developments in evolutionary theory seem to challenge the strong adaptationism underlying the arguments of evolutionary psychologists.

One possible option is to see a much closer integration of cognition and culture in human evolution and development along the lines of niche-construction or gene/culture coevolution theories.[1] This would mean, however, that we could not identify human nature with a set of innate cognitive mechanisms. Instead human nature should be sought from our flexible capacity to create and sustain culture and be shaped by it.

Another reason for the sustained interest in the idea of human nature has to do with human universals. Anthropologists have long sought to identify both universal and distinct features in human cultures. Are there patterns in human cultural diversity or not? If a common ground between cultures could be found, perhaps that could function as a basis for shared ethical views. If there indeed is a biologically determined universal human psychology as evolutionary psychologists suggest, we should expect to see some general patterns or structures.

....

1   These are parts of contemporary evolutionary theory. Niche construction argues that organisms have a hand in shaping their ecologies and thus their own evolutionary trajectories, and gene-culture co-evolution argues that biology and cultural processes mutually influence one another.

The quest for uniquely or distinctively human traits has also been of great interest to biologists, psychologists, and anthropologists. What, if anything, distinguishes humans from other animals? How are the psychological and biological traits that contemporary humans possess related to those of their long-dead ancestors?

Finally, one reason why human nature is relevant is that the notion carries with it strong ethical and political dimensions. Whether or not there is such a thing as human nature can surely make a difference in the way we live our lives. Take just one debate as an example.

Philosopher John Gray caused controversy in intellectual circles by arguing for a certain kind of nihilistic view of human nature. In his collection of essays *The Straw Dogs* (2002), Gray argues that the radical political and ethical consequences of human evolution have not been fully recognized. In his view, popular advocates of evolutionary naturalism, like Richard Dawkins, have failed to realize the radical consequences of their views; they hold onto a humanistic view of humans and human progress, even after giving up the metaphysical framework of Christian theism. For Gray, humanism and the faith in human progress are incompatible with an evolutionary view of humans. Given our biological imperatives, altruism and morality are both dropped at the first sign of trouble and self-preservation will take over. Our complex ethical systems are slaves to our passions and our passions are geared for survival and power, not collaboration or kindness.

For Gray, war and genocide are at least as deeply ingrained in human nature as art and prayer. Moral progress and technological progress do not necessarily go hand in hand: moral change is cyclical rather than linear. Technological progress can thus produce both better healthcare and more advanced tools of destruction.

It is not a surprise that Gray has received a lot of flak from his fellow intellectuals. One of his opponents, neurologist and philosopher Raymond Tallis, argues for a different interpretation for biological and neuroscientific results. Indeed, Tallis's *Aping Mankind: Neuromania, Darwinitis and the Misrepresentation of Humanity* (2009) offers a sustained critique of all who attempt to deny our freedom, morality, or consciousness on the basis of biology and neuroscience.

Tallis accuses Gray and others of unjustifiably reducing "human worlds" to crude biologically determined worlds. Tallis claims that humans have inherited a dual nature that includes tendencies towards both violence and cooperation. In addition, he emphasizes that our human nature is flexible and malleable; it is our ability to adapt to complex circumstances and shape ourselves via culture that makes moral progress possible. We are not slaves to our biology but are biologically adapted to develop ways to overcome physical, physiological, and ecological constraints.

This debate is a good example of why "human nature" is still a relevant concept. What does biology actually say about the origins of human morality and its flexibility? Is it true that we are slaves to our biological imperatives, or can we use our flexible minds to significantly change our behavior? These are clearly scientific issues of interest to biologists and psychologists.

But controversies about human nature do not end with biology and psychology: there are ethical, philosophical, and even theological assumptions being made. How do we ground human dignity? How should we go about forming ethical theories? Is there inherent teleology[2] to nature or not and what are the implications in each case?

Human Nature from Biology?
Evolution, Brains, and Human Nature

In our intuitive usage, human nature refers to something being essential, innate or shared among all human beings as opposed to being culturally specific. It seems that there is a rather robust, intuitive notion of human nature—a notion to which we might refer as the everyday or folk concept of human nature. It seems that our folk concept of human nature is a source of much confusion, because it lumps together a number of ideas that in principle could (and should) come apart.

Common notions of human nature assume a specific essence to being human, a kind of trans-historical core for all human beings.

----

2   Meaning an inherent design and purpose to nature.

If this were true, underlying all human diversity and variation, there would be something constant, some traits, tendencies and capacities that all humans shared. Usually this is cashed out in terms of distinguishing human biology from the influence of culture and upbringing: we have the same genes (ingredients) on top of which culture and upbringing bake into the "cake" that is our final form.

This folk concept of human nature seems to entail that the essential and universal human features have the same causal history. That is to say, there is something very deep in human biology or some sort of a plan in nature itself that causes the similarities. Traditionally, in western and many other societies, such causal powers were usually attributed to something like the Soul or the Self inside the individual or the purposes of God (or gods) or the brute purposefulness of nature. It is the innate essence that is causally responsible for our uniquely and universally human features.

The third aspect of the folk concept of human nature is a normative one: given that there is a purposeful human essence, some human actions, practices, or societies are more natural than others. Unnatural is not only bad, but also wrong, whereas natural is good and right.[3]

With Charles Darwin's writings, a new perspective on human nature emerged. Darwin was the first to offer systematic tools and theories linking human capacities, development, and history to that of other animals: the same kinds of causes that are driving change in animals also work in the human case. This put the whole question of human nature in a new light: the move from an essentialist notion of species to an evolutionary, Darwinian notion of species as populations seemed to cast strong doubt over there being an innate essence to humanity. The Darwinian turn also seemed to undermine the teleological or normative aspects of the folk notion of human nature. Natural selection, Darwin maintained, does not work with a goal or end in mind.

....

3 A very interesting empirical study on the folk concept of human nature is presented in Linquist, S. E., P. Machery, E. Griffiths and K. Stotz. 2011. Exploring the Folkbiological Conception of Innateness. Philosophical Transactions of the Royal Society B, 366 (1563):444-454.

While the Darwinian turn created a strong pressure to see human nature in biological, evolutionary terms, social sciences and humanities at the same time were going in a completely different direction. Nineteenth and twentieth century European thinking in philosophy and social theory had a strong tendency to reject both the everyday notion and the Darwinian notion of human nature. Marxists and existentialists, for instance, maintained that there is no such thing as a biologically given essence. For the Marxist, it is our institutions and relationships that make us what we are, and society is the sum of such relationships. However, these relationships are in no way given by nature but can be reorganized. Thus, by changing society, we change human nature. For the existentialist, it is not biology or society that determines our nature; it is instead our own will. We are thrown into the world and without the help of God or Nature must decide what we want to be. Both Marxism and existentialism, thus, point to a kind of anti-essentialism about human nature.

Hermeneutical and postmodern views propose that the proper subject of the study of humanity is the interpretation of human experience. Here a dividing line is introduced: since there is no essential, biologically conditioned human nature, human actions should not be scientifically explained but instead understood "from the inside." The sciences deal with facts, but since there are no discrete scientific facts about human behavior, another method is needed. The sciences study humans as physical and biological entities, whereas the humanities, philosophy, and theology account for the personal, the social and the religious world of humans. One of the reasons why contemporary debates about human nature have been so vitriolic is that some scientists have strongly criticized these no-nature views and sought to revitalize something like the folk view of human nature.

Although Darwinian ideas were developed after Darwin's death, the evolutionary perspective remained a minority view in the social sciences. Controversies began in the 1970s when ethologist Edward O. Wilson introduced the idea of *sociobiology* of humans. Working inside the Modern Synthesis,[4] Wilson adopted an uncompromisingly

---

4   The synthesis during the twentieth century of ideas from several fields of biology and ecology that provides a widely accepted account of evolution.

neo-Darwinian view of human social behavior, especially altruism: outwardly altruistic behavior can be explained by invoking the underlying fitness effects it has for individuals. In other words, human social behavior was not to be explained by invoking cultural influences or some such factors, but instead by seeing them as adaptations for survival and reproduction. Here Wilson envisaged a program under which the social sciences and psychology would ultimately be subsumed under evolutionary biology. In terms of human nature, Wilson's program amounted to a rather robust view: under the veneer of individual and cultural variation, humans share a set of biological dispositions and traits that is not too far from their primate cousins. So, not only is there a biologically driven innate human nature, there is no unique or distinct human nature to speak of.

Wilson's claims created a large-scale debate on various overlapping issues, sometimes known as the sociobiology debate. Some of Wilson's biologist opponents, like Steven Jay Gould, challenged his strong reliance on natural selection as the only possible explanation for traits of organisms. For many social scientists at the time, the explanations of human behavior were sought at the level of cultures, institutions, and individual motivations. Wilson turned this upside down: now it was our genetic inheritance shaped by our evolutionary past that held cultures, institutions, and motivations on a tight leash. Finally, the sociobiology debates could have not been so vitriolic were it not for the ethical and political implications of Wilson's work. Many of his opponents saw him as offering a pseudo-scientific defense of a rather conservative or traditionalist view of human nature, where human beings were naturally selfish.[5]

Subsequently, it was the evolutionary psychologist who took Wilson's basic idea and ran with it. Serious adjustments were made, though. Evolutionary psychologists like Steven Pinker, Leda Cosmides, and John Tooby maintained that we should not jump directly from the possible adaptive effects of social behaviors to the explanation of current behaviors. Instead, we should focus on the mechanisms of the

....

5   For a great introduction into the to the sociobiology debate, see Segerstrå-le, Ullica. 2002. Defenders of the Truth: The Battle for Science in the Sociobiology Debate and Beyond. New York: Oxford University Press.

human mind that are both products of natural selection and are the causes of current behaviors. Our minds are adapted to solve specific problems in our ancestral environment. Under the veneer of contemporary culture, we all still have these Stone Age minds.

Again, evolutionary psychology leads to a rather robust view of human nature. It is at this level of cognitive mechanisms where human nature is found. For Cosmides and Tooby, the modules of the mind are "the psychological universals that constitute human nature."[6] Regardless of culture, humans develop a rather unified set of psychological mechanisms, so Cosmides and Tooby can also claim that human nature is everywhere the same. This nature is innate in the sense that it is genetically coded and rather invariably produced by normal human development.

It is worth pointing out that sociobiology, evolutionary psychology, and their opponents are mainly interested in explaining human behavior. The controversy is ultimately about where to look for explanations of human behavior: from innate biology or psychology or from culture and experience. If there are kinds of human behavior that have pretty much the same biological and psychological causes regardless of cultural context, then a theory of human nature is viable. If there is no innate human nature and there are no general, scientifically tractable facts about human behavior (because human behavior is, say, so context sensitive), the scientific quest for human nature does not seem like a worthwhile enterprise.

Defenses and criticisms of evolutionary psychology have been one of the main driving forces behind the current scientific debates on human nature. Diverse fields of evolutionary human sciences have emerged in its wake. By the 2010s, the variety of theories and approaches is dizzying: Fuentes' *Evolution of Human Behavior* (2009) catalogs over thirty theories. The diversity of topics and issues can also be seen in a new collection of classic and new articles, *Arguing about Human Nature* (2013), edited by Stephen Downes and Edouard Machery. Many topics have their roots in the sociobiology debates but they also go beyond it. Here is the list that Downes and Machery give us:

....

6   Quoted in Buller, 2005, p. 71. See Buller, David. 2005. Adapting Minds: Evolutionary Psychology and the Persistent Quest for Human Nature. Cambridge, MA: MIT Press.

- Evolution of human nature, that is, whether biology can offer a robust view of human nature.
- The origin of the human mind and its fixity or plasticity. Is it the case, for instance, that our minds were formed and fixed during the Pleistocene period or have human minds changed since then? Can they change now?
- Issues having to do with innateness, that is, whether we have innate psychological mechanisms or traits and what this innateness might mean.
- Claims about genetic determinism and what the sciences say about the relationship between genes and human behavior.
- Universality of human traits and issues having to with individual variation.
- The nature of cultural and social categories, that is, whether these categories are natural kinds or socially constructed.
- The question of human genetic diversity and the concept of "race."
- Debates about the extent to which human sexual behavior can be explained in evolutionary terms.
- Numerous political and ethical issues revolving around health and the notions of "normality" and "species-typical functioning."

There is no doubt that the debates around human nature are diverse and invoke a range of possible inputs and outcomes. But at the very heart of the inquiry into human nature is the controversy over just what we are talking about, and what we are actually seeking.

Defining Human Nature

The issue of human nature is complicated because the word "nature" can be understood in several different ways: nature as opposed to culture, natural as opposed to unnatural, natural versus accidental, etc. We already outlined the everyday concept of human nature, how it was appropriated by sociobiology and evolutionary psychology and how it was subsequently criticized. The folk notion and many of its incarnations contain various separate components. For the sake of clarity, we should distinguish them.

The attempt to reveal our *universal human nature* has to do with, simply put, human universals. What are the invariant dispositions of human beings? Perhaps there are anatomical or physiological or psychological or social characteristics that all human individuals or societies share. If there are such features, then they constitute our nature. Candidates for human universals include language, music, marriage, play, and various other cultural institutions. The search for psychological universals that motivates cross-cultural and anthropological research like the work of Donald Brown[7] is an example of this quest. Many take this quest to be of great ethical and political importance, seeing commonality among human beings as the basis of human rights, for example.

The second notion of human nature is that of *human uniqueness*. What is it that distinguishes human beings from other things, including other animals? Is there, perhaps, a set of properties that, not just all, but only human beings share? Biologists might be interested in this question for taxonomic purposes; theologians might wonder what the Imago Dei[8] consists of. Many candidates for human uniqueness have been offered: language, rationality, self-consciousness, capacity for moral judgment, religion, and so on.

The problem is that we do not really have an idea what uniqueness means exactly. First of all, there is the uniqueness of certain human abilities. We doubt that anyone in their right mind would deny that humans could do a lot of things that no other animal can do. We can build space shuttles and satellites, write books about human nature, and design computers. What is more controversial is whether such abilities are based on unique capacities. In other words, do humans have capacities that other animals do not have? It is clear that we share most of our psychological capacities pretty much as they are with many other animals (sight, hearing, basic forms of reasoning, etc.). But do we have capacities that significantly differ from those of other animals? Traditionally, candidates for such capacities have included higher-level reasoning, the intellect, moral judgment, symbolic language, knowledge of God, and so on.

....

7   Brown, Donald E. 1991. Human Universals. New York: McGraw-Hill.

8   Literally "the image of God." It is the theological position that humans are created in God's image.

Finally, one could say that humans are unique in the sense that they are not products of the same causes as other animals. Here the uniqueness would be at the level of causes or factors that contribute to the emergence of humans. If it is the case that humans are products of the same causes as all other animals, then there is no human uniqueness is this sense. But if there are causes that contribute specifically to human evolution, say, gene-culture co-evolution or kinds of niche-construction that are not present in other animals, then we might be unique in this sense.

Notice that, in all these cases, uniqueness is a matter of degree and it is extremely difficult to draw sharp boundaries. So we think that we should be extremely critical of sweeping claims about similarities or dissimilarities between humans and other animals.

Finally, there is the idea of *innate human nature*. The fixity of traits across cultures has typically led to questions about whether such traits are "innate." The idea is that the traits that constitute human nature are somehow produced by innate tendencies or causes (genetically specified or other). However, it is far from clear what "innateness" consists in. A trait may be "innate" in the etymologically conservative sense that it is present at birth, for example. This is closely related to the notion that innate traits are those that are unlearned. If—and this is a big if—it makes sense to assign causality between genetic and environmental variables, an innate characteristic might be one that is wholly or mostly due to the genetic influence. We could also claim that a trait is innate if it is "environmentally canalized"; that is, if its development is insensitive to environmental variation. Candidates for innate nature consist again of the usual suspects of language, morality, religion, and reasoning. Many debates about human nature are actually about innateness, as we can see from, for example, Pinker and Prinz.

We should also remember that notions of human nature could include normative components. Typically, the folk concept of human nature has normative implications: natural behaviors and tendencies are good, non-natural are bad. A further normative claim would be that whatever powers and capacities human nature consists of, its realization would be something morally right. If we naturally act selfishly, this would be the right way for us to behave. Similarly, if we were naturally selfless, this is how we should act. Traditionally, some ethical theories, like natural law ethics, have drawn extensively on what they have considered to be "natural" for humans and in the process produced various definitions of human nature. Other ethical approaches, such as deontological ethics, have opposed this by arguing for a strong distinction between nature and the normative.

The Biocultural Ex-Ape: Evolution, Culture, and Human Nature

Although evolutionary psychology and the debates surrounding it have contributed significantly to the conversation on human nature, many want to steer clear of strong notions of innate or otherwise biologically determined human nature. Instead of seeking to separate cultural and biological influences and use human nature to refer to the biological only, many have argued that human nature consists of our ability to be shaped by a number of, broadly speaking, cultural influences. Indeed, it is our biology that makes us this way. If this is true, the quest for a biologically determined human nature might be futile. Philosopher Jesse Prinz summarizes the idea by telling us that:

> We must give up on approaches to social science that try to articulate how humans act or think by nature. Nature alone determines no pattern of behavior. Rather, the investigation of our natural constitution should be directed at explaining human plasticity.[9]

Emphasizing the biocultural core of human nature is to reject the existence of biology that is not already shaped by culture and culture that is not already shaped by biology. It is to reject the layer cake metaphor of human nature in which biology forms the bottom layer on top of which culture and environment build the rest of the cake. Given this interpenetration of biology, culture, and sociality in human existence, we might be left with a view of innate human nature that is rather slim: it is neither the robust views of many scientists (especially evolutionary psychology and sociobiology)

----

9   Prinz, Jesse. 2012. Beyond Human Nature: How Culture and Experience Shape the Human Mind. Pp. 367-368. New York: W. W. Norton & Company.

nor the no-nature (or nature as irrelevant) view of some humanists and social scientists.

There are many reasons why a number of anthropologists, biologists, and psychologists have moved in the biocultural direction. One
central one is the recent development of evolutionary theory itself.

First, modern evolutionary theory is not entirely reliant on
explanations that depend exclusively on natural and sexual selection: the whole of human evolutionary experience is not reducible
to variation in patterns of DNA and reproductive fitness.[10] Against
this, sociobiology and much evolutionary psychology still rely
wholly on natural (and sexual) selection as the only significant ar-
chitects of evolutionary change. The fact that modern evolutionary theory has moved substantially beyond this perspective is now
challenging the evolutionary assumptions of both sociobiology
and evolutionary psychology. Our contemporary view is that evolution goes way beyond "survival of the fittest."

Current understanding of evolution can be summarized as follows:
Mutation introduces genetic variation that, in interaction with genetic drift, epigenetic, and developmental processes, produces biological
variation in organisms that can be passed from generation to generation. Gene flow moves the genetic variation around and natural (and
sexual) selection shape variation in response to specific constraints and
pressures in the environment. Organism-environment interaction can
result in niche construction, changing the shape of natural selection
and creating ecological inheritance. For humans, social structures/
institutions, cultural patterns, behavioral actions, and perceptions can
impact these evolutionary processes. This in turn can affect developmental outcomes. Diverse systems of inheritance (genetic, epigenetic,
behavioral, and symbolic)[11] can all provide information that influence
biological change over time.

....

10 Laland, Kevin, N., Tobias Uller, Marc Feldman, Kim Sterelny, Gerd Müller,
    Armin Moczek, Eva Jabonka, and John Odling-Smee. 2014. Does Evolu-
    tionary Theory Need a Rethink? Yes, Urgently. Nature 514:161-164.

11 Jablonka, Lamb. 2005. Evolution in Four Dimensions: Genetic, Epigene-
    tic, Behavioral, and Symbolic Variation in the History of Life. Cambridge,
    MA : MIT Press.

In addition, the emergence of epigenetics[12] and the understanding of such processes have significantly changed our view of the relationship between evolution and the development of an organism. Epigenetic processes can affect gene function and regulation, but are not coded for in the DNA. These processes are initiated, regulated, and otherwise influenced by life experience, social stressors, perceptions, and a range of psychological variables, in addition to being affected by specific biotic and material ecological factors and having cross generational impacts. Thus, epigenetic variations can produce different outcomes even for organisms with identical DNA sequences.

Humans generate and transmit symbols, artifacts, institutions, and meaning, in addition to our ecological manipulations and genes. All of these processes are multi-directional, with humans, throughout their lifespans, both directing and directed by their own development.[13] Human reliance on learning, plasticity, and culture lends human niche construction a special potency. Niche construction includes the effects of the cultural context, social histories, and human behavior as an active part of our evolutionary dynamic.

These emerging perspectives put the relationship of evolution, development, and culture in a new light. It has become clear that human biology does not exist separate from our social and structural ecologies: our culture and cognition are constantly entangled with our biology.[14] The boundaries between our genes, epigenetic systems, bodies, ecologies, psychologies, societies, and histories are fluid and dynamic. Perception, meaning, and experience are as central in our evolutionary processes as are nutrients, hormones, and bone density—and all these elements can interact.

....

12 Epigenetics are the interactions in development above the level of the gene that can have broad impacts in an organism and its offspring.

13 Flynn, Emma G., Kevin N. Laland, Rachel L. Kendal, and Jeremy R. Kendal. 2013. Developmental Niche Construction. Developmental Science 16(2):296-313. Kendal, Jeremy. 2012. Cultural Niche Construction and Human Learning Environments: Investigating Sociocultural Perspectives. Biological Theory 6(3):241-250. doi: 10.1007/s13752-012-0038-2.

14 Fuentes, A. 2013. Blurring the Biological and Social in Human Becomings. In Biosocial Becomings: Integrating Social and Biological Anthropology. T. Ingold, and G. Paalson, eds. Pp. 42-58. Cambridge: Cambridge University Press.

Human Nature Eliminativism

If the biocultural approach to human evolution is correct, one might wonder whether all accounts of human nature are doomed. As we have seen, one reason for skepticism or eliminativism about human nature might be a strong methodological commitment to separating the sciences from the humanities. Related to this, radical forms of social constructivism or cultural relativism might also criticize the notion of human nature on ethical or political grounds: claims about essential human nature can be used as tools in the hands of oppressors.

The scientific arguments for eliminating the concept of human nature (from the sciences, at least) draw from biology itself. One commonly used argument is that of David Hull, which maintains that since Darwinian population thinking eliminates species essences, it makes no sense to talk about "human" or "human nature" from a biological point of view.[15] Another scientific argument has to do with criticisms of strong forms of evolutionary psychology. As we have seen, some representatives of evolutionary psychology, like Pinker, maintain that there are robustly innate cognitive mechanisms that are the basis of human nature. Critics of this line of thought might argue that, because there are no robustly innate and specified mental mechanisms, there is no human nature in any meaningful sense. In other words, there is no human nature, because there is no biologically or genetically given psychology. We could dub the former argument as the Anti-Essentialist Argument from Darwinism and the latter the Nurturist Argument.

There is a burgeoning philosophical debate going on about the prospects of a scientifically relevant notion of human nature. The philosophers of biology Grant Ramsey, Edouard Machery, Richard Samuels, and others have formulated notions of human nature that aim to survive the Anti-Essentialist Argument and the Nurturist Argument. Indeed, Ramsey and Machery explicitly re-

15 Hull's classic article On Human Nature is reprinted in Downes, S. M., and E. Machery, eds. 2013. Arguing about Human Nature: Contemporary Debates. New York: Routledge.

ject various forms of innateness and associated ideas of genetically specified cognitive mechanisms.[16]

Grant Ramsey points out that the enemy of anti-essentialist arguments is the everyday, essentialist view of human nature. In addition to David Hull and Ramsey, there are others that have pushed this objection against human nature essentialism. One is philosopher John Dupré, who puts the main claim like this:

> What has become increasingly clear to post-Darwinian biologists is that there can be no necessary and sufficient condition for being an organism of a certain species, and the characteristic properties of members of a species are, first, almost always typical rather than universal in the species and, second, to be explained in various different ways rather than by appeal to any simple or homogeneous underlying property.[17]

What Dupré is saying here is that the categorical understanding of species-membership receives no support from evolutionary biology. On the Darwinian view, even if there are, in fact, shared characteristics in a given species, they might not be and need not be uniform in the population. Most members of current *Homo sapiens* population have the capacity for walking upright or thinking about mathematics, but these features are not what make the individuals in the population *Homo sapiens*. Instead, they are *Homo sapiens* by virtue of being members of a specific historical population. Dupré's view also highlights the fact that population thinking demolishes essences as explanatory factors as well: whatever similarity there is across a population of individuals, the similarity might have various causes and those causes need not invoke any shared, essential factors inherent to the organisms themselves. If Dupré is correct, there is very little hope for a robust unique or universal human nature in biology.

....

16 See, e.g., Ramsey, G. 2013. Human Nature in a Post-Essentialist World. Philosophy of Science 80(5):983-993; Machery, E. 2008. A Plea for Human Nature. Philosophical Psychology 21(3):321-9; and Samuels, Richard. 2012. Science and human nature. *In* Royal Institute of Philosophy Supplement 70(112):1-28.

17 Dupre, John. 2002. Humans and Other Animals. P. 155. New York: Oxford University Press.

Closely linked to the Darwinian argument is the Nurturist Argument. In his recent book *Beyond Human Nature: How Culture and Experience Shape the Human Mind* (2012), philosopher Jesse Prinz argues against Steven Pinker and others. For Prinz, the question of human nature has to do with the relationship of cultural and biological influence on human behavior, that is, whether there is an innate component to human behavior. His main argument against there being such a thing as human nature is that most human capacities and behaviors are not innate in the sense of having a specialized psychological mechanism as a base. Prinz himself defends what he calls a rather thoroughgoing *Nurturism* (as opposed to *Naturism* or *nativism*):

> The mind comes furnished with few, if any, innate ideas, and the innate rules of thought can be used for a wide range of different cognitive capacities. Most of our specific capacities are learned, and the cognitive differences between humans and our close animals stem largely from small improvements in the general-purpose mechanisms that we share with them. Character traits, vocational dispositions, and aptitude may be influenced by our genes, but they are also heavily influenced by experience.[18]

Prinz then goes on to examine various aspects of human cognition, including language, moral emotions, and reasoning, while arguing that no robustly innate "modules" or "specialized mechanisms" need to be assumed in order to explain our performance.

Notice that the Anti-essentialist and Nurturist arguments locate "human nature" in different places. On Hull's view, human nature, if it exists, has to do with human uniqueness or distinctiveness. If individual members of *Homo sapiens* population are not characterized by a set of distinctively *Homo sapiens* traits, there is no human nature. On the nurturist view, human nature is understood somewhat differently. For Prinz, the issue is whether we can meaningfully distinguish traits and cognitive mechanisms that have genetic causes from those that are products of culture and the environment. He then provides reasons for why this is very difficult or impossible.

....

18 Prinz, Jesse. 2012. Beyond Human Nature: How Culture and Experience Shape the Human Mind. P. 11. New York: W. W. Norton & Company.

Most people whose interviews are presented in this book seek a meaningful middle-way between strong nativism and eliminativism about human nature. They believe that there could be a meaningful use for the concept "human nature." We believe that by exploring the interfaces of cultural and biological evolution, human nature, and personality and the flexibility of the human mind such a middle way can be found.

It is also worth pointing out that even if the scientific quest for human nature ends up being futile, who is to say that there cannot be an account of human nature that is not scientific. Indeed, many a philosopher (and theologian) might say that there is an essential human nature but it is not accessible in any direct way by science. One could, for instance, claim that humans are essentially self-conscious persons with a certain kind of moral standing.

Philosophical Perspectives on Human Nature: Freedom

As we have already pointed out, scientific perspectives are far from being the only ones when it comes to human nature. Indeed, we have a host of perennial philosophical, ethical, and theological issues. Before the emergence of modern biology, psychology, and social science, philosophy and theology were the main sources of reflection about what humans are and what they are like. If one looks, for example, at Louis Pojman's *Who Are We* (2005), which offers an overview of the philosophical debates in the Western tradition, one finds a plethora of topics, including the following.

- Do humans have souls and what are those souls like?
- What is human psychology like?
- What are the essential features of human beings as opposed to animals?
- Are we free and what is the nature of our freedom?
- Are we naturally good or evil, selfless or selfish?
- Where did we come from? What is our ultimate end?
- What kind of society is good for us?
- What should our proper relationship to God be?

In the contemporary scene, these topics are often discussed separately in respective branches of psychology, political theory, philosophy, and theology. In this context, it is futile to try to summarize the vast literature on all the philosophical perspectives. It is enough to point out that the reflection of these questions is still very much part of at least some discourses, albeit more philosophical than scientific, about human nature.

There are three main philosophical issues that come up in the discussions in this book. The first has to do with the nature of human freedom. Are we free and what does it mean? The second is the nature of morality and its evolution. How should we understand moral norms and their truth? It seems clear that the kind of human morality we have is shaped by evolution, but what does this mean? Third, there is the basic question about what kinds of beings we are. What is this "human" whose nature we want to find out? Is it an organism and are we that organism or is it something else, perhaps a person, soul, brain, or a first-person perspective?

Let us begin with freedom.[19] By freedom we can refer to a number of different things. When we can talk about freedom in a political or social sense, we are referring to the autonomy of individuals or human groups to set their own legal and moral standards. To be free in this sense is to be independent from legal control (or oppression) that comes from outside the individual (or the group). This implies that there is an underlying, basic notion of freedom: to be free is to be able to realize one's desires without external constraint. It is this deeper issue that interests us in the context of human nature.

Freedom has played a major role in the debates about human nature, because of its connection to moral responsibility. Most people agree that we cannot be held responsible for actions that were not under our control, actions that we could not have decided not to do. Normally, humans think that they are free to choose what they want. The implicit assumption here is that there are alternative possible futures. Further, to be free one must be in control of one's actions and

----

19 For an excellent introduction to contemporary free will debates, see Kane, Robert. 2005. A Contemporary Introduction to Free Will. New York: Oxford University Press.

choices. Even if we do not have alternatives available, we must be the author or the source of our own actions to be responsible for them.

The contemporary debate on free will is driven by the realization that this everyday view of free will seems to be in tension with what the sciences tell us. The progress of biology, social sciences, neurosciences, and psychology has produced massive amounts of information about the genetic, cognitive, social, and neurological influences on human behavior. The main issue, it seems, is not really whether determinism or indeterminism is supported by contemporary physics, but rather the suggestion of contemporary neurosciences, biology, and social sciences that there are many different kinds of non-voluntary influences on our decisions. Does this mean that our actions are not really under our control? Does this take away our freedom?

Consider the following argument for neurobiological determinism. If we reject the existence of non-natural factors influencing human organisms (souls, etc.), then we must conclude that human brains are physical systems. As with all other physical systems, everything that goes on in the brain has sufficient physical causes—causes that are explicable in terms of neuroscience or other sciences. Since every mental event is also a physical event with sufficient physical causes, the mental events themselves make no difference to what happens next. Our thoughts and acts are, thus, necessitated by the physical functions of our brains and their environment, not by our choices, reflections, or deliberations.

Three central positions have emerged in the debate: soft determinism, hard determinism, and libertarianism. According to libertarianism, freedom is not compatible with the view that my actions are ultimately determined by non-conscious causes. Such actions are not in my control so they cannot be said to be free. However, libertarians will argue that we are indeed free and that cognitive science, biology, or neuroscience has not demonstrated that the causes of our actions are indeed out of our control. Libertarianism comes in many forms but all acknowledge that we are indeed authors of our actions, usually via some kind of influence over our basic cognitive and brain mechanisms.

Soft determinists or compatibilists argue that freedom is compatible with the causes of our actions being out of our control. Thus, we can be free even if our actions and decisions are determined by non-voluntary causes. Compatibilism also comes in many different forms but they are united by the insistence that freedom is a matter of having the right kind of connection between our beliefs, reasons, and actions. When our actions flow out of our beliefs and reasons, we are free. Freedom, therefore, does not depend on whether we have ultimate control over our beliefs and reasons or whether there are alternative futures available. Because of their less demanding notion of free will, the compatibilists can adapt and accept the results of the biological and behavioral sciences more easily than their libertarian colleagues.

Finally, there are hard determinists who, like the libertarians, insist that freedom is incompatible with our actions being determined by causes outside our control. However, unlike the libertarians, hard determinists buy into the argument from neurobiological determinism: our actions are determined by various psychological and biological causes that out of our control. Therefore, we are not free.

Philosophical Perspectives on Human Nature: Morality and the Foundational Question

The second issue we want to briefly introduce here is the emerging philosophical and scientific debate about the nature of morality and its evolution. Morality as a topic features prominently in the debates about human nature. How is morality linked to our nature? As we have already seen, how we think about our basic moral tendencies leaves us with different views about ethics and politics (Gray versus Tallis).

To get a basic idea about the nature of these debates, consider, for instance, three authors, Frans de Waal, Jonathan Haidt, and Jesse Prinz. There is considerable agreement as to how they approach morality: our capacity for morality is an evolved, biological trait and is not based on objective moral facts. Nevertheless, they end up seeing morality and its relationship to human nature in different ways.

Primatologist de Waal has famously argued that human morality is very closely related to a morality in other animals, and especially our primate cousins. In de Waal's view, the same causal factors that are responsible for the altruistic and group-well-being-oriented behaviors of our primate relatives are also responsible for similar behaviors in humans.[20] De Waal sees the central establishment of social norms connected to emotional and even cooperative physiologies and behaviors in highly social mammals as an indication of the evolutionary (and thus biological) template for morality.

For de Waal, the moral law is not imposed from above or derived from well-reasoned principles; rather, it arises from ingrained values that have been there since the beginning of time. In other words, on the level of causes, the difference between human and primate morality is rather small. If this were true, one could agree with de Waal and acknowledge that morality is deeply embedded in human (and primate) nature. Naturally, the next question would be: what sense of human nature is being employed here? It surely cannot be human uniqueness, since de Waal's argument seems to be directed against the uniqueness of human morality. For him, morality is part of human nature, just because it is not uniquely human. Rather, human morality should be considered innate and universal, because it has deep evolutionary roots.

Psychologist Jonathan Haidt has presented a theory of moral psychology that resonates, to an extent, with de Waal's notions and is strongly inspired by a multipartite version of brain structure and function (similar to that found in much evolutionary psychology). De Waal seems more interested in moral behaviors, while Haidt is more interested in the origins of moral judgments. In Haidt's view, our moral responses are again based on our moral emotions, which are, in turn, caused by very specific and distinct cognitive systems. These "moral modules" have evolved to deal with various challenges in our ancestral environments that have had to do with sharing, justice, trading and such. For Haidt there is a constant conflict between the active analytic aspects of our reasoning and the ancient, emotional, and gut-level reactions that permeate the majority of our neurological and physiological functioning.

At the other end of the spectrum, there are views about morality that on the surface seem rather close to de Waal's and Haidt's, but

----

20 de Waal, Frans. 2009. *Primates and Philosophers: How Morality Evolved.* Princeton, NJ: Princeton University Press.

underneath are revealed to be quite different. Philosopher Jesse Prinz, for instance, has argued, like de Waal and Haidt, that our moral judgments are based on our moral emotions. But unlike the two, Prinz maintains that our moral emotions are neither directly under biological direction nor products of any kind of deep-rooted adaptive modular systems. Instead, the way in which we acquire emotions involves a complex interaction between our experiences, biological development, and cultural environment. Our emotional responses are mostly independent from biological imperatives or innate psychological mechanisms. Moral emotions are instead culturally constructed.

The difference between de Waal and Haidt is that they have different accounts of the evolutionary history of our morality. Furthermore, they differ in their views about the universality of human morality: for de Waal, core human morality is a rather uniform phenomenon, whereas Haidt acknowledges greater cultural variation along predictable lines. Finally, according to Prinz, morality is not innate to humans in any robust sense. Our moral systems and behaviors are based much more on our cultural environment and experiences than any biological grounding. In this view, it is true that humans universally develop moral systems, but there is no single, underlying moral system across cultures. So morality is neither innate nor universal for Prinz.

Finally, we want to discuss the third philosophical issue that has to do with what kinds of beings we actually are. We already saw how the "nature" part of human nature can be understood in different ways. The same is true about the "human" part. This might seem somewhat counterintuitive at first, so let us explain. We take it for granted that whatever quest for human nature we embark upon we are ourselves the subject of that quest. In other words, the "human" in human nature refers to us, not to some obscure beings across the galaxy. We are the ones whose nature is in question. However, it is far from clear what we are, what kinds of beings we are. What counts as a human being?

There seem to be two different starting points here, both supported by a basic set of human intuitions. On the one hand, we identify ourselves as a specific kind of animal, *Homo sapiens*. In this case, the quest for human nature is the quest for the psychological, social, or biological features of our species. In contemporary philosophical literature, this view is often called *animalism*. Surprisingly, animalism has not been very popular in the Western philosophical tradition. Indeed, it has been more typical to think of "us" as animals only accidentally (that is, non-essentially). That is, while it is true that we are animals—by virtue of the bodies we have, the behaviors we exhibit, etc.—we are, philosophers and theologians have historically maintained, essentially persons, thinking things.

There have been various options along these lines but we mention only two: dualism and constitutionalism. On the dualist view, a human individual is identical with a non-physical soul. We only accidentally have bodies and *Homo sapiens* species membership; we could have different kinds of bodies altogether, non-*Homo sapiens* bodies. Some forms of physicalism also maintain that we are essentially persons, and that human personhood is not just membership into the species *Homo sapiens*. According to constitutionalism, what makes us persons is that we have a first-person perspective; that is, we are self-conscious and can refer to ourselves with the first-person pronoun "I." Further, to have this capacity for first-person perspective is essential for us; we would not exist without it. Nevertheless, we are not identical to a non-physical soul, nor are we identical to a particular *Homo sapiens*. Rather, the *Homo sapiens* with which we share all our parts constitutes us.

In his interview in this book, philosopher Carl Gillett defends an alternative view to dualism, constitutionalism, and animalism. In his view, we are identical to a specific part of *Homo sapiens*, brains. The brain view, as Gillett points out, resembles dualism and constitutionalism in the sense that it takes the mental as essential for our existence: we are things that think. Animalism, however, does not do this: our existence as animals does not essentially involve thinking or mentality. The brain view differs from dualism and constitutionalism in the crucial respect that instead of attributing thinking to the soul or to the first-person perspective, it attributes thinking to the brain. Since we are thinking things and the brain is the part of the *Homo sapiens* that thinks, the brain view claims that we are identical with brains.

Homo Religiosus:
Religion, Theology, and Human Nature

Whether we are atheists, agnostics, theists, or something else, we must acknowledge the central role of religion in human history and (perhaps) human prehistory. There is no doubt that religion has been and is one of the basic features of human existence. One reason why the notion of human nature has become so interesting lately is the emergence of evolutionary and cognitive study of religion. Evolutionary and cognitive study of religion has had two main areas of focus: the biological functions of religious belief and behavior and the cognitive foundation of religious thinking.

Contemporary explanations of religious belief are informed by recent scientific developments in biology, psychology, anthropology, and cognitive science. They are naturalistic, since they assume that only causes, effects, powers, and entities can be understood in terms of current theories of natural and behavioral sciences. As a side effect of these methodological choices, most naturalistic explanations of religion are very critical towards more traditional hermeneutical and socio-cultural approaches to religious belief that tend to make a strong distinction between explaining the natural world and understanding the "human" or the "social" world. Drawing—but more cautiously—on E. O. Wilson's legacy, the assumption of the naturalist is that the findings of biology, neuroscience, and cognitive science are relevant for explaining socio-cultural phenomena, such as religion, and the psychological phenomena of religious belief.

"Religion" and "religious belief" are defined here very broadly to include all beliefs and behaviors that have to do with culturally postulated supernatural agents. Supernatural agents can include gods, spirits, ghosts, goblins, or any other similar entity that is understood personally. In addition to the idea that explanations of religious belief should be naturalistic, there is also another concept of "natural" at work here. Naturalistic explanations of religious beliefs argue that religious belief is part of our nature as human beings, as opposed to something we have constructed; it might serve a biological function or it might be a by-product of our cognition, but nevertheless the tendency to form religious beliefs is a part of universal human nature, rather than simply being a product of religious individuals' history and cultural environment.

Questions that these explanations attempt to answer are something like this: How did this panhuman tendency to form religious beliefs emerge? and How does it persist and operate? Answers come in two basic types: biological explanations and cognitive explanations.

On the biological side, consider Ara Norenzayan's evolutionary approach that summarizes a number of recent theories and studies.[21] This approach, popular amongst social and biological scientists, is the perspective that to understand religion one must understand the evolutionary function religion serves. Norenzayan proposes the thesis that "Big" Gods (moralizing and interventionist deities associated with large-scale religions, particularly the Abrahamic traditions) emerged alongside the initial increases in social complexity and coordination over the last ~10,000-15,000 years of human evolution. As human populations became more socially and materially complex, their Gods became more moralizing and powerful. It was the belief-ritual complexes (religions) associated with these Gods that then facilitated large-scale hyper-cooperation and coordination, which in turn enabled the emergence of large scale, complex societies (states). Norenzayan explicitly states that "Big God" religions are responsible for "Big Groups": modern human societies, including large-scale intragroup coordination and large-scale intergroup warfare.

This approach is not new, as Dominic Johnson and Jesse Bering,[22] and others, have proposed specific adaptive scenarios for the emergence of Big Gods and the role of supernatural punishment in facilitating both hyper-cooperation within human groups and warfare between them. They make the case that large scale religions and their strong tendency for moral policing and punishing God(s) are the product of the natural selection of specific cognitive (neurological and perceptual) characteristics. However, unlike Johnson's and Bering's

21 Norenzayan, A. 2013. Big Gods: How Religion Transformed Cooperation and Conflict. Princeton, NJ: Princeton University Press.

22 Johnson, D. D. P., and J. M. Bering. 2006. Hand of God, Mind of Man: Punishment and Cognition in the Evolution of Cooperation. Evolutionary Psychology 4:219-233.

proposals, Norenzayan argues that strong cultural evolutionary processes have resulted in a system that links prosociality, morality, ritual, and "deep commitment" to "Big Gods" who are powerful, interventionist, and punishing and require hard-to-fake commitment.

A core aspect missing from Norenzayan's approach is the individual believer's experience of religious faith and their interpretation of what that faith means. The cognitive, physiological, and perceptual realities of people who believe in Big God religions vary, and in that variation there might be an evolutionarily relevant complexity that is missed in the larger scale functional treatment of what religion does. These are aspects of religion about which the cognitive science of religion has more to say.

Cognitive explanations are attempts to account for the emergence of religious belief by examining the cognitive mechanisms underlying all belief-formation. Popular theories along these lines include the minimal counterintuitiveness (MCI) theory of Pascal Boyer and the hypersensitive agency detection device (HADD) theory of Justin Barrett.[23]

Many have suggested that the fault line between adaptive and cognitive approaches lies in the way in which they understand the evolutionary role of religious belief: some claim that religious belief has never had a biological function, but is a pure by-product of the evolution of cognition, whereas others claim that religious belief has indeed been favored by natural selection because it has provided (or provides) certain survival advantages. This corresponds to a fault line in evolutionary biology between adaptationists who hold that all important physical and behavioral traits are governed by natural selection and pluralists or 'spandrelists' who hold that certain seemingly functional traits of an organism might be accidental consequences of some other traits. The adaptationist assumption that natural selection is causally omnipresent in evolution underwrites evolutionary and co-evolutionary approaches to religion, whereas a methodological preference for "constraint-based" explanations tends to underwrite the more "cognitivist" approaches.

---

23 Boyer, Pascal. 2001. Religion Explained: The Human Instincts That Fashion Gods, Spirits and Ancestors. New York: Basic Books. Barrett, Justin. 2004. Why Would Anyone Believe in God? Walnut Creek, CA: AltaMira Press.

Finally, we want to highlight a topic of disagreement that has to do with broad metaphysical and epistemological views. Both Agustín Fuentes and Wentzel van Huyssteen (in this book) point out that what we think about metaphysics and epistemology in general might have important implications regarding our view of human nature. This is nowhere more evident than in the debates between religious, theological, and naturalistic views of human nature. For theists and non-naturalists, there might be aspects o f human nature that are not scientifically tractable. Some theologians have suggested that only revelation tells us what human beings ultimately are. Scientific study of humans might be useful in many ways but it does not, in this view, tell us much about our essential nature. Theologians, however, are not the only non-naturalists. Some philosophers have also maintained that certain aspects of human nature, such as self-consciousness, reason, and freedom, might be inaccessible to science (for instance, Thomas Nagel's 2012 book *Mind and Cosmos: Why The Materialist Neo-Darwinian View of Nature is Almost Certainly False*).

It seems to us that many debates about human nature exhibit a kind of naturalistic bias. There is an implicit assumption that scientific results and debates about human nature are free of philosophical or conceptual assumptions. The truth of animalism, for instance, is often assumed without any further argument. Similarly, it is often assumed that whatever human nature is, it is scientifically and empirically tractable, making a theory of human nature naturalistic. We are not trying to say that these views are necessarily false and that naturalism must be false as well. Instead, what we are saying is that these assumptions need to be made explicit and argued for. The naturalist cannot come to the transdisciplinary table to discuss human nature and simply assume that everyone else will agree with her on these issues.

Our background assumptions also have an implicit or explicit impact on how we understand the questions: biological accounts of how *Homo sapiens* emerged, for instance, do not necessarily answer all our questions about what human nature means. We do not want to say that there is a necessary contradiction between asking biological questions and asking other kinds of questions about human beings.

Instead, we want to point out that posing the questions biologically might end up obscuring or completely sidelining other ways of addressing and understanding what humanity is and what its nature is like.

Our intention is not to enter or adjudicate complex philosophical and worldview issues of epistemological and metaphysical nature. Instead, we wanted to make two points: first, there is a widespread (and, in our view, rational) disagreement about basic metaphysical and epistemological questions (such as the existence of God, the nature of scientific knowledge, existence of essences, etc.); and second, we must be cautious and try to explicate and identify where our own assumptions come in when we talk about human nature. Nevertheless, we want to emphasize that we should not give up seeking convergence on human nature, because of our metaphysical disagreements. If convergence eludes us and common ground cannot be found, this is already a relevant result itself: it would reveal to us how deeply our questions about ourselves are connected to our basic metaphysical assumptions.

The Conversations on Human Nature

Having set the stage and established the range of contexts we will cover, we are now primed to move on to the interviews and hear what this collection of excellent scholars from the fields of anthropology, biology, philosophy, psychology, and theology[24] have to say about the topic.

Each interview here presents an edited segment of a larger interview. We edited for content and for flow in order to keep the narratives engaging and as on-topic as possible (with the recognition that this is a very, very broad topic). In order to help structure the interviews we

----

24 Here we only present a set of perspectives from Christian theologians as those were the focus of the theological aspects of the research project from which this book emerged. However, we are cognizant that a more comprehensive account should also include theological perspectives from other religions and for that matter a broader range of academic disciplines than represented in this book, but that is beyond the scope of this project.

attempted to direct the discussion by asking questions that focused on definitions and descriptions of human nature, on the processes and philosophies that go into human nature, and on the personal viewpoints of each interviewee. We reproduce the interviews with some of the questions so that you (the reader) get a flavor of the back and forth, the conversation that elicited the fascinating and engaging perspectives of the interviewees. All of the interviewees were able to see and make minor edits on their interviews and approved the final texts.

CHAPTER 2

Evolution, Brains, and Human Nature

Interviewee: Francisco Ayala

Bio. Dr. Ayala is a biologist and philosopher with the University of California, Irvine. He received his doctorate from Columbia University, studying under Theodosius Dobzhansky, and his own research in evolutionary biology includes work in population and evolutionary genetics. Known for his work on the cloning of *Trypanosoma cruzi* (Chagas Disease), his defense of embryonic stem cell research, and his critique of creationism and intelligent design, Ayala is a former President and Chairman of the Board for the American Association for the Advancement of Science. His many awards and honors include the National Medal of Science (2001), the President's Award of the American Institute of Biological Sciences (2007), The William Proctor Prize for Scientific Achievement from Sigma Xi (2000), and the Templeton Prize (2010).

Slogan. *"We adapt to the environment by cultural changes, not biological changes, and that is what defines humanity. That is what accounts for the great success of humankind."*

Agustín Fuentes and Aku Visala, *Conversations on Human Nature*, pp. 43-104. © 2016 Left Coast Press, Inc. All rights reserved.

Agustín: *The first question I have asked everyone is the most diffi-cult one, but it is the one that is a logical beginning. That is, if you were questioned or queried by a student or a colleague or someone in the public for a definition or a description of a human nature, how do you respond?*

Francisco: Well, depending on how much time I have in front of me, I would say we have two components. One is the biological ba-sis of human nature, which shows continuity from non-human an-cestors, and then we have the human lineage, that separates us from our relatives, the chimps, about seven or eight million years ago.

Then, many things started to happen in the lineage: especially the evolution of our hands. Hands allowed our ancestors to make tools, which in turn led to an enlargement of the brain and finally to the enormous intelligence that we have.

Due to the enormous increase in intelligence, a new kind of dis-tinctively human evolution appeared: cultural evolution—cultural adaptation to the environment. It is cultural evolution rather than biological evolution that now defines what humans are and what our future might be.

Cultural adaptations occur in the scale of years, months, some-times it seems almost days. You have an iPhone invented, and in a year, millions of people have it, and so on with other inventions from the past and of the present. These are adaptations to the en-vironment, while biological adaptations take thousands and thou-sands of generations.

We have adapted to travel in rivers and the oceans, and we do it more effectively than any fish, despite the fact that we do not have gills or fins, and we fly better than any bird and longer distances, but we do not have wings either. We adapt to the environment by cul-tural changes, not biological changes, and that is what defines hu-manity. That is what accounts for the great success of humankind.

Nevertheless, we are still biological and tropical animals. Our *Homo sapiens* ancestors left tropical Africa, maybe 100,000 years ago, probably a little less. This is not a long time on an evolution-ary scale, perhaps 4,000 generations or so. Consider people living in Alaska and Siberia, in Scandinavia. These people have not adapted to live in the cold climates physiologically. They have not changed physiologically. They do not have fuller hair, which would allow them biologically to survive in these cold climates. Instead their adaptation is cultural. We have invented a whole world just by cultural adaptation, clothing, and housing.

This is what has made us the most successful living species and the most powerful, and of course we also have destructive power. That is another side of the coin.

Agustín: *Do you think that our nature in this sense, the broad sense, is a result of biological and cultural evolution and that it sets humans apart as unique from the rest of the planet, or is it just more of a distinction amongst commonalities?*

Francisco: I think in a strict sense, we are distinct. There are some behaviors that can be identified as cultural in chimpanzees and in some birds, like making nests and cracking nuts. One famous place is Monkey Island in Japan. Apparently one chimp discovered how to wash potatoes from the fields, and then all others learned from him, but only the young ones learned. The older ones never learned.

Some non-human primates occasionally have imitation and learning, of course, so not everything is biologically transmitted. However, this is so trivial in the big scale of things, that it is quite justified to speak of culture in the proper sense being a distinctively human phenomenon.

Agustín: *How do you see, or do you see, a presence or absence of a role for free will in this?*

Francisco: As you know, the matter of free will is very difficult philosophically. It is surprising to me that philosophers often argue against free will, on the grounds that we are made of atoms and molecules and nothing but atoms and molecules. Those molecules do not have free will, so we therefore cannot have free will.

I think there is a confusion here between two kinds of, I am going to use a big word, reductionism. Metaphysically, ontologically, in terms of what we are made of, we can be reduced to atoms and molecules and nothing else, because if we remove all the atoms and molecules that make me, nothing is left. One does not need to believe in souls, or at least I do not.

But ontological reductionism does not imply elimination of higher-level properties. That is, being able to have new attributes, new properties, and in fact, one can establish this by very simple examples. Water is hydrogen and oxygen. Neither hydrogen nor oxygen has the properties of water, and yet you put them together and you have water, with distinctive properties.

I think it is possible, in the particular sets of combinations of atoms and molecules and organization, as well as the biological developments of the brain and the like, that new attributes arise. Atoms and molecules do not have intelligence, we do, and they do not write books, we do. I believe that free will is one of the cases where the phenomenon is emergent in this sense. Some people call these "the missing properties," but we should not worry about this: water has missing properties and table salt does. Neither sodium nor chlorine has the properties of salt.

Agustín: *This notion of emergence that's been bandied around quite a bit is a very interesting one. Is your use of the notion related to what Nancey Murphy and others, like Warren Brown, say about non-reductive physicalism?* [1]

Francisco: Yeah. It is a very similar position. I am not sure of this, but I think it is the case. I wrote these things about reduction already in 1972. Non-reductive physicalism is still physicalism. There is nothing there in reality but basic physical parts. However, it is anti-reductionist at the epistemological level: we cannot reduce these new properties to anything present already in the components.

Agustín: *You have also written about this very recently. Maybe a few years ago, the John Templeton Foundation put out a few statements on evolution, and you conclude that statement by saying that evolution tells us a lot about our bodies and our cells and about being human, but it does not tell us everything.*

----

1 See Murphy, Nancey, and Warren S. Brown. 2007. Did My Neurons Make Me Do It?: Philosophical and Neurobiological Perspectives on Moral Responsibility and Free Will. Oxford: Oxford University Press.

Francisco: Of course not.

Agustín: *How do you see the role and relationship of morality then, as tying into this broader human nature?*

Francisco: Morality has, in my view, two components, one which is biological another one which is cultural. When people talk about morality and when they argue different points of view, very often they are talking about two different things.

One is that we are moral beings. That is to say that we evaluate actions as being right or wrong in the moral sense, which is a very distinctive way of evaluating actions. You can evaluate them in many ways. This capacity is determined by our biology and it is grounded in our intelligence and the fact that we can anticipate the future. This is actually the fundament of our culture: the ability to anticipate the future.

But, anticipating the future makes it possible to anticipate the consequences of our own actions, and therefore, we cannot avoid judging an action as right or wrong because of its consequences. Pulling the trigger by itself is not a moral action, but if I know that when I pull the trigger, it is going to shoot a bullet into an enemy, it becomes a moral action.

Now, the rules, the norms, according to which we decide what is right and what is wrong, they are largely products of culture and they are non-biological. There are some foundations in biology, there are some people who say that there are moral facts, that killing a human being is evil and that stealing is evil, adultery is evil.

You start to go around the line, and you very soon realize it is not that clear that these are determined naturally. Perhaps one could say that there are some predispositions for some moral norms in our biology, but largely they are cultural products. Property rights or prohibitions against stealing are not in our biology.

Let me draw a parallel with language. The capacity to have articulate language, creative language, which humans have and only humans have, is determined by our excellent intelligence, determined by our biology, but the languages we actually speak are determined by culture. People like Noam Chomsky claim that there is an underlying grammar to all languages. Well, similarly there might an underlying moral grammar but the norms of morality are cultural products.

Agustín: *Do you think someone like Frans de Waal would argue for an underlying moral grammar?*[2]

Francisco: I think so, probably more so than I would, although his way of thinking is probably not very different from mine. We know each other quite well. Our emphases are different, because he tends to emphasize the animal side and the biological side of things. Nevertheless, he does not go along with people who think that everything has to be judged in terms of the utility. There are people who think that morality is just utility calculus and is all biologically determined.

Agustín: *What do you think about the role of malleability or plasticity in human nature? You talk really a lot about humans using culture as our adaptive zone. Would you say that there is no human nature but human natures?*

Francisco: Again, it is fine to say something like that, so long as you explain what you mean. Yes, we have tremendous plasticity, which we have precisely because of our extraordinary intelligence, and again, you can trace the biological roots of that. It is intelligence, which gives us culture, cultural adaptation, our plasticity, and the multiple faces of human nature that we are able to create.

Agustín: *In addition to morality, there has been a lot of recent work on the role of faith in human societies and how it relates to culture; not necessarily a particular religious faith, but the role of religion and the role of faith in human culture or moving it forward. Do you have any thoughts on that?*

Francisco: This is an interesting issue. Foundations of religion can be discussed from two points of view, historical, like ten thousand years, and evolutionary, which is more like millions of years.

I think one aspect of religion has to do with our need to understand things. We often refer to forces that are extra natural, supernatural or outside nature to explain things that are not able to explain by natural processes.

---

2   See, e.g., de Waal, Frans. 1996. Good Natured: The Origins of Right and Wrong in Humans and Other Animals. Cambridge, MA: Harvard University Press.

It rains because these farmers are good people, and Vesuvius erupted because the people in Pompeii were bad people, and therefore God wanted to destroy them. Of course, now we have natural explanations for such things, continents and clouds move and all that.

The reference to extra natural forces and entities, such as God, is, I think, one of the bases of religion. The other one has to do with our self-awareness. We know we exist as individuals; other animals do not get this, although Frans might challenge me here a little bit. He gives animals more credit than I do, but I say we are self-aware, we are death-aware. If a species is self-aware, they know that members of the same species die. Therefore, they are aware they are going to die.

That, of course, creates anxiety and stimulates us to find meaning in life and perhaps even in some versions a future life. I think that self-awareness, which is a biological attribute, an attribute coming from our biology, leads us to death-awareness, which leads to various cultural practices around death. This introduces religious rituals, not only concerning the dead, but other ones around life, trying again to find meaning and to relieve the anxiety that we experience as a consequence of knowing that we are going to die.

In our modern societies, there is, of course, this debate about religion going on. We do not use religion to explain natural processes, or at least most of us do not, but many people still need to have some form of faith or have some hope that life has meaning in some way, either through good deeds, or as I said, in some cases, through future life after death.

Agustín: *The role of cooperation or cooperative systems in human evolution has received a lot of attention recently, and some are even arguing that it is not just cooperation within a group for competition between groups, but maybe a larger kind of cooperation that characterizes humans relative to other forms of life. We understand the consequences of our actions and therefore understand that cooperating with other individuals, even if from other groups, may benefit us as well.*

Francisco: Yes, my old friend David S. Wilson argued against my other friend, Edward O. Wilson, the father of sociobiology, for such group selection already in the '70s, even when group selection was denied by sociobiologists and people like Richard Dawkins, again another friend with different views from mine. I actually gave D. S. Wilson his first job, back when I was chairman of the division of environmental sciences at UC Davis, and I wrote the introduction to his first book.

By the way, I have managed to be friends with everybody, even with some scientists who have very different views and who know I do not agree with them in many things.

I just wrote a review of Wilson's new book, *The Social Conquest of Earth* (2013).

Agustín: *Yeah, the article on group selection by Edward O. Wilson and David Sloan Wilson from four or five years ago was pretty groundbreaking, because they basically took back the whole last chapter of Sociobiology.*[3] *[Laughter]*

Francisco: E. O. Wilson has also given up on the views of many of his later books, *On Human Nature*, for example.[4] I disagree very much with E. O. Wilson, but he is also a good, dear friend. In *The Social Conquest of Earth*, Wilson actually gives up on many ideas that made him famous, like inclusive fitness and gene selection.[5] His followers, as well as those who challenged his theories since the '70s, will read his most recent book with astonishment. He admits that the foundations of the general theory of inclusive fitness, based on the assumptions of gene selection, have crumbled. The beautiful theory never worked well anyway, and now it has collapsed.

....

3   E. O. Wilson's groundbreaking Sociobiology (1975) develops a model to explain animal cooperation. For the most part the book examines various insects and other animals, but in the last chapter of the book Wilson extends his model to cover humans as well. The book and the subsequent field of sociobiology created an enormous scientific and ethical debate in the '70s and '80s. For an exciting historical account, see Segerstråle, Ullica. 2002. Defenders of the Truth: The Battle for Science in the Sociobiology Debate and Beyond. New York: Oxford University Press. See also the first chapter of this book.

4   This was a follow-up to Sociobiology and dealt mostly with human sociobiology. See also Wilson, E. O. 2013. The Social Conquest of Earth. New York: W. W. Norton & Co.

5   Inclusive fitness is the argument that one's evolutionary success is related to the succes of one's close biological relatives. Gene selection occurs when the actual action of evolutionary forces is targeted at the genetic level.

He is still a strong reductionist, though. He thinks science is all there is: everything—including music, literature, art, and morality—can all be reduced to the science way of doing things, scientific discourse.

He thinks there are two components in human life: individual's relationship to other individuals in the individual's group and individual's relationship to other individuals in other groups. But when you have different groups, you can have collaboration or competition between groups. So far so good, but then Wilson says that the human genome mirrors this: we have some genes for behavior between individuals in the same group and others for behavior between groups. Believe it or not, he then says that individual selection is mostly responsible for sin and selection among groups, mostly for virtue.

Agustín: *Wow!*

Francisco: He is amazing. As I said, I love him very dearly and admire him. The statements he makes are still amazing. He will get away with these, because he is so distinguished. He writes very well, also, and he has given it a lot of thought and he will fight for his ideas. Good for him!

Anyway, so there you have it: we have to also consider the interactions between groups in evolution, not just the interaction between individuals. There is no question that groups have played a major role. The way I see it, one critical step here into human social life was cryptic ovulation. A chimp, or a primate in general, a male that has opportunity to mate with a female mate, he knows she is receptive because when the female is in estrous, her sexual swellings are large and usually a bright color. The male comes and mates.

There is no reason for the male to stay around, since it is 95 percent-plus probable that she will be pregnant. Thus, the female carries the male's genes. Any genes that will move a male not to stay there, but to go somewhere else, would be favored by selection, because those genes will allow the opportunity to inseminate another female.

Now, cryptic ovulation came about, and we do not know when, but now in the human case the male does not know whether the female is in estrous or not. Therefore, the only way to make sure that the female is going to carry his genes is to stay with her and mate repeatedly. That gives rise to the nuclear family, which does not exist in other primates, at least not very well established: father, mother and children, and sometimes more generations. Once you have a family, you can have groups of families that collaborate, and when you have groups you can have relations with other groups and the formation of larger and larger groups.

I think selection favored this development. Because in this, E. O. Wilson says different families can collaborate for the benefit of everybody. Groups, larger groups, tribes, he calls them, include some tribes that also collaborate with other tribes. This has started to happen on a grand scale in humans in more recent times, leading to nations and the like.

Agustín: *One common theme that seems to be arising across multiple disciplines when people think about human nature is community. There is something about being around other humans that makes you human. Perhaps this is human nature?*

Francisco: To be fully human, you need a human mind, to be able to think and be creative. You can have a computer that, for example, translates, but it does not mean it understands anything. It is transforming symbols and that is it. Computers that play chess better than the world class champions, the masters. It does not make them human, because still they are not thinking. They are not being creative.

One can conceive of computers that collaborate with each other in some way and accomplish new things that had not been planned. I think that is possible, but to me there is a very long way from that to having a creative mind.

Agustín: *Robin Dunbar and others, for example, have talked about this in terms of extended brain, social mind, and the social brain context.[6] Do you think there's something about our exalted intelligence, as he put it that requires the social?*

Francisco: I think so. Collaboration will be favored by natural selection and by adaptation through culture and otherwise, because as we were saying, families can collaborate and form a tribe and

6   See Robin Dunbar's interview in this chapter.

tribes can collaborate. That makes them more human, because it offers a number of possibilities. The horizon of possibilities expands tremendously when we move from groups of a couple of families to large, modern societies, like ours.

But we must remember that even tribal groups have not been around for that long and it is difficult to say how much adaptation has happened in that time. Tribalism probably starts just about, at most, 100,000 years ago, with the origin of our species in Africa. Then, with the migrations out of Africa, at least there was already something more than family units, because you had to imagine going from Africa all the way to reaching Australia eventually, and to Beijing and eventually to the Americas, as individual families is possible, but there had to have been collaboration, because of all the activities that only larger groups could do, like navigation.

There is no question that group life has been favored by natural selection, because it allows humans to accomplish these things, to survive and reproduce better, which is natural selection.

Agustín: *You often focus on natural selection as the cause of evolutionary change. What do you think about the recent work by Boyd and Richerson and Henrich and others in cultural evolution suggesting that there are other, central forces of evolutionary change? Laland and Feldman have also said this as well as the niche construction theorists.[7]*

Francisco: I will have to go back to my early definition of human nature, not that I can provide a definition in a few words. I think most adaptation now does not happen by natural selection. It is not biological adaptation. It is adaptation by culture, so surely we have gone beyond natural selection. People often ask me in public lectures, if evolution continues in humans, biological evolution, and the answer is yes. It can be demonstrated that it does, but it is so trivial compared to adaptation by culture.

Adaptation now happens via cultural evolution, not natural selection. You could even talk of cultural selection: culture is hereditary and has variation and selection, so it has all the attributes of natural selection.

....
7   See Kevin Laland's interview in this chapter.

Agustín: *It is a very exciting time, I think, to be thinking about human evolution, and a very interdisciplinary time.*

Francisco: That's right, and of course, in ten years it will be even more exciting, and twenty years even more exciting. That is the great thing about cultural adaptation, you see, that we keep on growing. The rate of cultural evolution is accelerating, no question. The rate of change in technology is constantly growing: the change that took place during the twenty years after my childhood was insignificant compared to, say, the last five years.

Agustín: *I think that is very interesting. One of the reasons I have enjoyed talking with you is that it is still difficult to find individuals well trained in the biological sciences, who are open to the fact that philosophy and other humanities can tell us something, that there is a way to think together on these topics. E. O. Wilson is a good example of someone, and Richard Dawkins is another one, in many ways, who argue that all of this is good, but at the bottom line, only the materialistic, biological account can succeed. I am optimistic that scientists' views are opening up a little bit more.*

Francisco: Yeah, I think it is opening up. There is more exchange between the humanities, including philosophy and the arts, and the sciences, now than ten years ago or twenty years ago. These dialogues now are very frequent.

Suggested Readings

Ayala, F. J. 2012. The Big Questions: Evolution. London: Quercus Publishing.

Ayala, F. J. 2010. Am I a Monkey? Six Big Questions about Evolution. Baltimore: Johns Hopkins University Press.

Ayala, F. J. 2007. Darwin's Gift to Science and Religion. Washington, DC: Joseph Henry Press.

Ayala, F. J. and J. C. Avise, eds. 2014. Essential Readings in Evolutionary Biology. Baltimore: Johns Hopkins University Press.

Ayala, F. J. and R. Arp, eds. 2010. Contemporary Debates in Philosophy of Biology. Malden, MA: Wiley-Blackwell.

Interviewee: Edouard Machery

Bio. Edouard Machery, PhD, is Professor in the Department of History and Philosophy of Science at the University of Pittsburgh as well as a resident fellow of the Center for Philosophy of Science (University of Pittsburgh) and a member of the Center for the Neural Basis of Cognition (Carnegie Mellon University and University of Pittsburgh). His research focuses on the philosophical issues raised by the cognitive sciences. He has published on a wide range of topics in the philosophy of psychology, including the nature of concepts, racial cognition, evolutionary psychology, innateness, moral psychology, and methodological issues in cognitive science and neuroscience. He is the author of *Doing without Concepts* from Oxford University Press, the editor of *The Oxford Handbook of Compositionality* from Oxford University Press, *La Philosophie Expérimentale* from Vuibert, *Arguing about Human Nature* from Routledge, and *Current Controversies in Experimental Philosophy* from Routledge. He is the current editor of the Naturalistic Philosophy section of *Philosophy Compass*. He is also one of the leading contributors to the development of experimental philosophy.

Slogan. *"Critics of the notion of human nature are losing track of this very interesting fact about human beings, that you can go to many cultures and you can look throughout history, and you are going to find many things that people have in common. That is not a necessary feature of any species. We need a notion to make sense of that feature. The notion of human nature is exactly that notion."*

Aku: *You work on human nature. Would you like to tell us a little bit about, in terms of background, how you came to write about human nature?*

Edouard: I approach human behavior from an evolutionary point of view, and my original focus was on the philosophical questions raised by evolutionary psychology and human behavioral ecology. Evolutionary psychologists and human behavioral ecologists talk about human nature all the time; they often present their science as a science of human nature. The question was then, "Well, what do they really mean by human nature?" This notion is used all over the place, but it is never really explained. As a philosopher of science, my job is, at least in part, to identify unclear scientific notions and to try to clarify them. The notion of human nature seems to play a very important role in some scientific projects despite being on its face quite unclear. For that reason, I wanted to look at it more carefully.

For example, I have long been influenced by Robert Boyd and Peter Richerson's work.[8] In their view, we are a cultural species: humans are animals that get a lot of things through culture, through cultural learning. When they defend this idea, Boyd and Richerson are actually employing what I think is a notion of human nature, and they are committing themselves to a very specific view about what human nature really is. Nonetheless, when I told Peter about the reader on human nature I published with Routledge,[9] which contains one of his papers, he was somewhat dismayed by my efforts to clarify and defend the notion of human nature.

Aku: *Perhaps it is because he associates human nature with the layer-cake model of human nature. First there is biology, and then culture comes on top of it. Human nature is the biology bit, not the culture bit.*

Edouard: That is probably the way he thinks about human nature, but there is no reason to think about it that way. There are plenty of better ways of thinking about human nature. In fact, in my opinion, philosophers, biologists, geneticists, and anthropologists should work together to redefine human nature, to propose a conception

....

8   E.g., Richerson, Peter R., and Robert Boyd. 2005. Not by Genes Alone: How Culture Transformed Human Evolution. Chicago: University of Chicago Press.

9   Downes, Stephen M., and Edouard Machery, eds. 2013. Arguing about Human Nature: Contemporary Debates. New York: Routledge.

of what it means to talk about human nature that is compatible with our modern understanding of biology, psychology, and culture. This is a genuine interdisciplinary project. It is intellectually exciting, and it also matters socially: Problematic notions of human nature are often used by the lay public, and we should be able to offer a novel, scientifically grounded conception of human nature.

Aku: *You said that scientists might easily end up rejecting one concept and accepting another. What kinds of human nature concepts do you think are out there?*

Edouard: There are probably a few. The most obvious one is the "bad" concept of human nature, the one almost everybody rejects. This is sometimes called the essentialist notion of human nature. Roughly, the idea behind this notion is that human nature is a set of properties that all human beings have and only human beings have. These necessary and sufficient properties explain the way we are; they are explanatory. Some say the essentialist notion of human nature comes from Aristotle, but that is probably false, according anyway to recent scholarship. In any case, many people would say, and I agree with them, that this notion is incompatible with a truly evolutionary view about human beings. Conspecifics do not share any intrinsic essence that distinguishes them from members of other species, and diversity is an essential feature of populations in an evolutionary framework.

Aku: *Would the essentialist notion of human nature be related to our folk notions of human nature and essences?*

Edouard: In my view, that notion of human nature is an outgrowth of the way people spontaneously think about animals in general, including human beings—what psychologists call "folk biology."

There is a small complication about connecting folk essentialism (that is, roughly, ordinary people's tendency to ascribe essences to kinds) with human nature. Folk essentialism is probably a universal feature of the human mind. It is found in many different cultures, and it has probably been around for quite some time. In contrast, the notion of human nature itself is not that old. One reason, of course, is that the idea that all human beings form some kind of unified group is actually recent. For a long time, people have been thinking about human groups in terms of "them versus us," and as a result they have not thought of human beings as a unified kind. So, while the notion of human nature is indeed an outgrowth of folk essentialism, it is not a necessary outgrowth. For a long time, people just did not have any idea of human nature.

Personally, I do not have a very good sense of when the essentialist notion of human nature emerged. As I said earlier, people often say it is found in Aristotle, but scholarship on Aristotle shows that this claim is actually a mistake. It is probably a more recent invention.

I have been arguing for a distinct, novel notion of human nature, which I call the nomological notion of human nature. It is a very simple idea. In brief, human nature consists of the numerous properties that human beings tend to have by virtue of evolutionary processes.

The notion of human nature allows us to characterize humans as a homogeneous group, at least in some respects, in virtue of evolution. There are things to say about human beings in general in virtue of evolutionary processes. This is really the key insight into the notion of human nature. This is why the notion of human nature is valuable and worth keeping and why there is almost invariably a theory of human nature embedded in the evolutionary study of human behavior.

When you look at human beings, you can see the human species through diversity. Essentially, you can see patterns of behavior, patterns of social interactions, which tend to be common, which are almost universal, present in many cultures. Diversity is important, but we should not forget that there are aspects of the human species that are, roughly, invariant all over the world. We all speak. We all have very similar patterns of social interaction.

It is very important not to lose track of this shared aspect of human existence, and the whole point of the notion of human nature is to highlight it. Critics of the notion of human nature are losing track of this very interesting fact about us human beings: that you can go to many cultures and you can look throughout history, and you are going to find things that people have in common.

I also want to say that the nomological notion of human nature implicitly underlies most of the work in what I call the evolutionary behavioral sciences. For instance, this is the notion used by Boyd and Richerson when they say that humans are a cultural species. What they say is that we humans have this dependence on culture by virtue of evolutionary processes.

Aku: *I think many people who deny the existence of human nature have a specific worry. They are afraid that if you use the notion, you are imply-ing some sort of biological determinism or a strong form of adaptation-ism[10] where natural selection makes some human traits inevitable.*

Edouard: I think that is right, but eliminating human nature be-cause of this worry is just throwing the baby out with the bathwater.

I am probably more an adaptationist than the critics of human nature you are referring to. Adaptationism has been a very successful strategy to study animal behavior, perhaps even the most successful strategy until quite recently. It is also a useful research strategy to study human behavior. But it is not the whole thing. It is just one way to try to explain biological traits, including human behavior.

In any case, I do not want the notion of human nature to be nec-essarily linked to adaptationism. I fully acknowledge the diversity of evolutionary processes: drift, adaptation, phylogenetic constraints, etc. All these evolutionary processes happen to have produced a shared human nature.

Another interesting thing about human nature is that it is rich or thick. There are many things that people tend to have in common because of evolutionary processes. This richness, so to speak, is not a necessary feature of a species. Some species have a much poorer or thinner nature because for whatever evolutionary or ecological reasons, there are fewer things in common between conspecifics or between groups of conspecifics. Human beings are not like that.

I speculate that the richness of human nature is related to the fact that there is very little genetic diversity among human beings.

....

10 Adaptationism is the view that natural selection is the most central cause of evolutionary change.

Compared to many other mammals, humans are actually on the low end of genetic diversity. Perhaps this low genetic diversity and this richness of human nature are in part due to the existence of a population bottleneck at some point during human evolution. There were very few hominids, and we human beings are all their descendants.

Aku: *It seems that we have to navigate between two extremes here. On the one hand, some anthropologists claim that there is too much diversity to say that there is a nature. Then, on the other hand, we have some biologists like Edward O. Wilson, especially in the '70s and the '80s, saying that whatever human nature is, it is very robust and it is somehow very strongly innate and it is really rooted in biology and has nothing to do with culture or learning.*

Edouard: We do need to find something between these two extremes. I do not want to say that human nature has nothing to do with culture. That would be really a mistake. I do not want to say either that human nature has to be connected with innateness because I am very critical of the notion of innateness. For me, the characteristics that are part of human nature can be acquired through learning and culture. Their acquisition is a very complex process.

That said, if I imagine a continuum between a cultural anthropologist who denies there is any such thing as human nature and an extreme sociobiologist from the 1970s, even though I disagree with the extreme sociobiologists about many issues—for instance their commitment to innateness was a mistake—I am closer to the sociobiologist's side than to the cultural anthropologist's.

Despite their mistakes, sociobiologists got something right. What they got right, and that is of fundamental importance, is the idea that if you want to understand human beings, you need to do it through the lens of evolutionary biology. This lens is going to give you very important insights about what it means to be a human being. Their problem was that their idea of evolutionary biology was too limited.

Aku: *Yes, I get that. You mentioned another concept that is often associated with human nature, innateness. This is interesting because a lot of people think that if innateness does not make sense, then human nature does not make sense. It is interesting that you are* *critical of innateness but not of human nature. Could you explain a little bit what kind of different things innateness is usually used to refer to and why you are critical of it?*

Edouard: In my view, innateness is really a folk or a lay concept, although it is also used by scientists. Many scientists use the word "innateness" in their scientific writings, but I do not think it is a technical notion.

When people talk about innateness, they really have three ideas in mind. One thing they want to say is that a feature or a trait is universal: It is found in every human being or in most human beings. Second, they want to say that the development of a trait does not depend on its environment: Its environment can change a lot, and the trait will still be there. Third, they want to say that the trait in question has a function.

There are several problems with these three ideas. Most important, the notion that the development of a trait could be independent from its environment is just bad biology. This is a view about development that everybody now rejects. This notion also contrasts traits that are the expression of an organism's inner nature and those that result from the influence of the environment, an untenable dualism.

Aku: *That sounds like essentialist human nature again: a trait that expresses itself no matter what, because it is a part of your essence.*

Edouard: Yes, the notion of innateness is really connected to the essentialist notion of human nature. As we just saw, the first problem is that it makes no sense to conceive of traits as developing independently from their environment.

Furthermore, the notion of innateness rests on the assumptions that traits that are universal must be adaptations and that adaptations must be universal, but these assumptions are just mistaken. Biology does not work that way: Some universal traits may be adaptations while others may be byproducts of adaptations or something else; furthermore, some adaptations may be local.

As I said, the notion of human nature embodies an insight about humans that is worth keeping, and we do not have an array of other concepts that could be used to capture this important insight. In contrast, there is little to be said on behalf of the notion of innateness. When I look at the way both lay people and scientists talk about innateness, or at the way they use the expressions "in his DNA," or "in her DNA," I see no insight about human beings that would be worth preserving. On the contrary, what I see is just drawbacks, just problems, just a very deeply misguided view about human development. So, we should just get rid of the notion of innateness. We should stop talking about innate traits!

The upshot is that we should teach people to stop thinking about human nature through the lens of innateness. People should come to understand that there are many traits which are part of the nature of the human species, that are learned or culturally transmitted.

Aku: *You maintain that human nature consists of shared patterns of traits and behaviors we have due to our evolution. How fixed would you say that these patterns are? It seems that one dimension of human nature is this fixed/malleability contrast. A lot of people, like nativists, think that human nature traits have to be very fixed. If there are no fixed traits and humans are extremely malleable, there is no human nature.*

Edouard: It is a bit complicated. You do find a lot of diversity in the human species, but this diversity is often variation on common themes. Family is a good example. There is tremendous diversity in family organization across cultures, and the specifics of kinship systems vary across cultures, sometimes in surprising ways, but you find some kinship system in every culture, and you find distinct sets of norms governing kin and non-kin relations.

My hunch is that the common themes that underlie variation may be hard to eliminate or radically transform, although I do not want to say they cannot be changed. After all, we can change a lot of things in human behavior. For instance, my hunch is that it would be hard to create a human culture without a familial organization, a kinship system, and a distinction between kin and non-kin.

Of course, human nature can change by means of evolution. No doubt about that. What it means to be a human being now is plausibly different from what it meant to be a human being 200,000 years ago, when *Homo sapiens* emerged. Probably our species could evolve in such a way that various aspects of human life would be changed. That is perfectly possible.

I already explained. Human nature may often be quite stubborn. The themes that underlie variation may be resilient. This is probably why human beings are interestingly similar.

Aku: *[Chuckle] That could be the tag line for your interview: Human Beings are Interestingly Similar.*

Edouard: Yes, this slogan does capture the real motivation behind my project.

Aku: *We already talked about universality and innateness. The third notion that is associated with human nature is human uniqueness. A lot of discussion about human nature seems to be about the differences between humans and non-human animals.*

Edouard: Traditionally one of the functions of the notion of human nature has been to demarcate human beings from non-human animals. There is no doubt about that, but I do not care very much for that function. Human beings are animals, and many aspects of human behavior are aspects of primate or even mammalian behavior in general.

Aku: *The way that you build up your concept of human nature, it does not really matter whether human nature traits are uniquely human or not.*

Edouard: Plenty of traits that are, in my view, part of human nature are actually characteristic of all primates or of all mammals. Some scientists, like Michael Tomasello, are really interested in what distinguishes humans from non-human animals.[11] They try to find what I like to call the magic bullet that distinguishes human beings from non-human animals. I have never found that goal incredibly interesting. Tomasello's work is always exciting, but the whole idea that we need to find what distinguishes us from them strikes me as

....

11 E.g., Tomasello, Michael. 2009. The Cultural Origins of Human Cognition. Cambridge: Cambridge University Press.

misguided. On the one hand, most, if not all, human traits are going to be homologous to traits found in other species. On the other, I am sure there are traits that, at least under some description, only human beings have. That claim is almost certain to be true, but why is it so important? I just cannot see it.

Aku: *There seems to be an extra-scientific motivation for this work. Perhaps there is a moral worry. If you read Frans De Waal, for instance, it seems quite clear. He wants to connect human morality with animal morality, because in his mind this connection will have certain good consequences.*

Edouard: It is plausible that philosophers and scientists may be driven to search for the magic bullet distinguishing human beings from non-human animals by a nonscientific concern, perhaps indeed by a moral concern. For De Waal the idea of continuity is clearly connected with some of his moral views.

Aku: *You have recently edited a volume called* Arguing about Human Nature.[12] *What's the story behind that?*

Edouard: The philosophical debate about human nature took a weird turn in the 1980s. In 1986 David Hull, an influential philosopher of biology, wrote a really good paper arguing against human nature, and that paper killed the philosophical debate about human nature for about twenty years.[13]

A few years ago—in 2007, I believe—Paul Griffiths, Karola Stotz, and others organized a workshop at Indiana University that brought together philosophers, psychologists, and behavioral ecologists. I realized at this workshop that, while Hull's paper was really quite good, it was a mistake to treat it as the last word on human nature. There was much more to be said about this topic than he had said in his paper. This realization led me to write my own paper on human nature, "A plea for human nature," which I published in

----

12 Downes, Stephen M., and Edouard Machery, eds. 2013. Arguing about Human Nature: Contemporary Debates. New York: Routledge. A very useful resource.

13 Hull 1986. The article is reprinted in Downes and Machery (2013).

Philosophical Psychology in 2008.[14] My paper responded to Hull and developed the nomological notion of human nature.

All in all, despite his positive contributions and his debunking of the bad, essentialist notion of human nature, Hull has had a negative impact on theorizing about human nature. He smashed philosophers' interest in human nature for a long time, and he prevented philosophers and, to some extent, scientists from developing new notions of human nature compatible with both evolutionary biology and genetics. We philosophers are just waking up from our dogmatic slumber about human nature, but there are encouraging signs that interest in human nature is picking up again: The 2015 conference of the International Society for the History, Philosophy, and Social Studies of Biology has many sessions on human nature; the University of Cambridge is organizing a conference on human nature at the end of 2015 and a book will result from this conference; and there is a summer school on human nature and biology next year in Germany. This is an exciting time to think about human nature.

Anyway, after having published my article in 2008, my next goal was to find a way to get other people excited about human nature, to bring back human nature as an important topic of discussion within philosophy and also more broadly within science. One idea was to publish a reader on human nature that would bring together the key articles from a forty-year period (roughly1970-2012). I wanted this reader to include the key texts that someone should have read in order to talk about human nature knowledgeably, starting with the sociobiology controversy and ending with recent controversies. Finally, I wanted it to be broad: It had to include various perspectives and to reflect live disagreements within science and philosophy. I think Steve Downes, my co-editor, and I have been quite successful.

There is another reason for the book. Many colleges in the United States have a course called "Theories of Human Nature." It is a common undergraduate course, which typically uses books going through conceptions of human nature since the ancient Greeks. These books summarize the Bible on human nature, Confucius on human nature, and so on.

....
14   Machery 2008. The article is reprinted in Downes and Machery (2013).

I have nothing against the Bible or Confucius or Plato. Quite the contrary, these are very interesting thinkers or traditions and from a historical point of view there is some value in being acquainted with them. But I do not think they are the kind of things we should be teaching undergraduates when we teach about human nature. An undergraduate course on human nature is a great occasion to expose students to what we know about human beings and to the live controversies about human beings in psychology, linguistics, evolutionary theory, biology, physiology, and anthropology. Basically, when we teach undergraduates about human nature, we should find inspiration in the sciences instead of outdated humanistic traditions.

On my view, we learn more about human nature from reading behavioral sciences or human behavioral ecology than from reading stories drawn from the Bible or Freud's misguided psychology.

Faculty teaching a course on human nature have the option of assigning *Arguing About Human Nature* in undergraduate courses about human nature. I hope that reader will be widely used.

Aku: *Sounds good. I have myself found the book an extremely good resource. Now, for my final question. We have talked a lot about the sciences. What might philosophy be able to contribute? You already talked about the methodological contributions, making sense of the concepts, and so on. Is there some content coming from philosophy that can contribute to the discussion?*

Edouard: I tend to have a relatively modest view of the role and contributions of philosophy. What philosophers are really good at is clarifying concepts. Helping lay people and scientists think more clearly about some issues is really an important and worthwhile contribution.

Of course, that does not mean that philosophers are limited to clarifying ideas. Another thing philosophers are pretty good at is synthesizing large swaths of literature to extract the big picture. Basically they attempt to abstract and articulate clearly a consistent, meaningful big picture out of messy, complex scientific areas. This is a second function philosophers are actually well equipped to fulfill. We rarely do the hard work of collecting and analyzing data as scientists do, and we have more time to read more broadly. That is a very useful contribution.

Aku: *It seems to me that in evolutionary behavioral, evolutionary social sciences, whatever you want to call them, there is a lot of theoretical, a lot of conceptual issues that have not been thought through.*

Edouard: It is one reason why, for a philosopher, the evolutionary behavioral sciences are such an exciting area. A lot of things are up for grabs conceptually. We can debate, engage, think through things, disagree. Scientists, some scientists anyway, are quite interested and sometimes receptive to philosophical contributions on these matters. Being a philosopher of science, I like to be able to do philosophy that interests scientists. I would be really disappointed if none of my work were ever of interest to scientists.

Aku: *The new generation of philosophers of science seems much more interested in interacting with the scientists than the old style philosophy of science in which scientists are like a foreign tribe to an anthropologist. The anthropologist says what they are actually doing. Similarly the philosopher says to the scientist, "Well, you're doing all sorts of things, but this is what you're actually doing. I'm giving you the theory of what you're actually doing."*

Edouard: It is indeed progress when philosophers can interact and work with scientists themselves instead of treating them only, as you rightly put it, as a tribe they need to study.

Suggested Readings

Downes, S. M., and E. Machery. 2013. Arguing about Human Nature: Contemporary Debates. New York: Routledge.

Griffiths, P., E. Machery, and S. Linquist. 2009. The Vernacular Concept of Innateness. Mind & Language 24:605-630.

Hull, D. L. 1986. On human nature. PSA: Proceedings of the Biennial Meeting of the Philosophy of Science Association 2:3-13. East Lansing, MI, 1984.

Jaggar, A. M. 1983. Feminist Politics and Human Nature. Blue Ridge Summit, PA: Rowman & Littlefield.

Machery, E. 2008. A Plea for Human Nature. Philosophical Psychology 21:321-330.

Richerson, P. J., and R. Boyd. 2008. Not by Genes Alone: How Culture Transformed Human Evolution. Chicago: University of Chicago Press.

Wilson, E. O. 2012. On Human Nature. Cambridge, MA: Harvard University Press.

 ## Interviewee: Kevin Laland

Bio. Kevin Laland is Professor of Behavioural and Evolutionary Biology at the University of St Andrews, where he is a member of the Centre for Social Learning and Cognitive Evolution, the Centre for Biological Diversity, the Institute for Behavioral and Neural Sciences, and the Scottish Primate Research Group. After completing his PhD at University College London, Laland held a Human Frontier Science Programme fellowship at UC Berkeley, followed by Biotechnology and Biological Sciences Research Council and Royal Society University Research fellowships at the University of Cambridge, before moving to St Andrews in 2002. He has published over 200 scientific articles and ten books on a wide range of topics related to animal behavior and evolution, particularly social learning, cultural evolution, and niche construction. He is an elected Fellow of the Royal Society of Edinburgh, a Fellow of the Society of Biology, and the recipient of both a European Research Council Advanced Grant and a Royal Society Wolfson Research Merit Award.

Slogan. *"I really do not feel there is much utility to a concept of human nature in this day and age. There has been this constant interplay of hundreds and thousands and perhaps millions of years between our socially constructed worlds and selection acting on our genomes.... [W]e have minds that are fashioned to absorb social information and to learn from others, and indeed, to structure our worlds in a way which is conducive to passing on the information to others."*

Agustín: *If you were approached by a colleague or friend or a student, and they ask you, "How would you define or think about human nature? Is there a human nature?" What would you tell them?*

Kevin: I would ask them to be more specific about the question they were asking me. I do not think the term "human nature" has any utility, really. I think it is a bit of an anachronistic term. Back in the 1950s, perhaps, when you had people like Konrad Lorenz arguing that there was a biological part to behavior and a learned part to behavior, then it might have made sense.[15] His is one way to think about behavior and cognition: you think that nature consists of characteristic or core aspects of a species that have a specific genetic inheritance, separate from social and experiential influences.

Really, nobody thinks that way anymore. Certainly no behavioral, developmental-minded biologist thinks that way. It is widely recognized that it is an inextricably interwoven complex of internal/external factors which bring about the development of an individual. You cannot talk about some aspect of it being inherent or unlearned or evolved. Every aspect of it involves interplay of genes and environment and with other internal factors and other social factors.

There have been experiments where people have tried to raise chimpanzees in human-like environments, raising them in the same way they have raised their kids, and they have not turned into humans. There have equally been some rather tragic cases of kids who have been raised—I am not sure raised is the right term—but who have developed in the absence of any human influence on their personal development. Again, we have not seen classic human behavior emerging.

If you want to understand where the characteristic aspects of humanity come from, we need to recognize that inextricably interwoven complex of internal and external factors. Our genes are not operating in isolation. They are switched on and off by our environment, which is very much socially constructed. Our learning is not something that happens in the absence of our biology or

....

15 "According to Lorenz, an Austrian ethologist, we can distinguish "instinctive" human behavior from learned behavior. His *On Aggression* (1966) is a classic.

unconnected to our biology. Learning is reliant on gene expression. These are things that are inherently interwoven. You need the right biology and the social influence to get humans.

If you want to partition aspects of development, we have to look at differences between individuals. There you can partition the variance that you see in behavior and cognition, and isolate a component attributable to genetic variation, but that is different from human nature. Equally, if you are interested in the dynamical interplay between biological and social processes, you can explore those in a variety of different ways, experimentally, theoretically. Again, that is different from asking questions about human nature. I really do not feel there is much utility to a concept of human nature in this day and age.

Agustín: *Do you think that there is some core or template that you can begin with to think about humanity or being human in a broader sense?*

Kevin: Well, if the issue is what might be distinctive about humans, I think that is a sensible question. It is a more specific question than asking, what is human nature? You can begin to ask that by making comparisons with other species, say, "Well, in what respects are humans different from other species?" We make comparisons most obviously with our closest relatives amongst the primates.

It is pretty obvious to me that any answer along those lines will emphasize our capacity for social learning and culture, including our capability to teach and communicate using language. In other words, a distinctive feature of humanity is not some core, inherent feature of our genetics. It is the way in which we are uniquely reliant on social influences, including socially constructed environmental influences, which impact on our learning, and on the way we organize and structure our world to facilitate learning in others. What is distinctive about humans is the interplay between biology and our socially constructed developmental environments.

Our genome has essentially been constructed by ancestral selection, which itself was foisted upon us through our social and cultural activities. There has been this constant interplay of hundreds and thousands and perhaps millions of years between our socially constructed worlds and selection acting on our genomes. So a distinctive feature of humanity is that we have minds that are fashioned to absorb social information and to learn from others, and indeed, to structure our worlds in a way which is conducive to passing on the information to others.

Agustín: *Then, in a large sense, the world of human agency would be a place to start to think about that.*

Kevin: It would certainly be. I would want to emphasize human agency as a key aspect of understanding the interplay that we have between our biological tendencies and our social tendencies. I would not want to single out humans as being unique in possessing that agency. There is nothing mystical or vitalist about my use of the term agency—it merely implies goal directed. I see agency as a distinctive feature of animals, and they will act in various ways on their environments to structure them, often in ways that benefit themselves, often in ways that benefit their descendants, and often in ways that facilitate learning in others. The agency that we have is very important to both our development and our evolution, but we are not unique in possessing it.

Agustín: *Is this what psychological and biological debates about Theory of Mind are about? What about psychological and philosophical debates about free will?*

Kevin: Well, I would guess that people work around working hypotheses about the rules underlying other individuals' behavior. Those other individuals might include dogs or ants or cars or even things that we know do not possess any sort of capability to think for themselves and certainly not in the manner that we might interpret them. I think it is a rule of thumb that we humans utilize as an effective predictive vehicle to how entities are likely to behave. I have no reason for thinking that the predictive power of that is necessarily reliant on Theory of Mind, although Theory of Mind may have evolved because it enhances our ability to predict or comprehend others' behavior.

However, I can imagine one being able to function effectively in predicting the behavior of other individuals, largely on the basis of learned associations between events. It is not inconceivable to me that, over and above the effectiveness of such prior experience, the ability to understand the mental states of others might confer benefits and predictive power. Certainly when it comes to social learning and teaching, which is obviously very important to human development, I could see some utility in being able to understand the mental states of others. If you are trying to teach them to solve some problem, it helps to understand where they are at in their addressing the problem at that point in time.

Agustín: *Thinking also along these lines, a lot of talk about what it means to be human has also invoked the notion of morality. Do you think that this role of morality and human relationships is important in thinking about human nature?*

Kevin: Oh, gosh. This is not a topic to which I have given much thought in the past. I would say, once again, it comes down to definitions. It comes down to what is and what is not morality and moral behavior. You can use evolutionary principles and methods to make sense of some aspects of human moral behavior. For instance, there has been some really nice work on cultural evolution and gene-culture co-evolution. We can see in what circumstances norms specifying how individuals should behave might be expected to appear in human societies, and we can see some utility, some functional utility, to possessing norms.

Exactly what those norms should be will vary from one place to the next. These are historical questions. They are not really informed by evolutionary biology as I see it, except with respect to the general ability and motivation to acquire norms. I can understand, as an evolutionary biologist, why there might be some utility in having the capacity for morality, but I do not think that biology has really much to say about what, specifically, those morals will be.

Agustín: *What do you think about Frans de Waal's and related arguments of human morality emerging from primate sociality?*

Kevin: I think that there may be some subjective interpretation of the data, which is minimally contentious. My little experience with chimpanzees, and primates in general, has been very different from what one might expect having read the literature.

If you read much of the literature in this area, you get a vision of this sophisticated, rich social behavior of primates and the complex cognition, which is immediately apparent to researchers like de Waal, and extensive behaviors imbued with these human-like tendencies. I do not see that in my observations of chimpanzees. Certainly they are perfectly capable of learning from each other. There are more elaborate claims associated with their coalitions. I have yet to see any evidence for much of it.

I see some degree of discontinuity between what we are witnessing in other animals and the extensive cooperation of humans. This is very interesting, because if you go back to the late nineteenth century, the challenge for Darwin was to make the case for human evolution by demonstrating that mental continuity was plausible; physically, anatomically there was little problem with showing that humans could have evolved. It was the mind of humans that seemed so separate from other animals.

Of course, back then we were far more dominated by a Cartesian view of the world than we are now.[16] The line that Darwin and his followers took was to search for animal-like tendency, brutish tendencies in humanity and clever behavior in other animals. They showed that animals were not just instinct-driven machines. They were capable of learning sophisticated behavior. I think this set up a mindset which has stayed with us and stayed with animal behavior researchers: in order to be a good evolutionist, one ought to be willing to entertain the idea that animals can do clever things, and we are looking for a kind of continuity in the mental abilities of animals and humans. Conversely, it is not good form for evolutionists to emphasize human uniqueness.

That research agenda that was, of course, established way before we knew anything about genetics or human evolution, for instance.

....

16 Cartesianism (after René Descartes) refers here to the tendency of drawing a sharp distinction between the mental and the physical, or bodily aspects of human beings.

We now know that chimpanzees and humans share a common ancestor approximately seven million years ago and that there are many other species which have shared a common ancestor more recently than humans who could equally have, or more plausibly have, human-like cognition. There is no need to continue with this agenda of trying to prove human evolution and showing what good evolutionists we are by showing sophisticated cognition on the part of other apes. I think that is a historical legacy that somehow we have not quite wiggled out of.

We ought to be prepared to look objectively at the behavior of other non-human primates and say, "Okay, well there are aspects of this which are very impressive and rich, but there nonetheless is a big gap between what humans can do and what other animals can do," rather than trying to bridge that gap through exaggeration.

Agustín: *I absolutely agree. Continuing with this, your work evidently points to the notion of plasticity in outcomes of human development. Is this plasticity or malleability something that is intrinsic? Is the plasticity something context based and you need to be human to have such plasticity or do you see plasticity as being much deeper and broader?*

Kevin: Well, I should preface my answer by saying that I have studied very few of life's creatures. The impression I get is that if you look at many invertebrates, there is a degree of plasticity there, indeed current thinking in evolutionary biology is that plasticity may be universal. Nonetheless, we can understand the behavior of many creatures in the world as relatively inflexible in the face of a broad range of environmental influences.

If we look amongst animalia, particularly the vertebrates, we will see high levels of plasticity, and if we look in large-brained creatures, we will again see high levels of plasticity relative to smaller-brained animals. Hence in many other cognitively sophisticated animals, plasticity is a defining, characteristic feature. I think plasticity would probably become increasingly important if you were to take an anthropocentric perspective and follow up the history of our lineage going forward in time. That leaves human behavior uniquely flexible, and context dependent.

Agustín: *You have talked a lot about the role of culture in human evolution and the role of culture in humans and the gene-culture co-evolution. Recently, biologists, psychologists, and anthropologists, although in different ways, have been talking about faith or religion or some such communal belief systems as almost naturally emerging on humans. Do you have any thoughts on that?*

Kevin: Not really.

Agustín: *[Laughter]*

Kevin: I mean, I guess ought to, really. I imagine that these systems have multiple functions, but I would guess amongst those functions is the need to control information within society. Once one has populations of individuals whose behavior is dominated by tradition, then it is easy to envisage that norms will emerge that start being prescriptive about the right way to behave.

I think, probably, something like a couple millions years ago, a more general tendency to teach evolved. We see instances of teaching appearing in animals. I am using the term "teaching" quite broadly to refer to behavior that functions to pass on information. Somewhere in our own lineage, we see this general capability for teaching emerging, and we have done a little bit of theoretical work on the conditions that might favor that.

It seems like the capacity for cumulative culture probably co-evolved with the capacity for teaching. Each favors the other. Cumulative culture broadens the range of circumstances under which teaching is favored by selection. It does so because it makes information available in the population that would be very hard for individuals to invent themselves, and therefore gives potential tutors good stuff to pass on to their pupils.

A very effective means of teaching is verbal instruction. In fact, when we see instances of teaching in humans, they are very rarely disassociated with verbal instructions, which is both the most efficient and most accurate means of transmitting information. It seems to be a short step from imagining teaching occurring initially amongst close relatives to imagining small groups of individuals, all of whom are reasonably closely related, passing information amongst themselves about the best way to forage for food or dig for tubers or coordinating each others' actions in some coordination challenge, maybe hunting for large prey.

It is a short step to envisaging how those groups might start being prescriptive in how things ought to be done. We know this method works, so this is the way we should be doing things. Norms for functioning effectively within society get established as traditions. In many cases, these norms become established, and we do not necessarily know why they work. We know that they work. Some rationale, one can visage, has been devised for why they work, and this might well bring in explanations that seem mystical to us here and now. Such explanations could have had the functional utility of ensuring that the individuals in a particular society adhere to rules that are effective and functional and do not allow other members of society to undermine those rules and thereby undermine the efficiency with which society operates, but also help to delineate that society from other societies.

That is the kind of scenario in which I would imagine religions, faiths, and other prescriptive kinds of institutions got started. I would image that these capabilities are very, very universal because all societies need rules.

Suggested Readings

Dean, L. G., R. L. Kendal, S. J. Schapiro, B. Thierry, and K. N. Laland. 2012. Identification of the Social and Cognitive Processes Underlying Human Cumulative Culture. Science 335:1114-1118.

Fogarty, L., P. Strimling, and K. N. Laland. 2011. The Evolution of Teaching. Evolution. 65:2760-2770.

Laland, K. N., K. Sterelny, J. Odling-Smee, W. Hoppitt, and T. Uller. 2011 Cause and Effect in Biology Revisited: Is Mayr's Proximate-Ultimate Dichotomy Still Useful? Science 334:1512-1516.

Laland, K. N., F. J. Odling-Smee, and S. Myles. 2010. How Culture Has Shaped the Human Genome: Bringing Genetics and the Human Sciences Together. Nature Reviews Genetics 11:137–148.

O'Brien M., and K. N. Laland. 2012. Genes, Culture and Agriculture: An Example of Human Niche Construction. Current Anthropology 53:434-470.

Interviewee: Patrick Bateson

Bio. Professor Sir Patrick Bateson, FRS, (born 1938) is a biologist and science writer. Bateson is emeritus Professor of Ethology at Cambridge University, former Head of King's College, Cambridge from 1988 to 2003 and president of the Zoological Society of London from 2004 until 2014. He received his BA in zoology and PhD in animal behavior from Cambridge University. Previous academic positions include a Harkness Fellowship at Stanford University and ten years as head of the Cambridge sub-department of Animal Behaviour. He was elected a Fellow of the Royal Society in 1983. He was knighted by the Queen of England in 2003 for his services to biology. Bateson is a research scientist and science popularizer, who has written many books and articles on ethology, animal welfare, measuring behavior, developmental biology, and genetics and gives public lectures and broadcasts.

Slogan. *"I hate the dichotomy between nature and nurture!"*

Agustín: *The first question I put out is the vaguest but probably the most important. That is, if approached by a colleague, or a family member, or someone in the public, and asked, "What is a human nature to you," how would you respond to that?*

Patrick: Well, I guess the first thing I would say is that the kind of folk biology which reduces everything to either nature or nurture is something that I have been battling to get rid of. *[Laughter]* This is because what we find is a close intertwining between the robust characters of human development and its very plastic aspects. We have lots and lots of examples of how the various mechanisms which are involved in robustness and the various mechanisms which are involved in plasticity are closely intertwined all the way through development. I hate the dichotomy between nature and nurture—but recognize how strongly a love of such classifications persist. The resulting debates are sometimes farcical. Consider two philosophers talking about human nature, and one says, "There are two kinds of people—those who like dichotomies and those who don't." The other one says, "That's rubbish." *[Laughter]*

Agustín: *I think it is very interesting that most people really want to have a strong, biological notion of human nature. Where should we start, if we want to think about this in a broader, integrative way?*

Patrick: Well, I think we should start by looking at exactly what happens in human development. In essence, a human will develop very much according to cues they get fairly early in development. If the mother is on a low plane of nutrition, she will have a baby who is small at birth and has a metabolism which is adapted to a low-nutrition environment. Conversely, if she is on a high plane of nutrition, she will have a large baby and well adapted to a high-nutrition environment. If those babies then develop in a very different kind of environment— weather changes, as it were—then, they could be in bad shape.

We know now that lots of people who are born small are much more prone to obesity, to heart disease, Type 2 diabetes, and all that kind of thing. In a low-nutrition environment, none of that happens. Conversely, if somebody is born large, and then suddenly enters a famine condition, they are much more likely to die. The women are much more likely to get rickets and have real problems with reproduction. Here you have a wonderful example of how early development shapes us. You cannot separate a single human characteristic out of this, because the whole of genetics depends on local conditions. The adaptation that you get is appropriate to the environment, providing there is also a correlation between one environment and the next.

Agustín: *So you are saying that human culture is a component of human nature and human development?*

Patrick: Well, it seems to me that the propensity for developing culture is something which goes along with enormously increased brain size. In about two million years, the human brain increased from 500cc to 1500cc. That is an enormous increase. I believe that our adaptability was a crucial driving process of our rapid cognitive evolution.

Once you have this capacity to be highly adaptable and then respond to new conditions in ways which are appropriate and also tell other members of your own group about what is variable and adaptive, you are in a really good position. There is a significant co-social component to adaptability and there are famous examples of this from animals too. Of course, once you get that tremendous benefit of (a) being able to respond to new conditions, and (b) to be able to transmit it to fellow members of your social group, a tremendously strong evolutionary pressure is established. If you have the resource to build a big brain and incorporate an awful lot of what you have experienced into creativity and innovation, then you have a powerful mechanism for the development of culture.

Agustín: *What do you think about the recent edited volume that Robin Dunbar and colleagues put out,* Social Brain, Distributed Mind?[17]

Patrick: I liked it. One of the things that I have been writing about recently is how play can be very important in driving creativity.[18] Creativity in its turn boosts innovation, which may then become a public good.

Creativity is interesting as it can grow out of novel experiences. The creative process can throw out loads of nonsense, probably 90 percent of the time, but it seems that that might be necessary to be extremely creative. You will get a lot of junk, as well as a load of stuff which is very, very interesting.

Agustín: *Do you think that this cycling creativity has low cost in the sense of, on average it throws all kinds of stuff out? If something sticks, it then becomes quite resolute. Again, that is an argument that reductionists are going to not grasp onto, because there is so much malleability. I like it.*

Patrick: It is very obvious that a lot of the things that both animals and humans do in the course of play get them nowhere. You talk to

17 Dunbar, Robin, Clive Gamble, and John Gowlett, eds. 2010. Social Brain, Distributed Mind. Oxford: Oxford University Press. See also the interview with Robin Dunbar in this chapter.

18 Bateson, Patrick, and Paul Martin. 2013. Play, Playfulness, Creativity and Innovation. Cambridge: Cambridge University Press.

any highly creative person, they will say most of the time the ideas they have are worthless. Every so often, because of their extraordinary searching around and fooling about, they get somewhere. When you are engaging with somebody else, where the environment is protected, there is no authority involved, it is very much like an enjoyable game where lots of silly ideas come up, but every so often, something really good is generated. Then, that can lead to something very important.

Creativity and play can also reveal something important about intelligence. Nice examples from the animal kingdom illustrate extraordinary cognitive capacities which nobody really suspected existed. You probably know some of the crow examples.

Agustín: *Yes. I was just in New Zealand. [Laughter]*

Patrick: In one case a Eurasian Jay was given a column of water in a transparent tube with a mealworm floating on top of the water which it could not quite reach. It was then given a pile of stones and a pile of cork. The jay dropped some stones into the column, raising the water level and bringing the mealworm closer, but occasionally it would drop a piece of cork into the tube. It very quickly, stopped using the cork, because it did not affect the water level. By using stones alone it was able to reach the mealworm. Nobody would have guessed they could do that kind of thing. That kind of cognitive ability, I think, particularly when it is accompanied by social learning, provides an interesting new perspective on the benefits of sociality and culture itself.

Agustín: *What do you think about people like Frans de Waal taking cognition and social adaptation and connecting them to the evolutionary trajectory of morality?*

Patrick: On the negative side, I think that interpreting everything in terms of kin selection has not been helpful.

Agustín: *[Laughter]*

Patrick: In that respect, it has led to a rather reductionist approach to the whole field of evolution of morality. Some aspects of our social behavior could be regarded as an emergent property of people acting together. So the adaptation is not necessarily at the individual level, the adaptation is at the group level. If that is the case, then it cannot be subverted by individual selection. You can have natural selection operating on many different levels, but in the case of morality, where you have the real need to maintain social cohesion, some kind of group selection would follow.

Agustín: *What about the argument by Joe Heinrich and others that this is where faith comes from or religion?*[19]

Patrick: I think it is interesting that some kind of religion crops up in almost every culture, probably in every culture. It provides a mechanism for sustaining group behavior. Have you ever seen a stage hypnotist working?

Agustín: *Yes.*

Patrick: What is interesting is that when you talk to people who have been hypnotized, they had been perfectly aware about what was going on, but they thought that it was the right thing to do. They went along with the hypnotist. Once he has selected his subjects by suggesting tougher and tougher things, which they were asked to obey, he gets his group to obey to perform bizarre acts very readily. While they are highly hypnotizable, in other contexts you can see others agreeing to do things, readily accepting somebody else's commands to behave in a certain way. For example, people who go on organized trips will happily accept directions to do what they are told.

Agustín: *[Laughter]*

Patrick: This is a good way of maintaining social cohesion. You can think about religion in that context, as a way of establishing authority.

....
19 See Atran, Scott, and Joseph Henrich. 2010. The Evolution of Religion: How Cognitive By-Products, Adaptive Learning Heuristics, Ritual Displays, and Group Competition Generate Deep Commitments to Prosocial Religion. Biological Theory 5:18-30.

Suggested Readings

Bateson, Patrick. 2015. Q & A Patrick Bateson. Current Biology 25: R180-R181.

Bateson, Patrick. 2015. Ethology and Human Development. *In*: Handbook of Child Psychology and Developmental Science, vol.1, Theory and Method. 7th edition. W. F. Overton, and P. C. M. Molenaar, eds. Pp. 208-243. Hoboken, NJ: Wiley.

Bateson, Patrick. 2014. Why are Individuals so Different from Each Other? Heredity, doi:10.1038/hdy.2014.103.

Bateson, Patrick. 2015. Thirty Years of Collaboration with Gabriel Horn. Neuroscience and Biobehavioral Reviews, doi: org/10.1016/neubiorev. 2014. 09019.

Bateson, Patrick. 2013. Evolution, Epigenetics and Cooperation. Journal of Biosciences, 38:1-10, doi: 10.1007/s12038-013-9342-7.

Bateson, Patrick. 2013. New Thinking about Biological Evolution. Biological Journal of the Linnean Society 112, 268-275, doi: 10.1111/bij.12125.

Interviewee: Robin Dunbar

Bio. Robin Dunbar read Psychology and Philosophy (PPP) at Magdalen College, Oxford University (1966-1969), and afterwards studied for a PhD in Behavioral Ecology in the Psychology Department at Bristol University (1970-1973). After a period as a postdoc working on primate behavioral ecology, he was awarded an SERC (now BBSRC) University Research Fellowship, which he held in the Zoology Department, Cambridge University (1977-1982), while working on the behavioral ecology of ungulates (principally klipspringer in East Africa and feral goats in Scotland) in Sociobiology Project at the King's College Research Centre. Subsequently, he held a docent post in the Institute of Zoology, Stockholm University (1984) and a Research Fellowship in the Zoology Department, University of Liverpool (1985-1987), before taking up a lectureship and later a Chair in the Department of Anthropology, University College London (1987-1994). He then held chairs in the Psychology Department (1994-1998) and the School of Biology (1998-2007) at the University of Liverpool, before returning to Oxford as Professor of Evolutionary Anthropology in the School of Anthropology (2007-2012). He is now professor of Evolutionary Psychology in the Department of Experimental Psychology at the University of Oxford (2012-2017). His principal research interests are in social evolution in mammals, with particular reference to ungulates, primates, and humans, and the ways in which ecology, behavior, cognition, and neurobiology interact. He was Co-Director of the British Academy's Centenary Research Project "Lucy to Language: The Archaeology of the Social Brain" (2003-2010). He was elected a Fellow of the Psychology Section of the British Academy in 1998.

Slogan. "Brain is the engine of behavior."

Agustín: *If a colleague or friend or a student asked you how you would define or describe a human nature, what kind of response would you give them?*

Robin: I suppose, in the end, it is an interface between cognition and behavior that makes up humans. By definition, with humans human nature extends beyond the individual and encompasses at least some aspects of society and organizations, like religion.

Agustín: *What is the origin, the core or basal template for this view of human nature?*

Robin: For me, it comes from the brain and not many other places, because that is the engine of behavior. Of course, we learn certain kinds of things socially, but by virtue of becoming enculturated during childhood. At the end of the day, all that is still instilled in the individual's brain. It has to be. It's almost back to Tinbergen's four whys.[20] There are

....

20 Tinbergen's four questions divide up why something happens as follows: a) the evolutionary "why," b) the ontogenetic (developmental) "why," c) the proximate "why," and d) the functional "why."

different levels of explanation here, which are often seen as in conflict with each other, in opposition to each other. But in reality they are not: culture, learning and brains are just different levels of the same system.

Agustín: *A lot has been made recently about human distinctiveness or human uniqueness. How do you see that as playing into discussions on human nature?*

Robin: To quote Professor Foley, every species is unique.[21] Humans are just another unique species. I guess the bottom line is that we inevitably share lots of things in the way we work and behave, and how we function with the other primates unavoidably, by virtue of being a primate. Like every species, there are things we do that nobody else does. I suppose the best example of this is culture. One has to add, however, that although most other primates aspire to a kind of culture, it is not even close to the same league as human culture. This, of course, is something we have to explain. What can, let us say, great apes or monkeys or dolphins do and how does that differ from what humans do? The question is how similar are these species to humans and whether the same mechanisms we see in humans also work in these other species. In addition, there is another question about all those other things that humans do, but which clearly no other species does. You have to ask why and how.

Agustín: *Would you pin some of this distinctiveness or uniqueness to the brain?*

Robin: I am afraid so. With my psychologist's hat on, I have to say it is all in the brain. Well, in the sense that, clearly, it is the individual who is doing the behaving. That said, of course, there are aspects of behavior that are not in the brain—and I am not sure they are in anybody's definition—namely, the substantively social components of behavior. This is obviously true about many other species as well: for any monkey or great ape and other species, too, no doubt, anything an organism does is done in a social context. The social context imposes constraints and as such, it is part of the adaptive suite of things that they do. Since 1975 we have mainly been engaged in working out

---

21 By definition, a species is a unique branch in an evolutionary lineage.

the nuts and bolts of how individual-level behavior works. I think we can now once more begin to think seriously about putting the individual back into the group again. People are doing that now.

Agustín: *Excluding E. O. Wilson. [Laughter]*

Robin: I am not talking about just kin selection here. We need to account for the whole social context in which organisms' decision-making has to be done.

Agustín: *Just to push this slightly further. In the recent edited volume that you put out in 2010,* Social Brain, Distributed Mind, *you argue that there is a clearly distinctive human pattern that ratchets up in a way different from any other such pattern in social organisms.*

Robin: I think that's true. I think you actually see it already in primates. We should, perhaps, see humans as the kind of end point of a long sequence of jumps in the size and power of mental machinery. At the same time, however, these jumps in cognitive evolution build on deeply rooted universal primate capacities.

Agustín: *A lot of philosophers and theologians have talked about free will. Recently, psychologists have thought about human agency and human evolution, and sometimes there are connections drawn between those. What do you think about this concept?*

Robin: Once upon a time, I used to be a philosopher. *[Laughter]* That was my actual academic background a long time ago.

I just do not know what to say about free will. It is a slippery topic best left to philosophers. I suppose I now have a scientist's pragmatic view of it. Whatever free will is and whether we have it or not does have an answer, but in practice it actually does not impinge upon what I do when I analyze human behavior, or anybody else's behavior. I think I can get away with a view like that. It is a sort of classic jump, as it were, that we all do in evolutionary biology, or behavioral ecology: when we examine a particular behavior, we simply assume that there is a mechanism somewhere responsible for it. The mechanism itself could be learned or it could be genes, but we do not really have to answer that question. We can do a lot of work without having to worry about it.

Agustín: *Recently, people like Frans de Waal and others have used primate sociality and underlying social complexities to make an argument for the evolution of morality and ethics. How do you see this kind of argument about morality related to human nature?*

Robin: Well, in the human sense, the answer to me is obvious. Morality has to do with large-scale communal cohesion. This is the issue about putting the individual back into the social context. I think that it is critical with primates, because of their peculiarly bonded societies. The same argument would apply to any other taxonomy that has similarly bonded groups. How do you keep the group coherent and immune to freeriders? With humans, you've got a scale problem to deal with. It's a coordination problem on a large scale.

It seems to me—and this may be my primatologist's perspective, if you like—that your functional reasons for forming your community are the classic primate explanations, namely resource defense or predation avoidance, and these are mainly coordination problems. Your problem is exactly the issue of how to keep large numbers of individuals coordinated. We have that problem all the time in social, political, military and everyday life, on the football field, whatever. Morality simply comes into that, in my view, as one of the many mechanisms designed to try and force the members of the community to stick to the common agreement, an implicit social contract.

Agustín: *What do you think about the role or structure of plasticity in human nature?*

Robin: It is crucial. That's true of life in general, because the whole point of having a big brain is to be phenotypically plastic, right? The scale of that plasticity is simply a function, presumably, of the size of the computer you can bring to bear to do the everyday calculations you need to do or decide not to do. Otherwise, it is obviously better and cheaper to automate it, with everything done genetically. But for all social mammals—primates in particular and humans the more so—the plasticity of behavior is the beginning and the end of the story.

Agustín: *You mentioned this earlier, this idea of culture as being crucial for what humans do and how they do it. How do you see the relationship between cultural and evolutionary processes?*

Robin: Best ignored. *[Laughter]* It depends what your question is. For me, it is a trivial issue in the sense that if you are bringing to bear the classic behavioral ecologist's perspective, all you want to know is, "Is the organism acting optimally given the various constraints acting on it?" The choice is between the various tradeoffs and choices it has to make. It makes no difference at all whether your behavior is learned socially, by trial and error or determined genetically. Sure, it is an interesting question to ask for those who are interested in development. I do not very often ask developmental questions, because I'm mainly interested in what adults do—particularly in the social context. How you get there clearly is a major issue in the sense that it involves lots of plasticity. You, therefore, inevitably have a major learning process. But you want to take that as given. Tinbergen's four whys again.

This much has been very clear for a long time, especially in the context of the social brain. The length of the socialization period (weaning to first reproduction) is a better predictor of neocortex size in primates than the length of the period of parental investment (gestation plus lactation), even though the latter is the best predictor of total brain size. In other words, for species that have big brains, the hardware alone is about as useful as a computer with no software. The software programming that goes on during socialization—the learning of social skills by experience—is crucial. It is clear that in humans we consciously learn many of the things we do. I guess this goes back to the heart of the Santa Barbara perspective,[22] an extreme modular perspective versus the kind of evolutionary anthropology or behavioral ecology view, which tends to view the organism as infinitely flexible. The latter assumes that, unless we can prove otherwise, an organism can do anything, or at least evolve the capacity to do anything.

....

22 The perspectives in modularity of the mind and evolutionary psychology promulgated at University of California at Santa Barbara, home to theorists such as John Tooby and Leda Cosmides.

I feel sometimes there is a sense in which, at least in functional terms, behavior can appear to be modular, but it does not mean that it is modular in the instinctive sense—in other words, you were born with it. Rather, it may simply mean that the decision process has become automated through practice. This was well understood in rat learning psychology: behavior gets overlearned. If you overlearn something, it is very difficult to unlearn it because it becomes automated, and that's as true of humans as it is of rats. Functionally, one might say that such behaviors really are modular in a genuinely meaningful sense. In many ways, the whole argument about what is modular and what is not is a bit futile, because of terminological confusions. Well, Santa Barbara folk were probably a bit over the top in claiming modularity in a very strong sense.

In adults, you may well be able to point to bits of the brain that are always active when an individual is doing something, solving a coordination game or whatever. That does not, however, necessarily mean that it has always been like that since birth. A learning machine like the brain is quite capable of creating its own neural networks. I suppose, in a way, this issue comes down to one of the big questions underpinning this whole area: "Is human nature instinctive or do you learn it?" It is fine to argue about it, if this question bothers you. But for me, I really do not care much either way: functional explanations hold true either way: the developmental question simply places limits on how fast behavior can change. The danger is that you simply get into the same kind of unproductive sophistry as bedeviled the nature/nurture debate. Each party spends their time trying to outdo or undermine the other, and in the end getting nowhere.

There are, of course, potentially important implications that we might want to know about. If the brain is very hardwired and you cannot change behavior, then you will never be able to change human society significantly. If, on the other hand, brains are modestly flexible, then it is possible to change society and human behavior by education. And, as economists are well aware, people will do what you want them to do if you give them a big enough incentive. I guess the bottom line is that it probably does pay to have certain very basic cognitive processing functions genetically built in, but there is no point in paying the cost of having a massive brain if you can't use it to tweak your behavior to the momentary costs and benefits of the circumstances you happen to find yourself in.

Agustín: *That actually segues nicely to this next question. A lot of people across multiple disciplines have recently become very interested in this concept of belief systems, such as religion and the possible naturalness of it. What are your thoughts on that?*

Robin: For me, religion is part of the grand scheme needed to enforce a very large-scale coordination problem. Of course, basic mechanisms, like the cheat detector mechanism, are there and clearly work. Nevertheless, it always has struck me that you have two options with these large-scale coordination problems—two ways of enforcing conformity to the collective decision. One is essentially punishment. This is the military solution: you have draconian discipline, you force people to do what they are supposed to do. The other is the complete opposite: you persuade people to sign up to the grand project. If people sign up voluntarily to the grand project, they will toe the party line much more conscientiously than any form of punishment will ever make them. You can make laws as draconian as you like, but people will continue to break the law all the time if they see doing so as being to their advantage. It is the big problem that bedevils conservation, the so-called poacher's dilemma.[23]

You can impose the harshest penalties you like, but actually you will not stop people cutting down trees and shooting animals, if their need makes it worth their while taking the risk and they are not going to get caught every time. Such negative ways of enforcing conformity are always going to be imperfect and susceptible to being undermined. The alternative way of enforcing conformity,

....

23 The poacher's dilemma (Messer, K. D. 2000. The Poacher's Dilemma: The Economics of Poaching and Enforcement. Endangered Species Update 17:50-56) refers to the fact that it always pays to poach rather than adhere to the collective decision to preserve habitats or their wildlife because an immediate return from poaching is always preferable to a future benefit, especially in an uncertain world where you may not live to see the longer term benefit.

which involves persuading people to sign up to the grand project, are always going to be much more effective because people then conform of their own volition and are more committed to doing so. There is a paradox in there. Actually, you are forcing people to inhibit their rational selfish interests on the expectation, to be fair, that if you persuade them to do that everybody will benefit more in the long run. It is the classic motivation problem issue. It seems to me we just have a suite of things that allow us to engage in this positive strategy. There is a whole suite of mechanisms, built round the endorphin system, whose functions seem designed to create conformity by building a sense a belonging to the community. The endorphin system works in exactly the same way in humans as it does in all other primates: laughter, music in particular, and then the rituals of religion all create the same sense of intense relationships as grooming does in primates—they just do it on a bigger scale.

I am much less interested in the cognitive science of religion, which I find tediously boring, and I might even say very bad science for most part of it.[24] It ignores, it seems to me, the fundamental driver of evolution. Most people do not go around having great metaphysical discussions on cognitive issues; they "do" religion instinctively and emotionally. It is the rituals where the origins of religions clearly lay. All ancient religions are of a practical, experiential kind; they do not have metaphysics, they do not have a theology, they do not even have gods. They are just performance religions and they are mostly intensely emotional, and because of that they seem to be very powerful. It is clear that, in people like the !Kung,[25] trancedancing is used explicitly when things have got fractious in the community, as a mechanism for healing those rifts so that the community sticks together.

I think the problem is that we have not really understood how to deal with evolution in the context of religion. The actual function of

....

24 The cognitive science of religion is a field dominated by cognitive scientists, psychologists, and other social scientists and a few neuroscientists who seek to advance the naturalistic study of religion. See Chapter 1.

25 The !Kung are an ethnic group of foragers in Southern Africa who have been the subject of much anthropological study.

religion does not seem to fit well with the classic selfish gene model. I think it is precisely this selfish gene model of evolution that has caused a lot of people to say that religions are nonfunctional maladaptive byproducts. I just do not think that is right. The opposite, in fact: religions are actually incredibly well adapted and, for better or worse, have played a crucial role in human evolution. But in order to understand this, you have to take a multilevel selection perspective—not in a David Sloan Wilson kind of slightly muddied way, but as a proper multilevel selection process where the payoffs are still at the level of the individual gene ultimately. We could say the cost accounting is at the level of the gene, but the benefits accrue at the group level through the marginal benefits gained by group coordination. What that imposes on the individual is a classic coordination problem dilemma.

In order for the communal solution to work, the individuals have to be willing to sacrifice some of their own immediate selfish interests. Their engagement with the group is a tradeoff. This is all about short-term versus long-term perspectives. Humans are not good at taking long-term perspectives. It just seems to me you have to have mechanisms that make large scale coordination possible by constraining freeriders—this is my hypothesis, anyway—because we have needed to evolve these in order to evolve very large community sizes. Particularly so once you go beyond communities larger than about 150—when you start to get villages and things and kingdoms forming.[26] Every time the scale of human communities has been ramped up, we've had to evolve mechanisms that solve the coordination problem in order to get the system to work. Without the coordination problem being solved, the balance would have tipped back to the individual selfishness side and the whole thing would have fallen apart. Humans would have remained trapped at a lower level of community size.

In addition to religion, it seems to me that there is also another big communal bonding thing. This is the combination of storytelling and a common worldview. We pick this up really strongly, on a small scale, in the research on the nature of friendships. This is

26   150 is the famous Dunbar number.

the 'birds of a feather' model of friendship. It comes out of sociology, I think, but we have really nice data showing the effects of this at the level of dyadic friendships. Shared interests and worldview (moral views, political views, etc.) turn out to be two important dimensions that are really important in creating strong friendships. That is supportive friendships—friendships as opposed to kinship relationships. The only benefit of such relationships is in terms of mutual support. To me, friendships are all part of this wider story of community cohesion. This perhaps gives you a bit of a bridge into the theology side. You are sitting around the campfire and start the storytelling: moral tales, or origin stories, or stories about your experiences on spirit travels during trance dances. What you exchange and share in these contexts is probably more important than anything else in creating a sense of community, because they tell you why we hang together. We belong to the same community *because* we believe the same things. We know the rules of baseball or cricket, so we belong to the same community, we can trust each other.

Agustín: *Are you familiar with Brian Boyd's book?*[27]

Robin: Yes, but I confess that I have not read it. There are a number of people in the literature area who have been using an evolutionary perspective to understand literature. Anyway, it's always seemed to me there's a lot of really interesting questions one can ask about literature. One is whether stories—they say there are only six or seven plots for novels—relate to natural human fitness related interests. Are they just moral stories because one of the purposes of storytelling is the community creating ways of telling people what they mustn't do and what awful things will befall them if they do? That obviously slides very quickly into religious versions of the fire and brimstone variety.

Equally, there are intriguing things going on in the storyteller's mind, whether that is Shakespeare or a casual storyteller at a campfire—they are all trying to put across to other minds an interesting story. So what makes a good story? Why are some better at this and

27 Boyd, Brian. 2009. On the Origin of Stories: Evolution, Cognition, and Fiction. Cambridge, MA: Harvard University Press.

others not? Is it the extent to which the storyteller can push the audience to their cognitive limits of understanding? And is the difference between Shakespeare and a jobbing pulp novelist simply their capacity to push their audience to their limits—which probably means that the storyteller has to be in the super league cognitively? Everybody can enjoy a good novel, but very few people can write them. You really have to be exceptional in your ability to understand other minds to be a great novelist or dramatist. I think it's a hugely overlooked area that offers masses and masses of really interesting questions, both in terms of evolutionary function and in terms of psychological mechanisms.

This actually relates back to the religion issue. There is some suggestion from neuroimaging studies looking at romantic relationships that areas within the prefrontal cortex, in particular, get shut down when you are thinking of your romantic partner. What makes this interesting is that this is exactly the same bits of the brain that are involved in mindreading and allow us to figure out whether others are cheating on us. It's as though switching them off allows us just to get on with it and go for this relationship!

It looks like a classic case, to me, of the kind of tradeoff you have to make when you have to cope with multilevel selection on a big scale, a large-scale community level coordination problem. You have to be able to switch the rational side down somehow in order to just force people to adhere to the common good. Otherwise, it just wouldn't work. You have to have a mechanism that undermines a little bit of the heavy selfish gene mechanism in the brain that otherwise drives the system. It is really back to classic Hamilton,[28] whose original conception of inclusive fitness was in terms of neighborhood-modulated fitnesses, for which the conventional kin selection story is a useful (and usually more tractable) approximation.

....

28 In his two classic papers (Hamilton, W. D. 1964. The Genetical Evolution of Social Behavior, I and II. Journal of Theoretical Biology 7:1-52), the evolutionary biologist W. D. Hamilton revolutionized the way we think about the evolution of behavior by introducing the concepts of inclusive fitness and kin selection.

Suggested Readings

Dunbar, R. I. M. 2014. Human Evolution. Gretna, LA: Pelican Books.

Dunbar, R. I. M. 2014. The Social Brain: Psychological Underpinnings and Implications for the Structure of Organizations. Current Directions in Psychological Research 24:109-114.

Dunbar, R. I. M. 2012. Evolution of Social Networks. New Scientist 214:1-8 [Instant Expert #21].

Dunbar, R. I. M. 2010. How Many Friends Does One Person Need? Dunbar's Number and Other Evolutionary Quirks. Cambridge, MA: Harvard University Press.

Dunbar, R. I. M. 2006. We Believe.... New Scientist 189 (2536): 30-33.

Dunbar, R. I. M., L. Barrett, and J. Lycett. 2005. Evolutionary Psychology: A Beginner's Guide. Oxford: OneWorld.

Gamble, C., J. Gowlett, and R. I. M. Dunbar. 2014. Thinking Big: The Social Evolution of the Modern Mind. London: Thames & Hudson.

Interviewee: Phillip Sloan

Bio. Dr. Sloan is an Emeritus Professor in the Program of Liberal Studies and a Professor in the Program of History and Philosophy of Science at the University of Notre Dame. He was originally trained in marine biology and oceanography with a specialization in evolutionary biology, before moving into the history and philosophy of science. He received his doctorate in philosophy from the University of California, San Diego. He studies the history and philosophy of the life sciences in the modern period, and has written extensively on the history of evolutionary theory, Enlightenment natural history, and the history and philosophy of recent genetics and molecular biology. Dr. Sloan is a Fellow and past President of Section L of the American Association for the Advancement of Science and a Fellow of the Reilly Center for Science, Technology and Values at Notre Dame. His most recent publications include *Controlling Our Destinies: Histor-*

ical, Philosophical, Ethical, and Theological Perspectives on the Human Genome Project (2000) and *Creating a Biophysics of Life: The Three-Man Paper and Early Molecular Biology* (with Brandon Fogel) (2012), and he is the primary editor and contributor to *Darwin in the Twenty-First Century: Nature, Humanity, God* (with Gerald McKenny and Kathleen Eggleson) (due Fall, 2015).

Slogan. *"Human Nature has many dimensions. It is simultaneously a dynamic product of the unique kind of posture we have in the world and the remarkable phenomenon of self-reflection."*

Agustín: *What is your background and how did you get interested in the idea of human nature?*

Phillip: My original background is in zoology, biological oceanography, and ecology of the deep seas. I was a deep-sea biologist. I then moved into the history and philosophy of science. My primary area of work now is in the history and philosophy of life science, particularly eighteenth, nineteenth, and now into the twentieth century. I have in recent years been getting into some more recent issues of molecular biology, things like that.

I have been interested in the questions of anthropology and human nature since I was an undergraduate and heard Louis Leakey give a series of lectures on his way to the Chicago Darwin Symposium in 1959.[29] This initiated an interest in the human sciences.

Agustín: *If a student or colleague or family member asked you about human nature, what kind of response would you give them?*

Phillip: That is a very big, cosmic question. First of all, I will say I do believe there is a human nature. So I am not a pluralist here. I think human nature has a lot to do with the concept of species and things of this kind. Also, I am an evolutionist, so I also have an evolutionary view on human nature.

....

29 Louis Leakey (1903-1972) was British paleoanthropologist who was famous for his work on early human evolution in Africa.

Philosophically, I would say that my basic orientation would be considered neo-Aristotelian. Aristotle's analysis of soul/body relationship, the nature of life and so forth, still makes, to me, an awful lot of sense.[30]

I think that the Aristotelian framework also gives a foundation for ethical issues, the concept of natural law, and of natural rights.[31] I think it does also engage, in some ways, what I would call the etiological perspective on human beings, that is, it bears in some respect on where humans come from, even though he is not an "evolutionary" thinker.

I think that we cannot get the answer to the question "What is human nature?" simply from the natural sciences. I think that empirical data and the natural sciences have a lot to do with some of the ways we think about human nature, and it charts the changes in human evolution. I also think that fundamental philosophy, reflection, things like this are also very much components of any answer to that question.

Agustín: *Where would you say that the template or the core of human nature, if there is one, comes from? How would you go about describing the underpinnings of that core?*

Phillip: Well, I think fundamentally it is a dynamic product of a unique kind of posture we have in the world. That is one dimension, and a physical answer. The other dimension is the remarkable phenomenon of self-reflection. One might say that we can speak about all kinds of animals that know things and do things and have

....

30 According to Aristotelianism, all organisms consist of basic matter and forms or structures. It is the structure that provides the organisms with their distinctive capacities, powers, and goals. Most Aristotelians would agree that organisms, along with all other individual things, have natures or essences, which consist of features and powers that are essential to that particular class or kind. In the human case, the "soul" is the form or the structure of the body that gives the body the distinctive human capacities of thinking, willing, feeling, and so on.

31 Furthermore, Aristotelians often think that organisms have natural goals or ends and argue that the objectivity of these goals and ends forms the basis of natural functions, rights, and moral laws.

intentions. But I think only human beings know that they know, in other words, they are capable of many orders of intentionality. With that, the whole complex of language, expression, face-to-face contact, and so forth come into play with our unusual physical form of "being in the world."

If I would put this in Aristotelian terms, I would say that to be human involves an integration of both mental and physical aspects. However, those functions of thinking and knowing are the core of human nature. Of course, a person can be a human being and be lacking in those sorts of things. I am not excluding humanness from those who lack thinking and knowing. What I am saying is that there is something about a full realization of what it is to be human that essentially involves the actualization of such functions and activities.

Agustín: *Given your view, would you say that there is something like human uniqueness or distinctiveness?*

Phillip: Yes, I would say that. I do not mean that we are disembodied entities or minds floating around, so I am not a Cartesian in that respect.[32] What I mean to say is that we are not just simply our physical selves. I think to be human involves the integration of physical and mental and behavioral aspects. However that came about, I think that is what is remarkable about being human.

Agustín: *Recently, in philosophy and psychology, and of course in theology, there has been a re-emergence of the notion of free will. What do you think about free will and the extent to which human agency is linked with human nature?*

Phillip: I think free human agency is so fundamental that science itself would be impossible unless we recognize this freedom. Whenever I read views that say everything is determined, I am very interested to know exactly what is the status of that statement itself. Supposedly it is the action of a free agent who is not determined. I think that is certainly part of it: free agency is part of this remarkable freedom we have, and however it has emerged, it enables us to do science.

....

32 A Cartesian refers to one who follows the core ideas of the French philosopher René Descartes.

The person who has been important for some of my thinking on this is Immanuel Kant,[33] who comments in one place that "I see everything to be determined, yet I know myself to be free." I think there is an important insight there and it positions our science and scientific views.

I certainly am a person who believes in free will, although there are environmental determinants and things that happen—historical events, our own autobiography—that have a lot to do with how we react to things. None of these can be excluded, yet I think there is some sort of fundamental core of human freedom.

Agustín: *In relation to this sort of core and this idea of human distinctiveness or uniqueness, do you see a relationship or a role of morality in human nature?*

Phillip: Certainly. I mean, I'm not simply saying that morality simply comes out in biology in some way. I think that there is another component, and this involves the whole question of self-reflection. We can, for example, think about something like public executions, which may have once been popular. Now we reflect more deeply about such things as this, and no longer accept them. This is a result of moral reflection that emerges through the discussions of theology, philosophy, culture, aesthetics, and things of this kind.

I do think that there is some argument also emerging from a neo-Aristotelian view—and this is where I think even Darwin has some interesting insights—that there are ways in which we can respond and act ethically without reflection, as in the case of the person that throws himself or herself under the subway to save a child, actions that are not simply based on calculation and reasoning out some kind of moral theory. I think that ethics is certainly deeply involved in the question of what is human nature and the basis it supplies for ethics. I think that is where both the notion of natural rights and some kind of natural law ethic are involved.

Agustín: *What do you think about, given this context of where we've come so far in the conversation, the idea of a role instructor for malleability or plasticity in human nature?*

---

33   Immanuel Kant (1724-1804) was a major modern German philosopher.

Phillip: I think that you can't be an evolutionist without thinking that there has to be some on-going dialectic between historical context and reflection. If we talk about human nature as simply biological physiology, that is a pretty conservative, slow changing sort of thing. I think that the combination forms a very dynamic process.

Of course, there is a lot of cultural conditioning. I mean, anybody that studies other cultures or even experiences other cultures knows that the world is divided up differently on the basis of all sorts of linguistic and cultural factors. But one reason why I resist what I would call structuralism and post-structuralism is the fact that it leads to the dissolution of the human being into structures which have no grounding themselves, no permanence. In that sense, I'm not a hard essentialist, but I still think there is some sort of fundamental core of human nature that we can define and that is a reference point for political theory, ethical theory, the concept of natural rights, and so forth.

Agustín: *How then, when you position—I mean, there are those who argue that human nature is culture. How do you see this?*

Phillip: Well, I just think that is false in one respect. I mean, I think human nature has an enormously important cultural component. I think underneath there is still something that we can identify as unchanging, at least within a limited time-horizon.

To take one example, reading a Confucian text or a Taoist text leads me to feel that I'm in a totally different world than that of the author of that text. But there are some ways in which I think things can be translated such that there are certain fundamental human goods, human interests, and things like this that we can relate to, even in spite of what would be linguistic and cultural differences that one can emphasize. Of course, it would become more extreme if one is dealing with Aboriginal cultures. How they divide up the world and how their language relates to the world is quite unlike mine.

I said that is where I would reject what I think is the structuralist, post-structuralist view that one can simply dissolve human nature into culture and language and things of this kind without anything left.

Agustín: *What do you think about the sort of patterns or presence and interaction of faith and human nature, culture, and faith?*

Phillip: These are, of course, fairly enormous questions and they also take different configurations. I am a practicing Catholic Christian. I think that there is certainly an interaction of faith with these other factors. I think there's a lot of thinking that needs to be done on these matters, but I think that some kind of traditionalist, at least traditionalist Christian, Judeo-Christian point of view would be holding some notion that there is a concept of creation that's involved, something special about human beings that isn't just simply a product of natural forces and material. And I would accept this.

That is where I would break with Aristotle and the kind of naturalist thinking one can get from a certain reading of Aristotelian biology, so that I do think there's something more involved. How that gets worked out and interpreted is sometimes very clumsily discussed by people. I think there are some interesting, sophisticated discussions going on that are trying to work that point out within a different theological framework. I have been interested in even trying to explore a little bit of that, some of my own recent writings.

Agustín: *What do you think about the attempts by Atran and Henrich[34] and others to sort of apply this sort of evolutionary, psychological, mental module approach to explain faith?*

Phillip: These are efforts, you might say, to explain it away. I mean, ultimately it's a kind of debunking strategy. I don't think it's adequate for the same reason I do not think evolutionary ethics is adequate. Evolution may be able to give us some interesting insights, but it is not an explanation. It might be able to tell us conditions for religious faith and so forth, but it is not an explanation of these beliefs.

The problem I have with evolutionary ethics is that it gives some interesting insights but it doesn't really deal with the kind of questions that I think develop from philosophy, theology, and self-reflection about these questions. These lead us beyond simply giving, given the causal scientific accounts.

....

34 Atran, Scott, and Joseph Henrich. 2010. The Evolution of Religion: How Cognitive By-Products, Adaptive Learning Heuristics, Ritual Displays, and Group Competition Generate Deep Commitments to Prosocial Religions. Biological Theory 5(1):18-30.

Agustín: *Would you engage the recently popular gene culture evolution theory in the same way? What about the argument that there's a genic inheritance system and a cultural inheritance system and the two are not the same but influence one another?*

Phillip: I'm uneasy with what I would call strong gene-centered notions of evolution. I think the whole concept of the gene is such a complex idea and I'm much more a developmental biologist and consider the concept of genetics involved with developmental biology. I think developmental genetics is much more interesting to me than the kind of genetics that typically underlie these discussions of genetics and culture.

If you wanted to talk about whether there is some sort of determination of our physical being and our culture, there is an interesting connection between those two. I don't know if gene-talk, in the ordinary sense, is adequate. I think there is a dynamic relationship between culture in all of its ramifications and our biology.

I've been observing this connection with my great-grandchildren. I have a pair of identical twin great-grandchildren. I've become very interested in thinking about these questions of nature and culture, even the differentiations it makes, as I see the development these two genetically identical children.

It is clear that one could put a chimpanzee and an infant, at a certain level, together and see many similarities. There are many similarities. Then when the child stands up and realizes if I do that, I've got these hands free, things change remarkably. There is this remarkable transformation that begins to develop into such an enormous gap. It's still tied to the physical being, but also to a remarkable transformation that is occurring.

I think that there's something—I said that's why in a certain way I'm a neo-Aristotelian—in the concept of the soul-body relationship as a form-matter relationship in a teleological relationship. This is much more interesting than thinking of two substances stuck together. I think in child development is where one begins to see that. There's certainly something to that.

Agustín: *That leads to this: I'm working with this larger cluster of some other colleagues here at Notre Dame in this larger multimedia analysis on human nature and these projects. It's all centered around*

Frankenstein, both Mary Shelley's version and of course, the James Whale's movies. I've been asking many people, after having this discussion about human nature, do you see any comparisons or corollaries or ways to think through this using the themes put forward either in the novel or even the movies?

Phillip: In fact, I have even opened up a chapter in the book I am writing at the moment with a reference to the Frankenstein story. This is where I begin with the question of life and what is life? Here you have an assembly of a creature out of parts of a cadaver. This thing looks like a human being and then Dr. Frankenstein animates it with electricity, or electrical force, and it comes to life.

First of all, there are some interesting issues here. It gives us a very vitalistic conception of life, vitalistic in the sense that what makes living things alive is something from outside—vital forces or electrical forces. That is the kind of model you have—the notion of vitalization by external powers. I don't think it's a very good model of what is the living state. In my view, Aristotle is not a "vitalist" in this sense.

There's an interesting point in Aristotle's book two of *De Anima*, where he says, "A dead eye is not really an eye, because it doesn't have the function of an eye." I think that is an interesting point of relevance to your question, namely that a cadaver that has all the same parts is not a human being because it doesn't have the functions of a human being. In this case, the functions begin when the body is acted upon by an outside power or force.

This is still a very Cartesian model. You have this machine and then one sticks in a motivating force and it somehow works. The philosophical tradition has never been able to resolve the problem of relationship between these two entities.

Agustín: *Recently we've both been writing on Darwin, and obviously we're both proponents of an integrated approach to trying to think about these questions. Do you think there are particular avenues of approach that are interdisciplinary that are better than others or that work more or have a better chance?*

Phillip: Yes. One of the advantages of being retired is I can do reading in a wide range of literature outside my immediate specialty.

One area I want to explore more deeply is in German philosophical anthropology—the work of Arnold Gehlen, Max Scheler, Helmuth Plessner, Erwin Straus, and others who were writing in the '20s and early '30s at the intersection of philosophical anthropology and Continental phenomenology.

The approach of the philosophical anthropologists was consciously empirical. The problem with Continental phenomenology, it has been claimed, is that it doesn't really have anything to do with science. *[Laughter.]* It doesn't make any contact with contemporary science.

That is not necessarily true, but at least I think there are some reasons for this charge. But I also think that one of the bases for such charges is that critics of these approaches often have never engaged the Continental tradition, or dealt seriously with Kant.

Even though I'm not a Kantian, I think Kant really raises the critical questions: What is the status of our knowledge and reflection in our sciences? To begin from that point opens up some new ways of thinking about these issues. What I don't think is adequate is warmed over social Darwinism or attempts to develop an adequate human science out of logical empiricism or its progeny. I think that misses the need to reach a deeper philosophical level in dealing with the human question.

Suggested Readings

Dunbar, R. I. 2008. Mind the Gap: Or Why Humans are Not Just Great Apes. Proceedings of the British Academy 154:403-23.

Fischer, J. 2009. Exploring the Core Identity of Philosophical Anthropology through the Works of Max Scheler, Helmuth Plessner, and Arnold Gehlen. IRIS: European Journal of Philosophy and Public Debate 1:153-70, available at www.fupress.net/index.php/iris/article/view/2860/2992.

Grene, M. 1968. Approaches to a Philosophical Biology. New York: Basic Books.

Marks, J. 2002. What It Means to Be 98% Chimpanzee. Berkeley: University of California Press.

Sloan, P. R. 1995. The Gaze of Natural History. *In* Inventing Human Science., C. Fox, R. Porter, and R. Wokler, eds. Pp.112–151. Berkeley: University of California Press.

Sloan, P. R. 2015. Questioning the Zoological Gaze. *In* Darwin in the Twenty-First Century: Nature, Humanity, God. P. R. Sloan, G. McKenny, and K. Eggleson, eds. Pp. 232-266. Notre Dame: University of Notre Dame Press (publication due summer 2015).

Straus, E. 1952. The Upright Posture. Psychiatric Quarterly 26:529-61. Reprinted in Phenomenological Psychology: Selected Papers of Erwin W. Straus. New York: Basic Books, 1966.

CHAPTER 3

The Biocultural Animal

Interviewee: Tim Ingold

Bio. Dr. Ingold is Chair of Social Anthropo logy at the University of Aberdeen. He received both his BA and PhD in Social Anthropology at Cambridge University. Ingold's research and interests include environmental perception, ecological anthropology and psychology, human-animal relations, and the interface between biological, psychological, and anthropological approaches to understanding culture and society. His latest research has examined the dynamics of pedestrian movement, the creativity of practice, and the linearity of writing. In addition, Ingold is spearheading research and teaching on the connections between art, architecture, archaeology, and anthropology. He is Fellow of the British Academy and the Royal Society of Edinburgh.

Slogan. *"Turning 'nature' and 'culture' into monolithic entities and then talking about the interface between them has really impeded our thinking. We have to do something about this."*

Agustín Fuentes and Aku Visala, *Conversations on Human Nature*, pp. 105-169. © 2016 Left Coast Press, Inc. All rights reserved.

Agustín: *I am going to start with the most vague and probably most open-ended question. If you are talking with colleagues or friends or students or whomever and they ask you about human nature, what is your response? How would you define it or—*

Tim: My response is that human nature is the name of a question and not the answer. I give the same response if people ask about culture: that it is the name of a question and not the answer. Therefore to give human nature as the answer to any question, just as to give culture as the answer to any question, is circular. The question of human nature is—I suppose—what is it that humans have in common or what binds them together. The question about culture is what is it that makes them different. To say that they are bound together or have something in common because of human nature is a non-answer.

Agustín: *Do you think that there is a template or a core for these similarities?*

Tim: No I do not. We have to understand the human being or any kind of being as something that is historically constituted, the result of an epigenetic process—the process of development. I think the idea that there is some core that all human beings have in common, rather than a family resemblance, is a result of our trying to abstract or generalize, to extract a lowest common denominator from the pool of variation. We then insert those abstractions into human beings, as though they were concretely there. That is why (following Whitehead) I call it the Fallacy of Misplaced Concreteness. I think this fallacy underpins most discussions on human nature.

Agustín: *Do you think this fallacy prevents us from better formulating the question?*

Tim: Yes, it does, it does. It obscures the question, because we think we already have the answer. The question—the really interesting question is—why is there so much convergence? If you assert "There's no such thing as human nature. It all depends on development", then people will always respond "Then why do human beings have so much in common?" The reason they have so much in common is because there are significant convergences in processes of development. We need to ask why or how that happens. If we simply say "Oh, that's due to human nature," then the question is not even asked.

Agustín: *What about the idea of human distinctiveness or uniqueness that we find in the Western philosophical tradition?*

Tim: I take the point that many biological anthropologists make, which is that all species are unique in their own particular way. Simply to say that humans as a species are unique is of no particular interest. It only becomes interesting and therefore problematic if you say that humans are somehow unique in the way in which they are unique, that they are unique in a way that no other species is unique. Then you get to the usual argument about how humans possess thought and reason and so on. Darwin of course, and many other thinkers of his time, did not suppose that humans were unique in that regard. Their view was just that humans had greater faculties of reason than other creatures, not that such faculties were lacking in the latter. For my part I would want to get beyond this distinction between cognition and mechanism, to find another way of dealing with it. Clearly human beings do think, and I am pretty sure that other animals think as well. But I do not believe that you can draw a clear line separating such an activity as thought from other kinds of activity. That has been the problem.

Agustín: *It seems to connect to a certain extent with this issue about free will, the human ability to choose and to be shaped in a very specific way. Do you think that agency of this kind is a component of human nature?*

Tim: Well, it certainly influences the way many people, Western scholars in particular, talk about these things. I think it is a distraction. I do not buy the concept of free will, but that does not mean I go for determinism instead. You can trace the history of this opposition between free will and determinism in the history of Western thought. I think it is an unhelpful distinction, which covers up the creativity of life processes in general. Creativity is not about innovation, it is not about somebody suddenly doing something different from what anyone else had done before, and spontaneously exercising free will where everyone else was determined. Creativity is about growth. It is about the way in which new life is continually coming into being and finding its own way in a kind of improvisatory dynamic. This dynamic drives all life processes. I do believe that life is a creative process in which organisms make their own way, and that by thinking about creativity in terms of growth and development we have a way of breaking out of the straitjacket of the free will versus determinism debate.

Agustín: *Do you think it is connected with debates about morality and the evolution of morality in humans as compared with other animals?*

Tim: Yes it is, but I do not quite know how to deal with it. I think that if morality and ethics are to have any force, then they have to have a foundation in sentience, in sentient awareness, in what we feel is right. In a relationship between a mother and her offspring—maybe human, maybe non-human—the mother knows what feels right in relation to her offspring because of the very close bond of sentience between them. We might codify that bond in terms of morality and ethics, but it will not have any force unless it is rooted in sentient awareness. In talking about morality, I think we have to get back to that.

Agustín: *Is this in a sense what Frans De Waal has been arguing, or is he arguing something different in your view?*

Tim: I am not sure. I have not read his recent stuff. Sometimes it seems as though that is what he is saying, but from my recollection there are times when he talks about politics in the animal world as if the animal's political world were structured on Western political principles.

Agustín: *Recently he has argued that the origins of human morality can be traced to primate social complexity and social relations. He nevertheless tends to use political and social terminology drawn from modern Western society.*

Tim: That is the problem. Then again, it is a problem I have with the whole Machiavellian intelligence hypothesis.[1] It is as though life were conducted in the common room of a Cambridge college! Nicholas Humphrey actually drew this analogy. He compared the machinations of a Cambridge common room with those of a primate group. This is nonsense.

Agustín: *What do you think about the role of malleability and plasticity in human experience, as it relates to these kinds of discussions?*

Tim: Plasticity, yes, in the sense that I am convinced, for example, that there is a huge amount of neurological plasticity in development. In that sense, I am against any metaphors of "hard wiring." Yes, plasticity is crucial and that ties in with the emphasis on ontogenetic development. I am not quite so sure about malleability. Malleability makes it sound as if we are lumps of iron which get hammered, and I do not think that is quite how it works. We are talking about development, not about people being knocked into shape.

Agustín: *What do you think about Patrick Bateson's work on robustness and variation?[2] His idea is that there are trends and patterns in development, but within those patterns there is a lot of micro-flexibility.*

Tim: Well again, this gives us one possible way of describing things. However, there is always a temptation to turn our descriptions of

....

1   The Machiavellian intelligence hypothesis comes in many forms but the gist of it is that advanced cognitive processes (usually of primates) are primarily adaptations to the particular complexities of social lives, rather than to the general ecology. The argument is that primates often act as if they were following the advice that Niccolo Machiavelli offered to sixteenth-century Italian prince-politicians to enable them socially to manipulate their competitors and subjects. See Humphrey, N. K. 1976. The Social Function of Intellect. *In* Growing Points in Ethology. P. P. G. Bateson and R. A. Hinde, eds. Pp. 303-321 Cambridge: Cambridge University Press. Also see Byrne, R. W., and A. Whiten. 1988. Machiavellian Intelligence: Social Expertise and the Evolution of Intellect in Monkeys, Apes and Humans. Oxford: Oxford University Press.

2   See Bateson's interview in Chapter 2. Also see Bateson, P., and P. Gluckman. 2011. Plasticity, Robustness, Development and Evolution. Cambridge: Cambridge University Press.

things, which are ex post facto, into their generative causes. That is no kind of explanation. We might find robust patterns. We might find them cropping up with such regularity that we can say, for example, that the vast majority of human beings end up walking, being biped-al. You might say "Well, that's pretty robust. There may be all sorts of variations in how people actually go about walking and in how far they can walk without getting tired and so on, but they all walk." But that is only because we have already generalized the developmental condi-tions that make walking possible. If we all went to the moon or another planet, where the gravitational force is different, we would not be able to walk. It is easy to forget that even with such a robust thing there are elemental, environmental conditions involved.

Agustín: *Yes, absolutely. You started by talking about how we often use human nature or culture as ready-made answers, instead of tak-ing them as open-ended questions. What do you think is the rela-tionship between "nature" and "culture" and between the disciplines respectively dedicated to their study? There has been a strong tendency to think of "nature" and "culture" as two distinct domains. If you look across much of anthropology, practically all of psychology, a very large chunk of philosophy and most of biology, you will find that these two domains have taken on the status of monolithic entities. In your work, you have tried to break down the dualism of "nature" and "culture", and the idea that they interact across some kind of interface.*

Tim: I do think this has been a problem. Turning "nature" and "culture" into monolithic entities and then talking about the inter-face between them has really impeded our thinking. We have to do something about this. But it is an uphill struggle. By using words such as "interface" and "interaction," or by asserting that "there's a continual interaction between biology and culture," many biolo-gists and psychologists think they have solved the problem, while accusing critics like myself—who insist that they have not solved the problem at all—of reinventing the wheel. I really do not know how to break this impasse. Goodness me, I have tried! The only way forward, I think, is to focus on ontogenetic development, on how differences emerge, and to show by example how it is possible to do this without having to use awkward words like "nature" and "culture." To my mind, the key to this lies in the relative priority one accords to developmental as against evolutionary processes.

But even with approaches like evo/devo and some of the other alternatives that are coming up nowadays, there is still a tendency to say, "Well, development is important but we've got to have an evolutionary paradigm that builds it in." It is still putting the development after the evolution: the devo comes after the evo, when it should be the other way around.

Agustín: *In one sense, there are these massive semantic battles on development and evolution. There is also the idea that biology and culture both matter and we just have to find a way to think about them together. However neither "culture" nor "biology" is one thing; neither is a singular entity. There seems to be relatively broad agreement that it is all shorthand, and yet people fall back into the habit of saying, "Yes, it's all shorthand, but we're going to use it anyway."*

Tim: Use it anyway, and then the shorthand actually takes over. "Oh, that is just shorthand" is a stock response whenever you criticize the logic of the argument. This is how shorthand becomes reality. I think the stakes here are enormous: they have to do with the whole way in which we think about what evolution is and what it means. The rigid Darwinian way of thinking—it is not really Darwin's way but the way in which it has been rigidified by those who have adopted his name as a brand—has become a hindrance. We have to think of evolution itself in a quite different way, in a way that would imply that the life cycle of an organism, human or non-human, is itself part of an evolutionary process. It is part of the process wherein that organism establishes the conditions under which it and its successors will live their lives. This is not just about introducing a Lamarckian component to our modeling. It is really to think in terms of developmental systems, and I am convinced that that is the way forward.

Agustín: *Oh yes, I am with you and agree that the whole developmental systems perspective is very powerful. The most common complaint about it is that you cannot quantify it or apply it properly.*

Tim: Yes.

Agustín: *Some people have tried and are moving in a particular direction in quantifying some things. Take, for instance, the whole cluster of ideas around niche construction, some of the renewed Spencerian and Lamarckian ideas on the Baldwin effect and things like that.[3] Do you see these at all as—*

Tim: Well, I find that niche construction has just reached the point where anthropology was about thirty years ago. I can see the point, for example, in the work of people like Eva Jablonka (who is not a niche constructionist but still working in the same general area); I can see what they are getting at.[4] I remember having an argument with Eva about how she must stop using this word "inheritance." It is all very well to say that there is another strand of inheritance, which is the inheritance of the environment as opposed to, or parallel to, the inheritance of genes or cellular structures or whatever else. However, as soon as you use this word "inheritance" you buy metaphorically into the Western property model: that the environment of an animal in generation X is handed on to the animal in generation Y. The truth is that the environment is just there and that it is undergoes a continuous process of becoming just as does the life that goes on in it. Niche construction is an odd mixture of constructing and inheriting, and it doesn't really work for me.

I remember when, about twenty years ago, this stuff first became evident to some anthropologists. I was just thinking "We've been there, we've done that, we've moved on." I still think that biologists, even those who are trying to think this through, whether it is

....

3   Regarding the inheritance of non-genetic traits and their integration into the organism, see Lamarck, J. B. 1809. Exposition with Regard to the Natural History of Animals. Philosophie Zoologique: Museum d' Histoire Naturelle, Paris; Baldwin, J. M. 1896. A New Factor in Evolution. American Naturalist 30:441-451; Waddington, C. H. 1942. Canalization of Development and the Inheritance of Acquired Characteristics. Nature 3811:563-565.

4   See Jablonka, Eva, and Marion J. Lamb. 2005. Evolution in Four Dimensions: Genetic, Epigenetic, Behavioral, and Symbolic Variation in the History of Life. Cambridge, MA: MIT Press.

through Baldwin effect or niche construction or whatever, are still hamstrung by a vocabulary which they cannot quite see through. This is actually where social anthropologists can help because they do understand the baggage that some of these words can carry.

Agustín: *I agree and I think this is why I have been very interested in niche construction and trying to broaden these engagements. If you are going to argue that social anthropology brings something to this inquiry and to this quest, then what is it that social anthropology brings?*

Tim: In principle, social anthropology could bring something to the table, but it has so far failed miserably to do so. This is because for the most part my colleagues in social anthropology don't care a damn about the whole thing. They would not otherwise have been supinely accommodating to the worst kinds of Neo-Darwinism, as if to say "Oh well, you do that, and of course we understand what you do, but we do something different." They have not been very helpful in this regard. Social anthropologists are able to draw on conversations with a much wider range of people, and from a much wider range of backgrounds, than most practicing biological scientists. It means that they have continually to be hyper-alert to the ways in which the words and concepts we use structure our thinking. You have to do that if you are working with people who are thinking quite differently and using quite different language. You have to be thinking, "Is this word right for conveying what they're trying to tell me? How is what they're telling me challenging what I'm thinking?" It sometimes forces you to think about things in a completely different way.

That sort of challenge is not one to which biologists or psychologists are accustomed. There, I think social anthropologists really can help, but they are to some extent prevented from doing so. What prevents them—and this is another bee I have in my bonnet—is their commitment to ethnography. They muddle up speculative inquiry into what human life is and what it means with their ethnographic concern to offer an accurate and sensitive depiction of the ways of doing, thinking, and being of the people they have worked with. They are rightly concerned that these people should not be turned into unwitting mouthpieces for the researcher's own favored philosophy of life. But this concern actually prevents them from engaging in the kind of speculative inquiries that we would need to make an impact in psychology or biology.

Agustín: *What do you think about the idea of some evolutionary psychologists that faith is a core component of human nature or being human?*

Tim: I am not very impressed by that and I think it misunderstands the nature of religion, to which I am generally sympathetic. They confuse faith with belief. To talk seriously about religion, one has to admit that it is ultimately about commitment. It is about recognizing that not only does the world owe something of its existence to us, but also that our existence owes something to the world, and building our knowledge and understanding upon that foundation. We owe something to the world too; we have a duty towards the world in which we find ourselves. Our knowledge grows on the inside of that commitment. Regardless of what particular religion you are talking about, this I think is where the essence of religious sensibility lies. In the public discussion on religion versus science, and on whether there is something in humans that draws them towards religious faith, this idea of commitment has been displaced by the idea that religion is a corpus of unquestionable beliefs about the world, to be set against scientific beliefs. If that is the way the issue is presented, then of course science is bound to win and religion is bound to lose.

If we think of religion in terms of commitment and care, then the opposite of religion is not atheism but negligence. Not to have a religion is to not care about the world, to say we will do whatever we will do. Never mind what happens to our environment: "Let us test some nuclear bombs here, let us build some power stations there. Who cares?" That is negligence, and that is actually the opposite of religion. Not believing in God is a completely different matter.

Agustín: *That is a powerful point. It comes back again to this concept of process that you seem to return to time and time again. Coming back to niche construction and evolutionary processes, do you* *think there is an open window here to move beyond the worst kinds of Neo-Darwinism, the kind of move that, for example, Eva Jablonka and Marion Lamb are pushing for? Is there an open window or will disciplines keep going on their separate trajectories?*

Tim: My answer depends on whether I am having an optimistic day or a pessimistic one. I have my optimistic moments when I think that the whole biology-versus-culture discourse, evolutionary psychology, and the rest will sink like the Titanic, like a stone, and good riddance. Then we could actually work together and build an alternative. Again, in my optimistic moments I get the sense that all around the place there are people who are working on alternative ways of thinking. They feel a bit marginal, however. They do not feel they have institutional support, they do not have so much money, and they are scattered. If one could just bring them all together one could actually launch a revolution just as powerful as Darwin's in 1859. I think we are pretty close to that point. That is on my optimistic days.

On my pessimistic days, I find the establishment so powerful and so conservative that it just does not seem to budge. I do think the institutional structure of biological and psychological science is very heavy and very conservative, even down to such things as how students are trained and what they are taught and what they are supposed to write in order to pass their exams. Then I remember what a wonderful thing it is to be an anthropologist: because it is actually the discipline where you can do and think what the hell you like. There are very few disciplines left where you can do that.

Suggested Readings

Bergson, Henri. 1911. Creative Evolution. Arthur Mitchell, trans. London: Macmillan.

Hallowell, A. Irving. 1955. Culture and Experience. Philadelphia: University of Pennsylvania Press.

Leroi-Gourhan, André. 1993. Gesture and Speech. Anna Bostock Berger, trans. Randall White, intro. Cambridge, MA: MIT Press.

Marx, K. and F. Engels. 1977. The German Ideology. C. J. Arthur, ed. London: Lawrence & Wishart.

Ortega y Gasset. J. 1941. History as a System and Other Essays towards a Philosophy of History. New York: Norton.

Oyama, S. 1985. The Ontogeny of Information: Developmental Systems and Evolution. Cambridge: Cambridge University Press.

Sheets-Johnstone, M. 1998. The Primacy of Movement. Amsterdam: John Benjamins.

Interviewee: Jonathan (Jon) Marks

Bio. Dr. Marks is a Professor of Anthropology at the University of North Carolina at Charlotte. Marks's primary research is in molecular anthropology and his other research interests include the study of human evolution and diversity, the anthropology of science, and the intersection of anthropology, evolution, and genetics. Marks is a Fellow of the American Association for the Advancement of Science, and he has been a Visiting Research Fellow at the ESRC Genomics Forum in Edinburgh and at the Max Planck Institute for the History of Science in Berlin, as well as a 2013-2014 Templeton Fellow at the Notre Dame Institute for Advanced Studies. His many awards and honors include the W. W. Howells Book Prize from the American Anthropological Association's Biological Anthropology Section, the General Anthropology Division Prize for Exemplary Cross-Field Scholarship, and the J. I. Staley Prize from the School for Advanced Research.

Slogan. *"We are biocultural ex-apes whose 'natural' and 'cultural' aspects are thoroughly entangled."*

Jon: By "ex-apes" I mean that our ancestors were apes, and we are not our ancestors. I've written about evolutionary genetics, and the nature of science, and our relationship to the apes, human evolution, and bioethics and things like that. And well, unfortunately, I'm educated in a tradition that's dying out, namely, holistic or four-field anthropology.

One of the things I think that is nice about the older tradition is that it links the scientific aspects of anthropology with the humanistic, cultural traditions, which I think you have to come to grips with if you want to understand—as we'll talk about shortly—human nature.

Aku: *It seems to me that this has been one of the main themes that comes up in your writings, this anthropology as a kind of bridge between the sciences and humanities.*

Jon: Well, I think I would define anthropology as the study of people in groups—and the groups can be as small as family or as large as a species—and the relationship between those groups. A lot of us study the human species, in relation to other species. Cultural anthropologists focus on the level of, say, cultures or families. Ultimately, you have to come to grips with the bio-cultural nature of human existence, in that we're both organisms—like apes and like cheetahs—but we also live in these historical streams. Our lives are very much shaped by decisions that we didn't make.

Aku: *This brings us to the concept of human nature. One question that we ask is the definition of human nature, or, let us say, the concept of human nature. Do you think that there are several concepts of human nature, or just one, or how would you define the notion?*

Jon: My understanding of what people mean when they use the phrase human nature—which is not a concept that I work with, because I think it's kind of silly—is that, somehow, there is a core biological component to being human that is divorceable from the historical, cultural, learned, acquired attributes of being human. That, somehow, all we have to do is scrape off the latter, and we can find what that bestial nature of the human organism is.

I think, basically, it's a dead end—it's a contradiction in terms, because humans don't exist external to the historical circumstances of their lives, it's a silly thought experiment to imagine what a human nature would be, independently of, or separate from, culture.

Aku: *Let me read something for you. This is something that you have written. You can explain it to me: "What we get from all this is that the quest for human nature is itself an illusion, the result of an antiquated*

*way of thinking about humans scientifically—with culture as a ve-
neer overlying nature. Every human being that has ever lived has been
born into a culture. Culture preceded our species—our ancestor Homo
erectus certainly was a cultural species. In other words, culture is part
of our nature; you can't strip it away, scrape it off, pretend it doesn't
exist, or look for it in simpler forms. It's ubiquitous in human life; it's
programmed into human life."*

Jon: Wow, that's good. I said that?

Aku: *Yes. [Laughter]*

Jon: Certainly, technology is part of culture. Certainly, *Homo erectus*
had technology. They made stone tools—they made nice stone tools,
better stone tools than I can make. They had brains two-thirds the
size of ours. Presumably, they had kinship and other kinds of things
that, if we saw them interacting, we would recognize as not being in
the lives of chimpanzees or gorillas, but in the lives of humans.

Unfortunately, we don't have a time machine and we can't do
that. I think it's fair to say that culture precedes the human species,
and that, consequently, every human that's ever been born has been
born into this historical stream. We don't get up every morning
thinking about how to redo what our ancestors have given us. If
anything, I think that the survival of the human lineage is probably
due to *not* getting up every morning and saying to yourself, "Wow!
How can I do something differently with this stone ax?"

Aku: *Yes, reinvent the wheel.*

Jon: Exactly. The human condition involves learning how to do it
right, and using it, and surviving with it. That's why you find those
hand axes for a million years. They worked, and they permitted their
bearers to survive using them. I think that's fair to say. Part of the problem, I think, with the whole concept of human nature is that it tends
to imagine a human being as being autonomous and separate from
other human beings, walled in and disconnected. That's not the state of
human existence. Human existence is social, and it's particularly those
relationships between people that, I think, construct human life to a
much greater extent than psychologists or biologists tend to realize.

If you look at human evolution, or compare human society with, say, chimpanzee society, we have concepts that are critical to human survival, like father, like grandmother, like in-laws, that are not part of the chimpanzees' or gorillas' social life. It's probably those crucial kinds of relationships—in-laws being the product of marriage. Chimpanzees have mating, but not marriage, but marriage produces in-laws, and in-laws are people you can call on in emergencies. It's a social relationship not by blood, but by law. Of course, fatherhood is, again, a relationship of law and obligation. Grandmotherhood is the one that's been written about the most, but tied into the human life history.

Aku: *You're basically opposed to the cheesecake model of human nature, that there's the bottom, which is the biological or the psychological given, and on top of that you pile the cultural stuff. I've found that evolutionary psychologists would say that there is a kind of innate batch of psychological systems that are, then, the building blocks of culture. In that sense, there is something like human nature. There's something innate, something in-built, which is, then, like a funnel for culture.*

Jon: The evolutionary psychologists have discovered what anthropologists were doing seventy years ago. What they haven't quite realized yet is those building blocks are very much the constructs of the investigator, rather than the constructs of the people living the lives. A nice example of that is religion. We like to bracket religion as "something." There's all kinds of evolutionary psychology literature asking where does religion come from?

The fact is that by 1917, I think, Malinowski had realized that religion wasn't separate for the lives of the Trobriand islanders. Everything they did was suffused with religious kinds of acts and religious kinds of beliefs, but they didn't separate their lives out into the religious and the secular, as we in the modern world do. The ancient Greeks didn't have a word for religion. It's not because they weren't religious. It was because they didn't bracket it and set it off as we're accustomed to doing it, ourselves.

The idea that there are these modules that you can talk of and that are elements of human nature, rather than elements of discussions of human nature, is a fallacy that I think Alfred North Whitehead called the Fallacy of Misplaced Concreteness. I don't think it's particularly useful, scientifically, in understanding much about the human condition.

Aku: *I also hear you saying that science is not something that we should abandon here. Some anthropologists have thought that, again, according to the cheesecake model, that biology is irrelevant—that there's just a lot of cheesecake. I thought of cheesecake but there are other kinds of cake, right?*

Jon: A layer cake.

Aku: *Yeah, layer cake. Given the layer cake model, some say that there is the biological stuff, but let the scientists worry about that. Let us worry about culture. The reasons that human actions have are on a completely different level than the kind of processes that scientists are looking at. Let's forget science. Let's just focus on interpreting the human condition.*

Jon: Well, a lot of the human condition really does beg to be interpreted like that. So much of the things that occupy us politically now are the result of simply economic and political forces. Biology hardly enters into it. If biology enters into it, it's usually as a red herring to try and diffuse attention away from evil behavior on the part of greedy, rich people.

Biology can be a real red herring in the study of human society. Certainly, in the early twentieth century, when Franz Boas was building American anthropology, he very strongly conceptualized humans as both biological and cultural creatures. He found the cultural studies to be far more important and far more interesting than the biological studies. He began his career as measuring children and robbing bones from Eskimo graves. He came out of a very strong naturalistic German tradition.

The bigger problems were political things, like the Indians being dispossessed and living in poverty. Biology hardly entered into it. I think that's where a lot of that attitude comes from, that a lot of the things that anthropologists are studying really are the result of history and politics. In that sense, the biology's largely a constant. Can't use a constant to explain a variable.

Aku: *OK. Moving on to a slightly different issue, one of the things that have preoccupied people a lot is the human-animal boundary, or the distinction. Would you say that there is something distinctively human? Given your emphasis on humans as a biocultural species, you would probably say that it is culture that makes us different from other species.*

Jon: If you're asking what distinguishes us, naturalistically, from other species, yeah. If you give me the cells of a chimpanzee, I can tell the cells of a chimpanzee from the cells of a human 100 times out of 100. If you know what to look for, those markers are there.

One of the interesting moves right now is to try and reduce the difference—taxonomic difference—between humans and apes, on the grounds that the genetics is so similar between humans and apes. Actually, we've known that since the 1920s. This is not a new discovery. One of the big lies of molecular genetics is that we just discovered this in the 1980s with DNA, or in the 1960s with proteins. We actually knew that.

Aku: *It seems that, in the last two or three decades, there have been two big projects of unlocking the mysteries of human nature. One is through genetics. The other is through the brain. Somehow, if we go deep into the brain and understand how the brain works, then we will finally unlock the mysteries of human behavior. The argument seems to be that, because all of our actions and behaviors are mediated by our brains, it's finally the brain that's going to explain why we do what we do. Because everything goes through that.*

Jon: I think that's going to be subject to exactly the same fallacy as the genome project, which is going to be that, once you've got the brain, what you're going to discover is that what is really interesting about the human condition is the relationships between people, not the stuff within people. Then, we'll have the human sociome project. *[Laughter]*

Again, if you want to understand war in Somalia, if you want to understand Islam, what is the brain going to tell you that's interesting? The answer is obviously nothing. This is about economics. This is about politics. This is about history. This is about colonialism. The brain isn't going tell you anything about that.

There's an old saying that goes, "When the only tool that you have is a hammer, everything tends to look like a nail." Certainly, the Human Genome project is a very good example of that. We got dragged into the Human Genome Project because we could do it. We had the technology, and the technology was going to get better and better, so we might as well do it.

Aku: *Then, another topic that's related to the notion of human nature is freedom. Often, especially in the West, it's quite often said that humans have a specific kind of freedom. What do you think about this? Does it make any sense to talk about a specific kind of freedom, in the case of humans?*

Jon: I tend to think not. I think, again, the idea of free will is very theological, a very religious idea, going back to original sin and that kind of stuff. One of the things that the anthropological concept of culture from the nineteenth century does is that it shows you that there are fundamental constraints on free will that we take for granted; we don't realize they're there, but we're born into them.

In theory, but only in theory, I could walk around the streets naked—well, not today; it's only two degrees outside. I could teach my classes naked, but I can't do that. Why? Because there are cultural sanctions. There are rules about what I'm allowed to do and what I'm not allowed to do, and I have to abide by them if I want to be a functioning member of society.

The idea that I can either—psychologically, I guess—do anything I want, or there are naturalistic biases in what I can do, is a really false dichotomy. There are limitations on what I can do, but they're, again, historical, cultural, for the most part. I can't walk on my hands, I suppose, for biologically limiting reasons. Most of the constraints on my behavior—I tell my classes, "Look around. How many of you really think that you had the freedom to choose how you were going to dress today? Look around you. You're all dressed exactly the same. You're all wearing t-shirts. You're all wearing jeans." *[Laughter]*

Aku: *For us, free will means a lot of different things. From the classical or traditional point of view, to have free will is to be able to pursue what's good.*

Jon: Well, that gets to another interesting question, which is morality. Another interesting difference between humans and apes is humans are constrained to know good from evil, and to do what's good. As an anthropologist, I know that there are different ideas about what constitutes good and what constitutes evil, but the generalization is that you have to know the difference, or else you're not wanted around here. Anywhere.

Aku: *Morality has really been at the heart of the human nature debate, especially in the last thirty years. As with language and these other markers of humanity, it seems that the debate always takes the same route. There are two basic ways of arguing. The first guy's going to say, "Well, we are moral because there were some reasons, adaptive reasons in our history, why we developed these things. As a consequence, we have, let us say, a set of mechanisms, biological or psychological, that make us moral. Then, cultures put in their own little veneer on top of it."*

Jon: The icing, yeah.

Aku: *Yeah, it's like the icing on the cake.*

Jon: I think what's strange is why you would try to separate them out when there's clearly co-evolution going on there. I think a fairly useful example of that, that again, we have some material record on, is tool use. One of the interesting things is why don't chimpanzees make nice tools? Granted, they take little twigs and stick them in holes and stuff, but why don't chimps bang rocks together and make sharp edges, and do things like that?

The answer is, one, they have small, weak brains. Two, they have small, weak thumbs. I think it should be fairly obvious that tool use and tool manufacture co-evolved with the physical ability to make the tools. If you want to understand, say, the evolution of the human hand, that has to come with the evolution of human technology. It's the cultural and the biological together. To separate them out, technology without the intellectual or dexterous capabilities of doing it, you're only getting half the picture. If you talk about the organic properties without the technology, you're only getting half the picture.

Aku: *Morality would be the same, a conglomerate of certain biological functions and aims and dispositions. Then, the symbolic world, moral norms, so on and so on.*

Jon: I think so, yeah. To talk about them as if they're separable is the only mistake you can make, but it's the one everybody wants to make.

Aku: *What would this mean, in terms of animal morality, then? Can we talk about something like morality existing in animals? There's an English writer called Raymond Tallis.⁵ He's a doctor—he's a neurologist, originally, but he's written on a lot of issues. He has a book called* Aping Mankind. *He says that we have a problem that, on the one hand, we try to make animals too human-like. At the same time, when we're doing that, what we're doing is also making humans animal-like. By not tending to the differences properly, we might end up anthropomorphizing animals, but also making ourselves as a subset of chimpanzees, in a way which, especially on the level of a metaphor, might be quite problematic.*

Jon: Well, again, Jane Goodall has made a great career on anthropomorphizing chimpanzees. That is where her career began. Now, she's devoted to conservation, which is a very, very important driving issue now in primatology. The sociobiologists, the early sociobiologists incurred the criticism that what they were doing was animalizing human behavior, because what they were doing was simply focusing on the continuities and, again, trying to scrape away the surface, ignoring culture and talking about only imagined biological propensities as if economics and history and politics weren't a motivating force.

Aku: *This leads to another issue, which is the flexibility of human nature. If I understand you correctly, you would say that, if we talk about human nature as something biocultural, it's a conglomeration about what is biologically, psychologically there.*

Jon: I'd say we are historical creatures, and that the things that I take for granted in my life, today, would have been absolutely unthinkable and unfathomable in my ancestors, five generations ago. I think that's probably true of most of us. We imagine going back five generations

5   Tallis, Raymond. 2014. Aping Mankind: Neuromania, Darwinitis and the Misrepresentation of Humanity. London: Routledge.

and having a nice conversation with our great-great-great-great grand-parents, but for most of us, we wouldn't be even speaking the same language. You might've spoken the same language as your ancestors five generations ago. A lot of Americans wouldn't have been able to.

Aku: *My language goes back at least 500 years, so I could go back-wards a little bit, but not much.*

Jon: Again, for a lot of us—and, again, thinking of transnational immigration, people who have moved around not only wouldn't be able to communicate with their ancestors, but just making sense of your ancestors' lives—that might be a better example. For you, I'm sure that, five generations ago, your ancestors lived lives that were very, very different from yours.

Aku: *Yeah, very much so.*

Jon: You could at least talk to them *[laughter]*, unlike me. We're very much historical products. I think we tend to underestimate that. We always imagine time travel as being something that you would—you could have a conversation with Achilles, or something like that. You wouldn't have been able—it wouldn't have made sense, at all, to you.

Aku: *This is something that, if we take this point seriously, leads us to a kind of epistemic humility; at least, I hope it will, because—*

Jon: That's a good phrase.

Aku: *Especially when we're talking about, let us say, human prehistory and trying to understand the lives of our ancestors a long, long time ago, thousands and thousands of years ago. If we recognize the fact that, if we go back 200 years, it's difficult to understand how people were living at that time and what they were thinking, then how big is the difference between our ancestors that have died thousands and thousands of years ago? How are we supposed to understand their lives and what they were thinking and how they were living?*

Jon: We look at the Bible and we imagine that the people in Biblical times were just like us, except for the fact that they took slavery for granted. They took polygamy for granted in a lot of it. They thought nothing of stoning people and killing people without due process, and things like that. We'd have been appalled by that. Again, that's what anthropology is. It's the fieldwork of modern anthropology introducing cultural relativism to discussions of human nature that I think the biologists still haven't really internalized. Different people really do see the world really differently than other people do.

There's a classic story that we still love to assign to students called *Shakespeare in the Bush* by Laura Bohannan.[6] Do you know this one? She's trying to explain *Hamlet* to a West African tribe, and she can't get very far because they question every cultural assumption in the story, and all of Hamlet's motivations simply evaporate when they're interrogated like that.

Aku: *Another interesting issue related to this issue of flexibility of human nature is the idea—that some philosophers and scientists have pushed forward is that we should intentionally try to shape our nature. Especially some transhumanists[7] are arguing for this, that we should use all the tools at our disposal to change ourselves. Some even argue that we actually might have a moral obligation to enhance our cognitive capacities. Would you say that it's a viable idea to somehow shape the way that we are? Intentionally, I mean.*

Jon: Yeah. Well, again, we do want to take some—we want to take whatever steps we can to try and make the world better for our descendants, because we're doing a very—I think every generation screws up the world in certain ways, and leaves problems for the next generation to solve. Our parents did that for us, and we're trying to solve those problems now. We're going to try and deal with anthropogenic climate change for our children.

When it comes to improving the human animal, we have a really bad track record with that *[laughter]*. Again, the problem with that I don't think is necessarily the moral obligation, because I think there is something to be said for trying to make things better. The problem

----

6   See www.naturalhistorymag.com/picks-from-the-past/12476/shakespeare-in-the-bush.

7   A philosophical movement related to the transforming of the human condition via technologies to enhance human intellectual, physical, and psychological capacities.

is with the naïveté of not appreciating the limits of our knowledge. Of course, a big example of that is the eugenics movement in the 1920s, which took different forms in different countries, but it was all modern and scientific and altruistic. It was progressive. We're gonna make the world better.

Aku: *We're trying to make it—yeah, we're trying to make a better world, and we've got the scientific tools. The ethics should follow that.*

Jon: Certainly in America, which is where I'm most familiar with it, it was based on a lot of assumptions—first of all, about the role of genetics—that turned out to be false. It was also based on a lot of assumptions about politics. For example, there was no conception of what we would now think of as the fundamental aspects, now, of liberal democracies, that the role of government is to protect its most helpless people against the most powerful people or institutions. That doesn't really enter into it, until the '40s, '50s, the idea that there was some—that there is something out there called universal human rights, doesn't come until the end of the Second World War.

Now, without that, without the idea that the role of government is to protect its citizens, and of course, also, before the income tax, so that the government could actually do something if it wanted to— those ideas all came later than the American eugenics movement, the major text of which, in the United States, was a book called *A Passing of the Great Race* by Madison Grant, which was praised by both Theodore Roosevelt, who was a friend of the author's, and by Adolf Hitler, who was a foreign admirer.

What Madison Grant was saying is we can solve all these problems, scientifically. We've got all these urban slums being populated by poor people from southern Europe and eastern Europe—which was code for Italians and Jews. They speak weird languages and they eat weird foods, and they're disease-ridden and crime-ridden, and it's horrible. The very idea that we would need protection for these people against slumlords, and public health and hygiene stuff— no. What we need to do is sterilize them so they don't breed, because they're the problem.

In '48, when a German physician named Karl Brandt was being prosecuted at Nuremberg, he read that book into testimony, into the record, as saying, "Look, we were just doing what the Americans were saying in 1916." It didn't help; they hanged him, anyway.

In the case of genetic enhancement, we do know, for example—I mean, there's the case of India in the 1980s, I guess, when abortion was free on-demand in India. What they discovered is that 99.9 percent of all the fetuses that were being aborted were females. Why is that? Well, because, in a fiercely patriarchal society, essentially being born with two X chromosomes is a genetic defect.

The first thing you have to realize is that we need a cultural discussion of what a correctable genetic defect ought to be. Of course, those are very strongly cultural decisions. The other thing is how the genetic processes actually work. There is no gene that has only one effect. Everything works in systems, and those systems are physiological.

If we had, for example, a very low-risk way of adding fifteen IQ points to your child by some sort of genetic engineering process, most people would say, "Yeah, sure. That would give my kid a leg up, make 'em smarter. Yeah, let's do that. Okay." Of course, nothing's going to be like that. If it comes with a 50 percent greater chance of having brain cancer, then you say, "Wait just a minute. Time out." Of course, that's the kind of thing that we would need to think about.

James Watson is on record—what's the quote? "People think it would be a bad idea if we made all girls pretty. I think it would be a great idea." As a great father of molecular genetics, I don't know if you can take that at face value. Maybe it's just an example of nerd wit. Think about what that would entail. It would entail a genetic modification program based on his aesthetic judgments. Or, cutting the fallopian tubes of all ugly people. What are we talking about here?

One does have to recognize the limitations—or, not just the limitations, the actual positive knowledge we have about genetics, and the way in which the science does feed into the real issues, which are political and economic—if we want to make the world a better place.

Aku: *There's still one issue that I wanted to discuss, and it has to do with artificial life. Not just artificial life, but artificial intelligence. Of course, the history of the last, let's say, fifty and sixty years, when people have started thinking about artificial intelligence is actually quite informative.*

We see this process of failure after failure. We started when people came up computers. Then the idea was that our minds must be like computers, so let's build a computer to make a mind. That will be what intelligence is. This, of course, keeps going, this tradition.

I think one interesting aspect of this is that only now, in the last ten, fifteen years, people working in the area of artificial intelligence have actually started to think about other issues, like learning culture, relationship to bodies, and so on. Whereas, again, it seems that anthropologists have realized this a long time ago, that there is no such thing as disembodied logical intelligence. It's something that we have social group norms, we've got bodies—intelligence is embodied and relational, in this sense.

Jon: I don't know that much about artificial intelligence. I do know that I wouldn't want to be governed by someone who is entirely rational. I wouldn't want Vulcans[8] running the earth. Again, even *Star Trek* got into those issues of how, if you are purely rational, you're only half a person. I want there to be a conception of universal human rights that transcends rationality. It had to be put out there. The Enlightenment started it, but they didn't complete it until we realized, with the Nazis.

Again, even that—our conceptions of what constitutes rights are constantly changing. We're getting, now, away from colonialism. We haven't gotten away from imperialism yet. Maybe that's the next step. Maybe we'll deal with corporate greed at some point, as well. To leave things alone, or to be governed by purely rational interests, is probably not a good thing. I think that's probably the lesson of the last generation of economic theory.

Are you familiar with David Graeber's book *Debt?*[9] What Graeber's doing is using anthropology to beat up the economists—the economists who model human behavior, and especially human economic behavior, as being one of rational self-interest. Any economic interaction is predicated on the idea that I'm trying to minimize what I give you and maximize what I get back.

....

8   Highly intelligent species from the *Star Trek* universe who systematically seek to suppress their emotions. See http://en.wikipedia.org/wiki/Star_Trek.

9   Graeber, David. 2012. Debt: The First 5,000 Years. Brooklyn, NY: Melville House.

What Graeber is arguing is that, based on ethnography, no human— no successful human economic relationships are based on that. They're based on moral obligations, not trying to cheat your partner, but both people trying to be happy because they know they're going to encounter one another again, and that they're governed by common cooperative mutual interests. That gives you a very different view of how to model human economic behavior than what the economists have been working with. It's a very threatening and very interesting book.

Aku: *That sounds quite interesting, yeah. I was still thinking about the issue of artificial life. The reason why I brought it up is that it's a good benchmark for thinking about the human nature issue. When we're thinking about manufacturing life or manufacturing life like us, human life, then, the way that we are trying to produce it reflects what we think we're like. It's a reflection of our understanding of ourselves. If we think that our minds are computers, we'll end up with "artificial intelligences" that—*

Jon: We'll build Vulcans *[laughter]*.

Aku: *Yeah, and they'll look nothing like us. So we don't seem to be computers, after all, or at least don't seem to work like that at all. It's interesting how enticing, especially in the '50s and the '60s, this idea was. Many people still think that. If you talk to some psychologists, they will say, "Our minds are like computers, and we work like computers." It doesn't seem to be that way to me.*

Jon: It doesn't at all. I think it is a good time to go back to the beginning of this chat and tell you what I think we (humans) are: We are biocultural ex-apes.

Aku: *Biocultural ex-apes, okay. Yeah, that would be a good tagline.*

Jon: That's my tagline: We are biocultural ex-apes.

Suggested Readings

Dupré, J. 2001. Human Nature and the Limits of Science. New York: Oxford University Press.

Loomba, Ania. 2006. Human Nature or Human Difference? *In* Human Nature: Fact and Fiction. R. H. Wells, and J. McFadden, eds. Pp. 147-163. London: Continuum.

Malik, K. 2000. Man, Beast, and Zombie: What Science Can and Cannot Tell Us about Human Nature. London: Weidenfeld and Nicolson.

Marks, J. 2016. Tales of the Ex-Apes: How We Think about Human Evolution. Berkeley, CA: University of California Press.

Simpson, G. G. 1949. The Meaning of Evolution. New Haven: Yale University Press.

Terrell, J. E. 2015. A Talent for Friendship: Rediscovery of a Remarkable Trait. New York: Oxford University Press.

Interviewee: Barbara J. King

Bio. Barbara J. King graduated from Douglass College with a BA in Anthropology. She received her MA and PhD in Anthropology from the University of Oklahoma and is currently Chancellor Professor of Anthropology at the College of William & Mary. In addition to her recent book, *How Animals Grieve* (University of Chicago Press), which was translated into Japanese, French, and Portuguese, she has authored *Being With Animals* (Doubleday 2010), *Evolving God* (Doubleday 2007), *The Dynamic Dance* (Harvard University Press 2004), and a number of other books. King has studied monkeys in Kenya and great apes in captive settings in Africa and the United States. Her research has advanced the thesis that animals have deeper cognitive and emotional capacities than previously thought. Barbara is a popular guest on interview programs, including the Diane Rehm Show and National Geographic Radio, and has been interviewed on radio programs in Canada, Austria, Germany, the UK, and Australia. King is the recipient of numerous teaching awards from William and Mary and the state of Virginia. She writes weekly for NPR's 13.7 Cosmos and Culture blog and contributes regularly to *The Times Literary Supplement* (London); her 2013 article on animal mourning for *Scientific American* was chosen for inclusion in *The Best of Science and Nature Writing 2014.*

Slogan. *"It is not that there is a human nature so much as we create our lives as bio-cultural beings: we are a product of that very plasticity of our evolution. It is also about meaning-making, in humans and in other animals, and this is what lies at the heart of the conversation about human nature and animal nature."*

Agustín: *If you had to provide a description or definition of human nature or natures, what would it be?*

Barbara: Yes, I think I would consider myself an Ingoldian, if that's a word. In other words, I tend to follow the anthropologist Tim Ingold's perspective pretty much, and Tim Ingold says that human beings are not naturally pre-equipped for life, but that they create their lives through development. What I think of is not that there's a human nature so much as we create our lives as bio-cultural beings.

I do want to return to that point with some caveats certainly, but through what happens to us in ontogeny and through the force of social dynamics, I think we make our human nature. I'm really shocked and annoyed by how often in our discourse the term "hardwired" keeps coming up, again and again, in discussions of human behavior.

I basically want to rail against that, for example, in explaining differences between men and women. Maybe we can talk more about this in subsequent questions, but when I think about this original question, what comes to mind is: What does "hard-wired" even mean? Does it mean that our human nature is impervious to change? Does it mean that we're stuck with behaving in certain ways and that we can change those ways only with enormous effort?

Agustín: *Do you think that there's not a hardwiring, obviously, but do you think there's a kind of soft ranging wiring? I'm trying to think of the best way to say this. That there's a sort of broad flexible outline that humans then fill in, or do you think the outline itself is even created?*

Barbara: Yes, I do think there is an outline that humans fill in, because I'm comfortable to some extent with suggesting that we have a human nature in the sense that we're built around plasticity. I know this is kind of a common thing to say, but I think it's common because there's strength in it and truth to it.

We are social beings. We co-construct our world with others around us. We are ready and able to respond flexibly, and in a sense what I like so much about that point is that it refers to a cross-cultural universality, but even so we are visibly constructing inside those lines at every point.

Agustín: *Yeah. Do you think then this is a pattern that's unique to humans? I mean, a lot of people invoke a uniqueness when they talk about humans. Do you think this flexibility is unique to humans, or do you think even this discussion about a nature is unique to humans?*

Barbara: No. No, on both points. I don't think the discussion of nature should be unique to humans, and I don't think that this very active co-construction of our lives is unique to humans. I'm reading a book right now by Whitehead and Rendell called *The Cultural Lives of Whales and Dolphins.*[10]

I'm completely convinced that orcas, or killer whales, who live in these incredibly large dynamic cooperative societies, have something very similar happening with them. It is not just, okay, we know there's inter-specific variation, that's kind of old hat and old story. With orcas, we find individuals or individuals in subgroups who construct traditions and customs very, very culturally and who respond enormously to their preferred habitats and the other animals around them.

In fact, my work as you know involves the cognition and emotional expression of non-human primates and other animals. I think a lot about what's unique and where are we falling into misplaced claims of human exceptionalism. I was really positively influenced by Eduardo Kohn's work on this, for instance, for example in his book *How Forests Think.*[11] I don't think we have yet, as anthropologists or

10 Whitehead, Hal, and Luke Rendall. 2014. The Cultural Lives of Whales and Dolphins. Chicago: University of Chicago Press.

11 Kohn, Eduardo. 2013. How Forests Think: Toward an Anthropology Beyond the Human. Oakland, CA: University of California Press.

more broadly as social scientists, to really start engaging with asking these types of questions about other animals, not just to understand ourselves but also to understand them and their perceptions and understandings. What is going on in these cooperative societies? What are the social relationships going on that enable these cultural solutions to emerge?

Agustín: *How then do you think—I mean, this leads right into this issue of personhood. How do you relate personhood to all of this?*

Barbara: Yeah, it took me a long time to realize that what the conversation about personhood is trying to do is just break a link between "person" and "human," not to suggest that all other animals have to fit into a mold of being human. We don't have to start thinking of elephants, chimpanzees, dogs, whatever, in human terms, rather, I think that the entire personhood conversation is important for issues of animal welfare that concern me very, very deeply. I think it's less important for conversations about human nature, so that might be something that I can get back into later.

Agustín: *Yeah. Well, let me, actually, then going with the humans here, what do you think, to what extent, or to what role does human agency itself play in human nature? You alluded to this earlier a bit.*

Barbara: Yeah. Most socio-cultural anthropologists whom I know seem to believe that human agency is almost limitlessly powerful, so that with the right will and the right resources, we can overcome almost anything. We can overcome aggression and violence, let's say, or xenophobia, prejudice, intolerance, what have you. Of course, I think there's so much right with this view, this openhearted good view, because it's our responsibility to do everything we can to alleviate social injustice, but I think there is some degree of influence of our human evolved tendencies towards favoring one's own group, however that may be defined.

Of course, these are completely culturally constructed categories of who's considered "in" and who's considered "out" of a group, but I do worry about this, that we are in some ways very shaped by our history—indeed, I would even be willing to say by our biology—to define some as "in" and some as "out," and respond with at the very least suspicion and the at the very worst with terrible violence. I grapple with these questions.

I think there are limits to human plasticity in this way, or maybe not so much limits as an obligation to be incredibly vigilant about some of the tendencies that we may have.

Agustín: *That segues right into my next point. What do you think the role of morality is in this discussion?*

Barbara: Yeah. I think we are fundamentally moral beings in a sense that we continually assess what is going on socially, what is culturally acceptable or not, what is punishable or not, what is to be trusted and what is to be deemed as cheating. It goes back again to this sense that we are dependent on cooperation. I see the morality as being sort of naturally emergent from our evolved tendency to cooperation. In this way our morality then arises from the ground up, from being so incredibly social, and this works again for other animals also.

I think about the accounts that you're certainly familiar with, say the chimpanzee female who mediates between males in dispute, who punishes male leaders who go too far even in these male dominated societies. When something deeply offends us (humans) that we perceive according to our culturally constructed categories, we respond, and that's something that we do share with some other animals.

Agustín: *So this deep connectivity to other animals you would almost argue is part of the discussion of human nature?*

Barbara: Absolutely, and something that I write about a lot is that we're only human because we co-evolved with other animals, and I want to push that envelope a little bit. One of the things that I've been engaged in is trying to take some of Marshall Sahlins's concepts, concepts that he believes quite firmly and decidedly relate only to humans, and ask if that uniqueness is really true. I'm thinking here about the concept of mutuality of being that you may be familiar with.

In his book *What Kinship Is—and Is Not*, which came out in 2013, Sahlins says that we are so different than other animals because we are co-present in each other. In other words, when humans spend time together, we know that we affect each other, but there's something going on that's more profound when individuals that are no longer together, no longer present and in front of each other, may still be very emotionally and cognitively taken up with each other's lives. He talks about how we can make each other effective kin. We're not blood related, but we become kin through social processes.

I'm trying to make the argument that, in fact, it's profoundly in the nature of some animals to do this sort of thing, not in a language-dependent way, but through their own meaning-making. I do mean even when animal individuals are not necessarily right in front of each other. I think that changes the bounds of the conversation a little bit about human nature and animal nature.

Agustín: *What about—let's sidestep the controversy about how we use the term culture in a broader sense, but what about human culture in and of itself and that notion of this filling out the outlines as you've been referring to in human nature, this plasticity. What role does human culture play in making us human?*

Barbara: Yes, I can only go back here to the fundamental inseparability of biology and culture. I think that because other animals are cultural, other animals, too, create their natures. I like your term also very much. I use the term "biocultural" but your term is "naturenurtural" and they come together incredibly well.

I am concerned that evolutionary psychologists in some cases (or certain biological anthropologists) seem unable to understand the plasticity of this process, and what the bicultural part really means.

I remember when Steve Pinker[12] wrote years ago that the bonobo Kanzi was like a trained bear in the Moscow circus. We know that Kanzi had learned to comprehend spoken English. He learned to express himself in a symbolic way through lexigrams, and, yeah, that happened because he was enculturated, but Pinker could not possibly see how this could come about unless humans essentially *forced* Kanzi into this. In fact, Kanzi soaked it up readily, and for me that's the beauty of culture and ontogeny shifting the brain, the genetics, the very body, in learning all these new and exciting things. That's another example that I would use from the animal world.

<hr>

12 The Harvard evolutionary psychologist. See Chapter 1.

Agustín: *You touched on this right there in that answer, this relationship between culture and evolutionary processes, right? I agree that we can't understand culture and biology as dichotomies. That makes no sense, but do you see evolutionary processes as having developed or changed this malleable human nature?*

Barbara: Certainly yes. I think the reason I'm a biological anthropologist is that I do believe that there's power in what happens to us through natural selection and the other forces of evolution. I guess I would go back to some of what I said earlier about our evolved tendencies in violence and aggression that require our vigilance. Also, if we think about patterns of disease and health and wellness, clearly these are issues that are related to patterns of social justice, and we can't separate out who gets sick from what they suffer in terms of poverty and stress.

Yet there are, of course, gene-based diseases against which no amount of human agency will prevail. If you watch a family become devastated by Huntington's disease, you won't doubt this. This is just a very specific example.

There are times in teaching at William and Mary when I have students who've been steeped in cultural anthropology theory, and they come to me and they really, really believe that we can overcome *everything* that's happened to us in evolution, and I don't believe exactly that.

Agustín: *Yeah. Related to that is the idea of the interaction between concepts of human nature, human culture variability, and different faith practices. Do you see a role for this dialogue in this discussion?*

Barbara: I have thought a lot about that question. Obviously, I knew you were going to ask me that, and faith is such an interesting word for me; I come at it from a slightly different perspective, but it's not completely irrelevant, I hope. I've been interested in the evolution of religious ritual in human prehistory, so I've come to think, yes, every human society going way back has had religious ritual, but as an atheist I do resist suggesting that that necessarily means there's some kind of religious faith or supernatural faith as a necessary part of human nature.

I mean, the fact that there's religious ritual that, I do believe, is patterned into human society is not the same thing as saying faith is part of human nature. There's a continuum of people, some filled with profound faith in a god or gods or spirits, and some who enact religious rituals for very different sets of reasons, socio-emotional reasons that may relate to being part of a collective, and some who don't participate at all. Again, I'm brought back to thinking that cultural tradition completely influences the expression of faith. I'm not sure that that's what you're getting at, but that's how I'm thinking of it.

Agustín: *No, no. I think that's a very interesting take on it. Back to something you said earlier about meaning making. Do you think there's a role for meaning making in this part of the discussion?*

Barbara: Yeah, very much. In my book *Evolving God,*[13] I was interested in trying to look at the evolutionary history of meaning making, because I do believe there is one. Again, this idea of emergence just delights me in thinking about our evolved nature…I'm willing to use that word, because you have all these sort of building blocks, non-human primates being conscious rule followers, interested in *this* punishment angle and *that* mediation angle and *this* morality angle. There's this profound emergence of something that evolution, biological and cultural, has combined to produce in us. That is where the question of religious ritual and faith comes in. That whole process I just think is a stunning example of what evolution can do; it is rooted in evolution. Yet, there's this very big difference in what happens in our societies in this case, than what happens in animal societies.

Agustín: *Yeah. Do you think, given everything that we've just talked about, do you think people sometimes identify or, let's say, misidentify the term evolution with a particular set of biological markers or morphologies and miss this kind of rich discussion that you've just presented?*

Barbara: Oh, most definitely. I mean, one of the first things that I say in a related way to my students when they walk into my Evolutionary Perspectives on Gender class is "Get out of your mind what I think you may be bringing to the very terms 'biology' and 'evolution.'"

....

13   King, Barbara. 2007. Evolving God: A Provocative View on the Origins of Religion. New York: Doubleday.

Again, I'm mostly teaching students who come from feminist theory class, or cultural anthropology class, and they may think that biology means "hardwired," and that evolution refers to a fundamental human nature. I think that that's not because they're not smart students. They're very smart students, but they have been seduced by the discourse in this country, internationally, globally, about a very simplistic view of biology and evolution. That's a big point, a very important point.

Agustín: *Excellent. Barbara, this is a fantastic conversation. I just want to go briefly back to what you started with about humans and human nature really being about our bio-cultural nature, or as I like to say, our nature neutral reality. If you could drive that home, what do you think the difference is for people understanding that versus these hardwired concepts?*

Barbara: Well, I think I would point to epigenetics. I would point to the power of listening to each other, educating each other, and just suggesting that what we are primed for as evolved beings is to shift. I have talked about limits of the ability to shift, but the power of this ability is still absolutely enormous. We can look at this in terms of gender. I mean, that's what I teach in the class I mentioned, and I look at patterns in the past of differences between men and women and talk about how incredibly much that's changing. I'm fascinated with the conversations that we're all having in the world today as well, about sexual orientation and gender identity. That we're beginning to *really realize* that it's not that gender is a dichotomy, but rather there's this incredible spectrum both for how you identify and how you act in the world.

I think that that speaks to what evolution has been doing. It's not the kind of process that is very simply rooted in mating and reproduction and genes and brains, but in producing the ability to understand in new ways the world, to describe the world in new ways. The fact that we're able to do this is a product of the very plasticity of our evolution.

Agustín: *Fantastic. Well, that's it. That's the perfect closer right there.*

Suggested Readings:

Boesch, Christophe, and Hedwige Boesch-Achermann. 2000. The Chimpanzees of the Tai Forest: Behavioural Ecology and Evolution. London: Oxford University Press.

de Waal, Frans. 2013. The Bonobo and the Atheist. New York: W.W. Norton and Co.

Fausto-Sterling, Anne. 2000. Sexing the Body: Gender Politics and the Construction of Sexuality. New York: Basic Books.

Gruen, Lori. 2015. Entangled Empathy: An Alternative Ethic for our Relationships with Animals. Brooklyn, NY: Lantern Books.

Ingold, Tim. 2000. The Perception of the Environment: Essays in Livelihood, Dwelling, and Skill. London: Routledge.

King, Barbara J. 2013. How Animals Grieve. Chicago: University of Chicago Press.

Sorenson, John. 2009. Ape. London: Reaktion Books. (and any of the other numerous volumes in Reaktion's Animal series: Monkey, Pig, Oyster, Cat…)

Whitehead, Hal, and Luke Rendell. 2014. The Cultural Lives of Whales and Dolphins. Chicago: University of Chicago Press.

Interviewee: Robert Sussman

Bio. Dr. Sussman is a Professor of Anthropology at Washington University in St. Louis. He received his MA from the University of California-Los Angeles and his PhD from Duke University. Sussman's research has included the ecology, demography, and conservation of the ring-tailed lemur (*Lemur catta*) in the Beza Mahafaly Reserve in Madagascar, as well as the ecology, social organization, and genetics of introduced long-tailed macaques (*Macaca fascicularis*) in Mauritius and the community ecology and conservation of primates in Central and South America. More broadly, he is interested in the way in which studies of primate behavior and evolution can help us understand the basis of human behavior, as well as the history of physical (biological) anthropology. He has recently written *Man the Hunted: Primates, Predators and Human Evolution* (with Donna Hart) and *The Myth of Race: The Troublesome Persistence of an Unscientific Idea* as part of his interest in the history of anthropology.

Slogan. *"Chimpanzees are chimpanzees; they are unique. Humans are humans, and they are unique. We are not saying human uniqueness is anything better or worse. It is different because of our total potential and our evolution."*

Agustín: *If you are talking with colleagues, or friends, or family and someone asks you, "What is human nature," what kind of description or definition would you offer them?*

Robert: Oh, that is a big, wide question. Human nature is basically very variable, but there is a core to human nature. I think we have not been studying that core correctly, because the core is more like a game. For example, we could say that chimpanzees have a nature, and humans have a nature. Those natures are different. You might say that human nature and chimpanzee nature overlap: humans and chimps both live on earth and to some extent in similar environments, for instance. You might say that chimpanzees have a rulebook in their nature, that they can do certain things. You can look at the total potentiality of what they do, and you say, "That's the game, the game plan." Let us say chimpanzees play checkers on a checkerboard—but humans play chess. You could actually look at the game, and you could say chimpanzees have variability, a lot of variability, but it is much, much less variability than humans have in their nature, given the types of reactions these animals have to different stimuli.

Much of chimp reactions to stimuli is genetically based. Then, in humans, we also have genetically-based reactions to stimuli, but the variety of those reactions is much greater. The game is much more complex. What we have been doing so far is trying to look at all of the little movements or reactions on this "board" and then trying to figure out, from a external view, how we can describe all of these movements or reactions, and then trying to describe human nature.

We have not, I think, in most cases, looked at what is the structure of the game. What is the total potentiality? Then, do a statistical analysis of that total potentiality, so we would be able to say, "They can do all these things, but they do this 90 percent of the time." We can be, by nature, aggressive. We can be, by nature, cooperative, but what is the statistical variation? We are, by nature, aggressive. We are, by nature, cooperative. Yes, we are, but that does not tell you anything. That is a simplification, because we are both aggressive and cooperative. If you wanted to know what all of the total potential of human behavior is, you look at human history and variation—that is why anthropology is so important.

You look at paleontology. You look at archeology. You look at human cultures generally. You see all the things humans have done in the past. What are the things that they do now? Then, you make a map, or a structured pattern, and you try to say, "What's the percentage or proportion of all of these things?" If you did this, you could not say, "Humans are, by nature, aggressive," because a very, very small percentage of their time is spent in that behavior. They are aggressive. That is not their nature, but it is a proportion of their total potentiality. Then, you might learn the rules of the game, but we have not done that type of analysis yet. We need to know the rules of the game.

In fact, people like Claude Lévi-Strauss and Edmund Leach, I think, really were talking about these things.[14] Leach had this wonderful quote, where he said, "If you draw a series of lines on a rubber sheet you can stretch this rubber sheet around and the series of lines will change the manifest shape though the lines will remain the same." What we want to know is, when you stretch the rubber around, what happens to these same lines? What are the rules of the game? Right? What are the pieces, and how are they moved?

Agustín: *Where do you see the rules of the game arising? Are they spatial or something else?*

....

14 Claude Lévi-Strauss was a French social antropologist who was famous for instigating a structuralist approach to antropology. The idea was to examine underlying patterns and structures in the great diversity of human systems of symbols.

Robert: Well, my professor at UCLA, Jack Prost, would say something like this. When he looked at, let us say, locomotion, what he wanted to know is not what animals do at any one time, but what—if you took a picture of the joint—was the potential, the total potential of that joint? Then you could say, "Okay. This is what they can do. Now how do you restrict that? Why do you restrict it in different ways?" Again, what I am saying is, we do not know what the potentials are, except we know basically what humans can do and what they cannot do.

What we now need to do is try to put that behavior into some kind of a structure, so we can define when they do it, under what circumstances. It is like, if you could do a picture, say in sixteen dimensional space, and you could map that picture. You could say, "Okay, this is the total potential." Then, you could start doing statistical analysis within that total potential—of everything that they can do—what do they do? Then, if you looked at different cultures, where do these map on the space? You could actually create a really neat graph. In this culture, they do these things. In that culture, they do those things. You could say, "Out of the total potential, they divide up that specific potential space because of their particular cultural background."

Agustín: *Where do you see the role of human uniqueness or distinctiveness in all this?*

Robert: You are asking what the difference is between, say, humans and chimpanzees. Well, chimpanzees are chimpanzees; they are unique. Humans are humans, and they are unique. We are not saying human uniqueness is anything better or worse. It is different because of our total potential and our evolution. I would say the major difference that really makes us a different kind of animal is the ability to symbolize. What I mean by that is no other animal actually thinks about and can communicate something in the future; no other animals can communicate about something that is not where they are presently. Things that exist but exist elsewhere. For example, that is why kinship is so interesting, because kinship in primates, basically, is related directly to familiarity and presence. If you recognize your father, he has to be present. If he goes, you forget him. If it is matrilineal, you have got to recognize your mother—your mother's offspring—as those that are familiar—and that is where you develop these social relationships. In humans, if you have a father you have never met, he is still your father. No other animal has anything like that.

Agustín: *From what you are saying, it seems to me that variation, symbolization, and culture are the forces that shape human nature.*

Robert: Yes. Variability in humans is extremely great, because we have this ability to think outside the box, outside of familiarity.

Symbolization is the particular sort of biological reality that we have that makes us different from all other animals. Some animals have symbols. Some animals will think symbolically: if a dog wants outside, or a cat wants outside, they know it is outside. It is in their mind, but they cannot communicate that, and they cannot change it. They cannot make it into something else. It is another part of our symbolization that we cannot only think about what is outside, but we can think about what is outside in a way that it is not really there. We can imagine things that do not exist, and I do not think animals can do that. I do not think they can imagine things or create things that do not already exist in their minds. It is our collective, group symbolization that makes up our culture.

Agustín: *In that same vein then, a lot of people have tried to argue for human uniqueness or against it by continuities and discontinuities in morality between humans and animals. How do you see that related to your perspective on human nature?*

Robert: Ah, that is an interesting question. I have not thought about that much, but I do think there is an evolutionary connection between human morality/ethics and animal morality/ethics. That is not directly connected to symbolism, but we, again, create more complex ethics because we can symbolize ethical and moral thinking. I think ethics and morality actually derive from the need for certain animals, who in their evolutionary context are better off being social, to develop ways in which they can be social. We have just symbolized those things. We just create another level on top, but the biological ground is still there. Socialization is crucial with humans and other social animals. Just like Marc Bekoff's studies on play in animals have shown, through play animals learn to interact with each other, how to be friendly and cooperative with each other.[15] Individual animals are sometimes even killed within a group, if they do not cooperate. If you are going to be a socially-living animal, you have to have some kind of shared cooperative norms, or mores.

In other words, human morality is both similar and different from animal morality. We do something special with the same basic stuff that all social animals have. There are lots of shared emotions, lots of shared values, lots of shared cooperative behaviors. What we do, again, is put a layer of symbols on these behaviors. We transform them to another level. Now, I think this can often be dangerous for humans. Because of their evolution, in non-human animals, their behavior and environment are all integrated. They are integrated through trial and error through millions of years of evolution. This human symbolization, this creation that we have, makes us vulnerable, because we do not have the advantages of millions of years of evolution to put between us and our environment. If the environment changes radically, bad things can happen. Symbolization and flexible behavior give humans an advantage. They can adapt very quickly. However, it also gives us a disadvantage in that we think that we know what we are doing. Yet, what we are doing is trying to create our own reality, which does not necessarily fit into this evolutionary/environmental progression of millions of years. Causing global warming does not fit into our long-term environmental advantage.

Agustín: *You are saying that we humans can think our way into bad situations?*

Robert: We can think our way into being more variable and better able to adapt to the environment, but we can also create an environment that is not adaptable, that has nothing to do with our long-term evolutionary history.

---

15 See, e.g., Bekoff, Marc. 2008. Animals at Play: Rules of the Game. Philadelphia: Temple University Press.

Agustín: *This brings up two questions. If you look at philosophical treatments of human nature, they talk a lot about things like free will and faith. Given what we were just talking about, what do you think about that?*

Robert: I think it is a part of this layer of creation that we have put on top of our regular behavior. We have to adapt to the world. We have to adapt to other people, and we have to explain it to ourselves. Now, other animals do not have to explain it to themselves. We explain it to ourselves; in some cases, we create theology. We create morals. We create these things. Sometimes they are good, and sometimes they are bad. Again, we are not really adapting those creations to our evolutionary history. We are superimposing them on our evolutionary history. It could be, like we have both said, a good thing, and help us be adaptable. It could be a very bad thing and help us become extinct much quicker than most animals have ever become extinct.

Agustín: *[Laughter]*

Robert: Let me add one thing to that. In my introductory course, I often say, "Dinosaurs became extinct because they became too big for their brains. Okay? They couldn't adapt. Humans will become extinct because their brains are too big for their bodies." *[Laughter]*

Agustín: *[Laughter] What do you think about some of these popular ideas about the extended mind, the whole idea that the human brain is nothing by itself? It needs cultures and symbols to work with and connect out.*

Robert: I am not sure if I interpret it like that exactly, but I agree. I think you are right. I think many social animals are like this at certain levels, but humans even more so, because we cannot exist without interconnectivity. Our whole basis depends upon the symbols that we learn throughout our lives, because that is what creates our worldview. We do not have a genetic worldview. We do not come into the world ready to adapt to what we eat and all of that. Everything we do is basically given to us through our culture. I think we are the ultimate animal that is social, because we are completely dependent on everything being social and everything being interconnected. No human could ever exist outside of a human group, outside of their own human group.

Agustín: *Would it be fair to say then via symbols, cultures, and languages we actually create our own evolutionary context? I have called this social niche construction.*

Robert: Yes, I think that is extremely important because, basically, that is the difference between humans and other animals. Again, this ties right into this idea that most animals have an evolutionary history with their genetics that ties them into their environment, and their social interaction, and all of that. It is really the end product of trial and error of evolution over millions of years. We have stopped doing that. We basically have that as a starting point, but on top of it, we have this thing that makes us create our own niches, which gives us both an advantage and a disadvantage, given the situation and if we think correctly. Humans have created a level on top of evolution. When we think, we are not thinking with that millions years of trial and error. It is an on the spot *[laughter]* decision!

But this capacity to shape our own niche can also put us into trouble. Indeed, this is what we do constantly. Well, some people say, "Oh, it's great to go out and, say, drill for oil." Then, we begin getting more and more earthquakes. Of course, the Earth has adapted in a certain way and is balanced in a certain way. If you withdraw all of the shock absorbent within the earth (if oil does this), what will happen? We will create something that is going to be bad for us, for everybody. We do not think about this until after the fact, and usually, when it is too late. I think that this is the real problem with humans: we have created Frankenstein's monster. We are going to create an earth that is supposed to be our super earth, but one that is not adapted to longevity. I think there is a good chance that we will become extinct because of our brain being too big and because we create an environment that cannot sustain us in the long run.

Suggested Readings:

Fuentes, Agustín. 2012. Race, Monogamy, and Other Lies They Told You: Busting Myths about Human Nature. Berkeley: University of California.

Marks, Jonathan. 2003. What it Means to be 98% Chimpanzee: Apes, People, and their Genes. Berkeley: University of California Press.

Sussman, Robert W., ed. 1999. The Biological Basis of Human Behavior: A Critical Review. Saddle River, NJ: Prentice Hall.

Hart, Donna, and R. W. Sussman. 2009. Man the Hunted: Primate, Predators, and Human Evolution, enlarged, paperback edition. Boulder, CO: Westview Press.

Sussman, Robert W. 2010. Human Nature. American Anthropologist 112:514-515.

Sussman, Robert W., and Paul A. Garber. 2011. Cooperation, Collective Action, and Competition in Primate Social Interactions. In Primates in Perspective, 2nd edition. C. J. Campbell, A. Fuentes, K. C. Mackinnon, S. K. Bearder and R. S. M. Stumpf, eds. Pp. 587-599. New York: Oxford University Press.

Sussman, Robert W. 2013. Why the Legend of the Killer Ape Never Dies: The Enduring Power of Cultural Beliefs to Distort our View of Human Nature. In War, Peace, and Human Nature. Douglas P. Fry, ed. Pp. 97-111. London: Oxford University Press.

Interviewee: Kim Sterelny

Bio. After studying philosophy at Sydney University, Kim Sterelny taught philosophy in Australia at Sydney, Australian National University (where he was Research Fellow, and then Senior Research Fellow, in Philosophy at the Research School of Social Sciences [RSSS] from 1983 until 1987), and La Trobe University, before taking up a position at Victoria University in Wellington, where he held a Personal Chair in Philosophy. For a few years he spent half of each year at Victoria University and the other half with the Philosophy Program at RSSS, but from 2008 he has been full-time at ANU. His main research interests are the philosophy of biology, the philosophy of psychology, and the philosophy of mind. He is the author of *The*

Evolved Apprentice: How Evolution Made Us Unique, Thought in a Hostile World, and *The Representational Theory of Mind,* and he is co-author of *What is Biodiversity?* (with James Maclaurin), *Language and Reality* (with Michael Devitt), and *Sex and Death: An Introduction to Philosophy of Biology* (with Paul Griffiths). Sterelny is a Fellow of the Australian Academy of the Humanities and the Royal Society of New Zealand. In addition to philosophizing, he spends his time eating curries, drinking red wine, bushwalking, and bird watching.

Slogan. *"I'd try to think about human nature and its plasticity in ways that are not empirically empty."*

Agustín: *The first question I ask is the one that I don't know if I could answer myself, but it is an interesting one to lead with. That is, if a student or a colleague or a friend asked you about a human nature, or human natures, how do you respond?*

Kim: I respond by emphasizing the plasticity of human nature, but clearly not limitless plasticity. This is a really difficult question. I'd try to think about human nature and its plasticity in ways that are not empirically empty. Everyone will sign up for some form of interaction between genes and the environment. One could say that genes and the environment interact and the environment matters and so on and so forth. This way you get a kind of bland interaction, which doesn't really tell you enough for any kind of effective models. Biology sets certain limits for development: biology demarcates the boundaries of the river because it's a very broad and deep river and it's a cultured history that determines where you are.

Limit models aren't very satisfactory either. They do play some role, however: the fact that we have two sexes rather than three or none, for example. But there's more—limit models aren't interactive enough. Linguistics also offers some limit models but they aren't interactive enough either. I don't think anyone's come up with a model that isn't banal and recognizes interaction properly. So on the one hand you get switch models and the other hand limit models, neither of them seems satisfactory but I don't have a better one to offer.[16]

Agustín: *At the core then it's some hybrid or some interstitial (in-between) space.*

Kim: Yes.

Agustín: *Maybe then between these limits and these interactions.*

Kim: Yes. And I don't think we have a good, simple picture to guide us in thinking about where we should be. We have good pictures and we have simple pictures, but what we don't have is good, simple pictures.

Agustín: *What about human uniqueness or a human distinctiveness?*

Kim: I do think that's important. There is plausibility in the idea that we're very different from other great apes and that those differences have arisen with remarkable rapidity. Just think how controversial the genetic dates were when they were first articulated.[17] So people were surprised by how rapidly the phylogenetic differences between humans and other great apes have evolved. So there is something unusual going on. There's that lovely "all species are unique idea"—there is a famous book on human evolution called "Another Unique Species"—but some species are more unique than others. I think humans are ones which are more unique than others. In part that is because we have evolved through cultural as well as genetic inheritance, but explaining how and why we came to evolve culturally is part of the problem.

....

16 Nativist evolutionary psychologists defend a switch model of the interaction of genes and the environment; a particular kind of environment flicks a switch, and directs development down one pre-planned path rather than another. A very unsafe environment predisposed the development of a risk-taking, early breeding life history, for example. This is sometimes called the "jute-box" model of how genes and the environment interact. A limit model says (for example) that in any environment not utterly pathological, human phenotypes with respect to (say) prosocial cooperation will fall within a certain range.

17 The molecular and genetic dates were much more recent than the older version of divergence times based on moprhology.

Agustín: *What about a number of philosophers, theologians, even psychologists who lean on this idea of agency or free will if you will? Do you think there's some difference in the distinctiveness or uniqueness in humans that has to do with an agency or—*

Kim: I'm like many philosophers, I think agency in the sense of free will is just a recognition of the increase of complexity of human behavior and increased role of internal planning and the fact that we're more sensitive than many other creatures to what we learned about twenty years ago and so on. I don't think there's a qualitative difference or even close to a qualitative difference between humans and other great apes in this respect. I think our systems of decision and control are importantly different. We have learned a lot more skills of inhibition. We have learned skills that enable us to leverage our behavior with a lot more information sources and can lean on one another cognitively in a way that other great apes can't. And we support one another: one reason why our plans are relatively stable and reach forward in time is that we are sensitive to one another's expectations of what we are going to do. For us, thinking and deciding is partly collective. But that's all there is.

Agustín: *So what about Michael Tomasello's theory of mind approach to learning and all of this?[18]*

Kim: I think there's something there. He's on to something important with his "collective intentionality." In particular, there is a really important relationship between collective intentionality and human cooperation. In order to have all this human cooperation, we have to establish certain negative practices, like systems of punishment and norms. This makes us feel bad; we have bad things happen to others. None of this is bullshit. I'm sure it plays a role, but I think the role of positive affects is underestimated here.

Think how much fun people have when they're doing stuff together. Playing sport, for instance, is incredibly intrinsically rewarding to people. Other great apes play, but they have nothing like a team game. Tomasello and his people have done these very

18 See, e.g., Tomasello, Michael. 2014. A Natural History of Human Thinking. Cambridge: Harvard University Press.

cool experiments which showed basically that little kids would keep doing stuff, if they were doing it with someone else and you're mutually acknowledging that you're doing something together. They get much more of the intrinsic reward of doing that than the instrumental reward of what you're originally doing, whereas chimps don't.

I think it's not just sensitivity to other's minds. I mean it's clear that humans are better mind readers than other great apes, but that's not the only thing that's going on. It's this stuff about collective intentionality or joint action, and the intrinsically rewarding nature of joint action. This, I think, explains a lot about the distinctive nature of human cooperation. I don't think it's a big breakthrough. I don't think there's a single big breakthrough, but I think it's an important element of the stew, and a lot of approaches neglected such processes, because they concentrated on negative affect rather than positive affect in cooperation. There are bastards out there, and we need to control them. But the story of the evolution of human cooperation is not just a story of how we came to control our inner bastard.

Agustín: *I know I am going back here, but I need to throw this in: Could you riff a little off of Robin Dunbar's extended minds, social brain context?[19] Do you think that in some way is related to what you were just eluding to?*

Kim: The extended mind stuff certainly is. Now, whether or not you call it an extended mind or you call it environmental scaffolding, the terminology doesn't matter. But it is certainly true that the cognitive powers we have, we have in part because of environmental supports and tools including the stuff that goes on in other people's heads. That plays a tremendous role in human cognitive life. Whereas, again with great apes, it's not wholly every ape for themselves, but it's pretty close. So that's one aspect of the Dunbar stuff.

The other claim is that the evolution of human cognition is basically driven by group size. I'm much more skeptical about that. For one thing, we have very little evidence about group size in

---

19   See Robin Dunbar's interview in Chapter 2.

human evolution. On the other hand, in some of his very recent work, Dunbar has been emphasizing the complexity of human social life, with group size just being one element of complexity. I am more on board with that.

Agustín: *Moving on from that, a number of people have looked to human natures or human nature or some sort of intrinsic notion of becoming and being human and placed morality in a central position. How you do envision it?*

Kim: I'm a bit more—well it depends exactly what you mean by morality; if you have a very broad notion of morality, which includes pro-social emotions, then sure. If by morality, you mean more narrowly cognitive judgments of right and wrong, I'm more skeptical for two reasons. Firstly, cognitive judgments of right and wrong are almost certainly language dependent, and I think language presupposes an already highly cooperative world. Now, we evolved language because we were cooperators. We didn't become cooperators because we evolved language. So that's the first reason.

The second reason—there is all of this stuff in cognitive psychology of morality that's hard to evaluate. Work by Jonathan Haidt[20] and people like that basically says that a lot of moral judgment is confabulation. We'll do stuff and respond with moral emotions and then you ask them why and they tell you a story. But often it's a case of just a story. They unconsciously make up a story about their moral views that justifies their initial reaction—now, I think the extreme versions have got to be exaggerated. Nevertheless, you have to take seriously the background worry that the explicit process of moral thought plays less of a role in shaping our own behavior and the behavior of the people they're talking to than the moral centrality hypothesis supposes.

Where that argument ends up empirically, it's too early to tell. I certainly don't think that this applies to all cases of moral behavior. I'd be very surprised if that turned out to be right. Some more moderate version of that is where a lot of moral life is the result of

....
20 See, Haidt, Jonathan. 2013. The Righteous Mind: Why Good People Are Divided by Politics and Religion. London: Penguin Books.

moral habits and unconscious and subconscious processes and only a bit of that is caused by explicit moral judgment and reflection. I would not be too surprised if that turned out to be true.

Agustín: *What about the role of culture and evolution, beyond just this sort of idea of a simplistic gene-culture evolution or even a more complex co-evolution relationship? What do you see as central in the relationship or the interconnectivity or the lack thereof between the human cultural patterns and processes and evolutionary bodies?*

Kim: I think it's an incredibly complex set of feedback relationships of various kinds. So the initial establishment of culture probably didn't depend on distinctive adaptations for cultural learning and cultural teaching. They probably piggyback on environmental change and preexisting plasticity and just the redirection of learning capacities to cultural situations, but once those become important you had all sorts of effects of genetic assimilation, selection for tolerance, selection for attention to what others are doing, probably selection for looking at people's hands, probably selection for looking at people's faces. That would then feed back to how complex the culture could be, how much could be learned, how much could be learned accurately. Of the people whose work I know, Celia Heyes is probably the person who most minimizes the role of genetic changes and specific genetic adaptations for culture. She thinks we have learned culturally how to learn culturally, with fairly minor genetic changes to our cognitive equipment. The nativist evolutionary psychologists—Cosmides, Tooby, and their allies—in contrast place a huge weight on genetic changes and new cognitive adaptation.

I think it will be a very complicated sort of feedback process. Probably different elements mattered more or less in different times. At certain stages it was really important but probably earlier than that—the kinds of things that Merlin Donald is interested in, that have to do with mimicry would probably play a much more central role.[21] They still play a quite important role in *Homo sapiens* but they probably paid a really central role with *Homo erectus*.

....

21 Donald, Merlin. 2001. A Mind So Rare: The Evolution of Human Consciousness. New York: W. W. Norton & Co.

Agustín: *Going along with that, we've got Scott Atran and David Sloan Wilson and others talking about the evolution of religion.*[22]

Kim: Right.

Agustín: *So this whole idea of trying to integrate faith as a component of adaptation, what's your take on this?*

Kim: I'm a by-product man. I think most of the adaptive stories are implausible. For one thing, the defenders carry on about the benefits but they don't talk about the costs. The costs of religion are very significant indeed. This is especially true in David Sloan Wilson's model. The defenders of the "religion as an adaptation" thesis are very good at reminding you how much help religion would be either at the group level or the individual level to maintain cooperation with the unseen policeman who's always watching.[23]

However, they don't explain the credibility of the police and they don't take into account the immense costs of these social forms. Now, Scott Atran and others like that have run by-product thesis, where religion is basically a side effect of the theory of mind. I find that more plausible but I'm still a bit worried. And given what I've just said about the costs, why hasn't the hyperactive agency detector been selected against?[24]

....

22 Atran, Scott. 2002. In Gods We Trust: The Evolutionary Landscape of Religion. New York: Oxford University Press; Wilson, David Sloan. 2002. Darwin's Cathedral: Evolution, Religion and the Nature of Society. Chicago: University of Chicago Press. According to Wilson, religious behavior and thinking is an adaptation for inter-group integration. In Atran's view, religious thinking and behavior are mostly by-products of cognitive mechanisms that have other, adaptive purposes (e.g., the Theory of Mind mechanism).

23 For a thoroughgoing supernatural punishment theory, see Norenzayan, Ara. 2013. Big Gods: How Religion Transformed Cooperation and Conflict. Princeton: Princeton University Press.

24 Some representatives of the cognitive science of religion, like Justin Barrett and Stewart Guthrie, have argued that some religious beliefs are outcomes of a specific cognitive mechanism, the Hypersensitive Agency Detection Device (HADD). See Barrett, Justin. 2004. Why Would Anyone Believe in God? Walnut Creek: AltaMira Press; Guthrie, Stewart Elliott. 1995. Faces in the Clouds: A New Theory of Religion. New York: Oxford University Press.

One possibility is it's all a lot more recent than they think. There's not much sign of religion before 15,000 or 20,000 years ago. It may be—a lot of the people think this—that folks just take it for granted that Neanderthals had something like religion but maybe they didn't. Maybe religion is much more recent, a side effect prompted by increased social complexity and social size around the last demographic transition[25] that hasn't been weeded out by selection yet. Now, I certainly wouldn't go to the stake for that hypothesis. One problem for the idea that religion is very recent is that historically known forager societies—even those with low population densities, and apparently long isolation from any large social world—seem to have something like religion. Australian aborigines, for example, have elaborate creation myths. I would have to argue that this is a product of increased social complexity in Holocene Australia.

Agustín: *I haven't seen that claim in print yet. I don't think it's actually been positioned in that way.*

Kim: Right.

Agustín: *That's very interesting. Let me ask one that's a bit of a side question about definitions of humanness. When some people start to define what a human is, they go back to the Theory of Mind or that a human is more than the sum of the parts. That does not convince me.*

Kim: I don't think there's more to us than what is physically there; we're just organisms. We're organisms that have evolved in a certain way and socialized in a certain way and acculturated in a certain way and that's all there is. I'm not signing up for any extra parts to that.

Agustín: *I'm just going to drop back one more time to this very interesting idea of religion being a structural component of human existence. Do you think there's a facet of this plasticity or this malleability of the human experience that ties directly to religion?*

Kim: Yes. The susceptibility to overactivate your findings is presumably, on this picture, significantly deeper. Coevolution, you know,

---

25 The increase in human populations and the shift towards more complex and hierarchical societies associated with the advent of agriculture.

with a human mind as it's evolved, but what the human mind does is extremely dependent on its physical, social, and cultural environment. We know that there's a very dramatic transformation in the transition to agriculture, and one that must have imposed really quite intense stressors on the existing kind of cultural moral fabric, as you had this transition from small highly egalitarian unstructured environments to much larger, more structured and much more hierarchal social environments. So it was a traumatic transition and so it wouldn't surprise anyone, if something new appeared, if you think of human minds and social behavior as highly plastic. You think that you might have some genuinely novel phenomenon appearing around that time as a consequence of that transition. So the situation is dependent on this picture of the highly plastic nature of human cognition and human personality.

Suggested Readings

Barham, L. 2013. From Hand to Handle: The First Industrial Revolution. Oxford: Oxford University Press.

Boehm, C. 2012. Moral Origins: The Evolution of Virtue, Altruism and Shame. New York: Basic Books.

Downes, S., and E. Machery, eds. 2013. Arguing About Human Nature: Contemporary Debates. New York: Routledge.

Dunbar, R., C. Gamble, et al., eds. 2014. Lucy to Language: The Benchmark Papers. Oxford: Oxford University Press.

Fry, D. P., ed. 2013. War, Peace and Human Nature. Oxford: Oxford University Press.

Hrdy, S. B. (2009). Mothers and Others: The Evolutionary Origins of Mutual Understanding. Cambridge: Harvard University Press.

Morris, I. 2015. Foragers, Farmers and Fossil Fuels: How Human Values Evolve. Princeton, NJ: Princeton University Press.

Seabright, P. 2010. The Company of Strangers: A Natural History of Economic Life. Princeton, NJ: Princeton University Press.

Sterelny, K. 2012. The Evolved Apprentice. Cambridge: MIT Press.

Tomasello, M. 2014. A Natural History of Human Thinking. Cambridge: Harvard University Press.

Interviewee: Warren Brown

Bio. Dr. Brown is the director of the Lee Edward Travis Research Institute at Fuller Theological Seminary, a Professor of Psychology in the Graduate School of Psychology, and a past member of the UCLA Brain Research Institute. He is also one of the founding members of the International Society for Science and Religion. Brown received his doctorate in experimental physiological psychology from the University of Southern California. His research examines the functions of the corpus callosum of the brain and its relationship to higher cognitive processes in humans, in particular studying the cognitive and social disabilities of individuals with agenesis of the corpus callosum.

Slogan. *"I think human life will be richer the more we understand our entanglements and responsibilities for one another's formation and development."*

Agustín: *The first question is actually the most difficult one, but I ask it because it derives interesting responses. If you were asked for a definition or a description of a human nature or human natures what would you respond? How would you respond?*

Warren: From the neuropsychological standpoint, it would have to do with cognitive capacities: capacity for language, capacity for theory of mind, and deeper relational capacities. This would entail the deeply social mind now studied in social neuroscience. I think social neuroscience is helping us understand the degree to which humans are more deeply social even than a chimpanzee. I think that would be one part.

Then, along with that come communal forms of relating that creates culture. I think human nature would have to include recognition of the cultural milieu we build for each other.

Andy Clark says we make the world smart so that we can be dumb in peace.[26] I think we credit ourselves with more intelligence than we have on our own. We create an environment that allows us to be more intelligent than we can be on our own. Both our openness to formation from experience and the kind of world we have created have to be part of human nature.

I think, theologically, persons stand in a particular relationship with God that is different than the rest of creation. There is a certain divine call on human beings.

Agustín: *Where do you think the origin for such a nature lies?*

Warren: Well, I am a theological evolutionist, both a biological and a cultural evolutionist. I think the cognitive templates are there genetically, physically. But I also read Rene Girard[27] and I think Girard has some value for us in understanding the relationship of culture and religion to controlling our tendency to be violent, and allowing, larger assemblies of persons and more complex culture to become possible. That makes some sense to me. It does not explain everything, but it explains some things.

Some evolving biology and some evolving culture, and then, again, I think in mysterious ways God communicates into that. I guess I understand an important part of God's work in creation of human life and humanness as speaking into it.

Agustín: *Would you argue that there is a role and pattern for human uniqueness in these human capacities or would you not use that term at all?*

Warren: I have written a chapter on human uniqueness, but in that work I moved towards talking about distinctiveness rather than

26 Andy Clark is a philosopher and a well known defender of the extended mind thesis. See, e.g., Clark, Andy. 2010. Supersizing the Mind: Embodiment, Action, and Cognitive Extension. London: Oxford University Press.

27 Rene Girard is a philosopher who has written extensively on the origins of culture and religion. He is famous for his "scapegoat" theory of religion and violence.

uniqueness. I do not think there is anything specific that we can point to (outside of a theological statement about the call of God upon human nature) that you can say is entirely unique.

The capacities that constitute human nature are distinctively human but they do have roots. These are things that you find in a colony of chimpanzees, but they have become distinctive in the emergence of greater complexity and depth and richness. Primate anthropology keeps telling us this over and over again, but we keep making the mistake of saying this or that is unique to human beings. [*Laughter*] Of course, it is not unique. It is distinctive in its development, but not unique.

I do not think cognitive uniqueness is at all necessary theologically. For me, because I am a physicalist rather than a dualist, I can say that human beings are within God's physical creation. God speaks into that creation in a unique way, but the human being does not have to be unique compared to the physical and biological nature of the world…distinctive is sufficient.

Agustín: *You have been strongly associated with non-reductive physicalism. Where do you see that? Obviously it is very important in these discussions about human nature. Looking at neurobiology and neuropsychology, how do you see that as playing an important role?*

Warren: First of all, I think the term "non-reductive physicalism" is a minimalist philosophical description—minimalist in the sense that it says merely that we are physical systems with irreducible properties. It is totally overlapping and congruent with terms like "emergent monism" and many other similar labels. The problem with the terminology is it gets trapped in philosophical boxes that I do not think are necessary or helpful. These terms are open and overlapping to me.

Now, to the second part of the question. How does a physical system become more than just biology in the non-reductive sense? I think emergent properties, as defined by dynamical systems theory, make a lot of sense to me. We become persons in the context of being physically complex but then developing and organizing within a culture that causes organizational properties to emerge in us from our interaction with the culture that are not reducible to biological properties.

Agustín: *Do you think this organization in the brain itself is—*

Warren: The functional organization is at the micro level. You have to say that because, at the macro level, everybody's brain just about looks alike, and our brain looks pretty much like that of a chimpanzee, not all that different. So, we have to start out with a genetically formed system that provides a base level of possibilities.

From there, the microstructure of the brain, the synaptic organization, is highly self-organizing and that is not hard to demonstrate at all, even at the level of single cell neurobiology. Shaped by our culture and experience, the microstructure is self-organizing.

Then you get to some fuzzy lines. The harder question for me now is not physical determinism, but where are the boundaries between personal responsibility and environmental causes of behavior? I am not sure that this question is philosophically solvable. I think we are all nested in a mesh of environmental predispositions and influences. We cannot extract ourselves totally from these influences and say, "I made this completely independent decision." This is probably a naïve thought.

We are entangled in a web of meaning, environment, and other people, but we still are agents in that entanglement. I am entangled in a web, but I have some agentive properties. The other thing I do not think we can deny, then, is that my exercise of agency has inescapable ripple effects in other people's life, just as their exercising of agency has ripple effects on mine.

One of the things we try to do in our book *The Physical Nature of Christian Life* (2012, with Brad Strawn), with respect to the church, is to make it quite clear that, in some sense, holiness is a thing of congregations first, before it is a property of the individuals. Our idea about the church is that it cannot be a loose association of independently spiritual persons, because that is just not a church. *[Laughter]* That is not a body.

So, this entanglement of human agency is what I think about nowadays. I do not think biological reductionism is something I worry about anymore. What I do worry about is how to understand individual agency in the context of obvious entanglements with the rest of our social environment. Sometimes I am not even sure I need to be an independent agent, other than to open myself to certain entanglements, rather than some other entanglements. One way or another, I am going to be entangled.

Agustín: *That actually falls right into the next question I want to ask. I wonder about free will and morality in notion of human nature. You pretty much sort of said that already, but—*

Warren: Yes. What Nancey Murphy and I tried to do in *Did My Neurons Make Me Do It?* was to defeat the biological reductionism part of the argument against free will. We think that there are lots of reasons to believe that persons are agents in ways that cannot be reduced to biology. The degree to which that gets disentangled from your developmental environment is a harder question.

Where does the freedom lie? We did not want to use the word "free will" in the book at all, actually. *[Laughter]* The publishers wanted us to include it in the subtitle, at least, because you can sell more books that way. People know what you are talking about. We basically talk in the book about whole persons as agents. One way that some talk about agency is to say that we are agents only to the degree to which agency can be expressed entirely independent of the influence of others. I do not think so; this is not a good way to think about agency.

Agustín: *Given that position, then, would you say that there is a significant role for plasticity and malleability in human nature?*

Warren: Yes. That is what I was saying before about a self-organizing system. One thing to be aware of when comparing humans to non-human primates is the difference in the malleability and openness of the brain of a human over a more extended period of time, which allows much more of the microstructural organization of the brain to be influenced significantly by culture.

The thing we know that we did not know twenty years ago is that we have neurogenesis going on, so some important areas like a hippocampus are getting new neurons all the time. Being a London taxi driver will cause your posterior hippocampus to get larger because you are using your visual-spatial memory heavily, even as an adult. That kind of plasticity and environmental influence needs to be taken very seriously. I think human life, in the cultural sense, will be richer the more we understand our entanglements and responsibilities for one another's formation and development.

Agustín: *What do you think about the interaction between culture and faith as it relates to human nature or becoming human?*

Warren: I think faith is something that is more lived than propositional. If it is more lived than propositional, it is lived in a community of faith. Therefore, that community is formative of the person, exactly what I was talking about before. In that sense, the church, I think, needs to be a particular sort of culture—not a sect, but a particular kind of culture that forms people in ways that they are not formed, or not as likely to be formed, in other contexts. In some sense, the church needs to be a counter-culture of a special type. Then I think that culture needs to spill out.

Agustín: *The term "soulishness" or "soulish" appears in your writings. Do you still utilize it? What do you hope for that term to do?*

Warren: The origin of that term was an argument between Nancey and me. This was all in good fun. She was saying when we were doing *Whatever Happened to the Soul?* and *Did My Neurons Make Me Do It?* that "the word 'soul' is so contaminated by Cartesian dualism that we've got to ban the use of the term for at least twenty-five years." *[Laughter]*

I said, "But Nancey, it carries such important communicative value. Why don't we say something like at least "soulish," such that you can connect with conversations of the past?" I am not bothered by the idea that a "person" may be more like a centered set, rather than a bounded set. So it does not bother me to say that some people would be less soulish than others if we are forced to consider them as entirely independent persons.

My theological argument is that we become soulish primarily by God's decision to be in relationship to us, almost to the degree that a parent decides to be in relationship with an autistic child. Similarly we grant to one another soulishness, often beyond the other's ability to reciprocate. In my chapter in *Whatever Happened to the Soul?*, the careful reader notices that I painted myself in a corner. I had described all these cognitive capacities that are required for soulishness, and the obvious response was, "Well, what about the person who is developmentally or cognitively disabled?"

I had to think about that for a while. It struck me that relationships are seldom symmetric. Asymmetric relatedness is probably more the rule than the exception, and therefore, in persons with lesser capacity, it is the moral obligation—and I think this is the primary moral obligation of humankind—to bring out soulishness or humanness in other persons, and that is particularly an important moral call with respect to people who are disabled or disenfranchised.

Soulishness was, first of all, something I was trying to *describe*. Then in the end it was, for me, a property we try to *instill* in others and bring out of others, even at times when they are incapable of reciprocating the relationships that would bring that out.

Agustín: *I have been thinking about human and non-human animal interactions. What do you think—can you extend this soulishness maybe to other aspects of creation, of the natural world?*

Warren: I would say our moral obligations get fuzzier in that respect. I do not feel a moral obligation to bring out in every chimpanzee the same level of soulishness that is the potential that is inherent in a human baby. To my own species, I do think I have a moral obligation to foster soulishness, as best one can when one has the option to interface with other people.

When your friend is deeply incapacitated by Alzheimer's disease, are they no longer soulish or a person? Well, that is up to you to decide. Are you going to remain by their side, support their personhood through memory, sing to them familiar songs, and hold their hand when they cannot reciprocate? They may not know what is going on, but you can stand in for them as persons.

Agustín: *This just highlights how humans are deeply social. What do you think about the recent interest in social brains and distributed minds, like with Robin Dunbar?*

Warren: Here is a round-about answer: Systems theory suggests that groups of persons become bodies through processes of self-organization in much the same way that functional properties organize within individual persons. A group can become a body and an agent, and as groups of people become bodies they manifest emergent properties.

Again, I think that is something the church needs to take seriously. It is not sufficient to just gather a bunch of individual persons together. To be of any use in the world you have to become a body, through extended relational experiences. This sort of group embodiment is lived out very explicitly in the little church that I attend.

Within corporate bodies, there are emergent narratives, thinking, and language. If you share a language (like English), you use the same words, but smaller bodies of persons come to condition the meanings of those words. The term "group think" has been pejorative, but I do not think it is totally a pejorative term. For example, Fuller Seminary has a certain kind of group thinking going on and that is okay, because for Fuller Seminary to be a factor in the world, it has to have a certain degree of social embodiment and thus group thinking.

That is okay, as long as you are loose enough with your group think, willing enough to loosen and deconstruct your language at times to realize the degree to which you are talking to yourself in ways that are incomprehensible to anybody else in culture...too trapped in your own language set. You sometimes need somebody else's language set to solve your problem. Mind is not a thing, but an event. That event happens in groups. Groups 'mind' in the same way that individuals 'mind.' It is not that a group *has* a mind, because minding is a thing we *do*.

What I like from Robin Dunbar is the Dunbar Number—given human brain size, the size of a group that can sustain long-term relatedness.[28] We actually use that idea in our book (*The Physical Nature of Christian Life*) in order to say that formative groups have got to be somewhere close to the size that Dunbar talks about. Formative human interpersonal networks cannot be over a certain size or they lose effectiveness, or begin to break down into smaller groups.[29] That Dunbar's Number is not exactly about group thinking or group

....

28 See Robin Dunbar's interview in Chapter 2.

29 This is the famous Dunbar's number, usually calculated to be somewhere around 150.

mind, but it is a social networks of strong, interpersonal influence where you are strongly forming of each other. So that is what I have gotten out of Dunbar.

Agustín: *There is an interesting recent article in* American Anthropologist, *where a group of anthropologists looked at Dunbar's Number ethnographically and actually added a lot of twists to it.[30] The idea is still there, but they have expanded it and looked at different kinds of relationships and numbers.*

Warren: Yes. Different group sizes are better for different kinds of things. But when you get to a number that is somewhere between 75 and 145 things begin to top out with respect to what human beings can cope with in sustaining any kind of long-term, relational tracking of each other. However, within this, smaller groups are necessary for different kinds of relationships and tasks.

Agustín: *There has recently been a move towards trying to think about the actual role of groups, or better put, community, in human evolution. That is to say, people focus much more on relationships and roles that might have played a significant role throughout the course of evolution of the hominids through our species.*

Warren: Yes. We have cycled through, as you know better than I do, a whole lot of explanations of what was this evolutionary pressure on the human brain that made us smart. Language, tool use, upright walking, etc., have all been suggested. To some degree, the current best explanation is social complexity. That makes a whole lot more sense to me as a pressure to develop cognitive power in order to interact socially. Do you know John Allman's work at Caltech on Von Economo neurons?[31]

....

30 de Ruiter, Jan, Gavin Weston, and Stephen M. Lyon. 2011. Dunbar's Number: Group Size and Brain Physiology in Humans Reexamined. American Anthropologist 113(4):557-568.

31 See Allman J. M., N. A. Tetreault, A. Y. Hakeem, K. F. Manaye, K. Semendeferi, J. M. Erwin, S. Park, V. Goubert, and P. R. Hof. 2010. The Von Economo Neurons in Frontoinsular and Aanterior Cingulate Cortex in Great Apes and Humans. Brain Struct Funct 214:495-517.

Agustín: *Yes.*

Warren: There seems to be an exponential evolutionary expansion of these neurons from higher primates into human kind. Such neurons are there in higher primates, but in small quantities. They develop in humans between birth and about four years of age into a very large population of neurons. That incredible development seems to have important social implications. Because these neurons distribute information about bodily emotional states to the rest of the brain, they are likely involved in our emotional attunement with other persons.

Social information has a strong influence on many of our cognitive processes. When some thought or event makes me feel uncertain or blush or makes my heart rate go up, these neurons make the information very quickly available to all of my cognitive processes in ways that allow for behavioral and social adjustments. The need for this kind of social attunement provides a deeper, richer explanation for the evolutionary pressures that have contributed to human intelligence.

This might also make sense of some social and cognitive pathologies, like an autistic child. In these persons you see the absence of the abilities to be socially in tune, have a theory of mind, make social inferences, and understand what other people are thinking and feeling. That is a big deficit.

Allman's theory was that autism has to do with the failure of Von Economo neurons to develop. I do not know if that is true or not. I do not think he knows yet. If it is true, then it tells us that the neurobiology that has come along with human development or human cognition has a lot to do with interfacing emotional information with a whole lot of other forms of cognitive processing.

Agustín: *I am very drawn to this because it actually has components that are testable, which I really like. [Laughter]*

Warren: Allman published his thesis about autism several years ago, and research since has been at least partially supportive. If Allman's theory is true, it tells us something about the nature of autism. It also maybe tells us something important about human sociality and human nature.

Agustín: *I have a round-up question for you about technology and human nature. What are your thoughts on human enhancement or artificial humans?*

Warren: I get asked that question a lot with respect to robots. My response is that I have no idea whether the technology is there to develop a robotic system that can be as intelligent as a human being. However, the answer to the question as to whether a robot could be human or not has to be answered ahead of time. That is, you have to be willing to admit the robot into human society for a long enough period of time for it to develop as a human being in the same formative ways that human children develop—the long-term process of self-organization. You would have to answer that question ahead of time. Do we want and expect this robot to be a human being? If we want it to be a human being, and therefore admit it to human society as a potential person, then it *might* have some chance of becoming a human being.

Think of Frankenstein's monster. I guess there is a sense in which the monster is a person to a degree. There is the necessary apparatus that allows it. Then the question is whether the community is going to admit the monster into human society for some period of time, because that is the only way it would become a human person.

Agustín: *That is a fascinating answer and one that is becoming very prominent in many debates about robotics.*

Warren: I think there are two totally different questions here: one is about artificial intelligence and another about a mechanical-digital thing becoming a human being, because even a biological human being must be admitted to human society prior to its becoming fully personal. You have to decide ahead of time.

Suggested Readings

Brown, W. S., N. Murphy, and H. N. Malony, eds. 1998. Whatever Happened to the Soul? Scientific and Theological Portraits of Human Nature. Minneapolis: Fortress Press.

Clark, Andy. 1997. Being There: Putting Brain, Body, and World Together Again. Cambridge, MA: MIT Press.

Jeeves, M. A., and W. S. Brown. 2009. Neuroscience, Psychology and Religion: Illusions, Delusions, and Realities about Human Nature. Radnor, PA: Templeton Press.

Jeeves, Malcolm A., ed. 2015. The Emergence of Personhood: A Quantum Leap? Grand Rapids: Eerdmans Publishing.

Juarrero, Alicia. 2002. Dynamics in Action: Intentional Behavior as a Complex System. Cambridge, MA: Bradford Books.

Murphy, Nancey. Bodies and Souls, or Spirited Bodies? London: Cambridge.

Murphy, N., and W. S. Brown. 2007. Did My Neurons Make Me Do It? : Philosophical and Neurobiological Perspectives on Moral Responsibility and Free Will. London: Oxford University Press.

Quartz, Steven, and Terrence Sejnowski. 2002. Liars, Lovers and Heroes: What the New Brain Science Reveals about How We Become Who We Are. New York: Harper Collins.

Welker, Michael, ed. 2014. The Depth of the Human Person. Grand Rapids: Eerdmans Publishing.

CHAPTER 4

Persons and Human Nature

Interviewee: Christian Smith

Bio. Specializing in the sociology of religion and social theory, Christian Smith joined the Notre Dame faculty in fall 2006, coming from the University of North Carolina at Chapel Hill, where he served as the Stuart Chapin Distinguished Professor of Sociology. He is the author of several books, including *Lost in Transition: The Dark Side of Emerging Adulthood* (Oxford University Press, 2011), *What is a Person? Rethinking Humanity, Social Life, and Moral Good from the Person Up* (University of Chicago Press, 2010), *Souls in Transition: The Religious and Spiritual Lives of Emerging Adults* (Oxford University Press, 2009) and *Moral, Believing Animals: Human Personhood and Culture* (Oxford University Press, 2003). *What is a Person?* and *Souls in Transition* have received numerous awards and recognition. Smith earned his doctoral and master's degrees from Harvard University.

Slogan. *"The discourse on human nature has associations, historically, with theological language. Science does not want to go there, of course, so that makes science allergic to talk about human nature. I just think that is silly. We cannot get away from the question of human nature."*

Agustín Fuentes and Aku Visala, *Conversations on Human Nature*, pp. 171-231. © 2016 Left Coast Press, Inc. All rights reserved.

Aku: *In the beginning of your* What is a Person? *and also in your Moral, Believing Animals, you say that you believe in the existence of something like human nature. This might not be such a fashionable idea, in your context. Would you mind explaining what you mean by that?*

Christian: In philosophy of science and social science, I am coming to things as a critical realist, from the point of view of critical realism. That tells me that what science is about is trying to understand what exists in the world, and how it works. It is unlike a Humean approach to science, or a positivist approach where we try to describe regularities in events.

Critical realists are not primarily interested in associations between events, but in the ontological being of things in existence and what their properties and capacities are, what their tendencies are, what their finitudes and limits are, and how they all developmentally, over time, interact with each other to make the world happen as it does. That is what critical realism is in the most basic form. It is ultimately an Aristotelian approach. It focuses, causally, on powers, and not temporally ordered associations between events.[1]

That kind of orientation gives me a high comfort level with the idea that reality consists of entities of different sorts of things. They can be very different from each other, but let us just use the word "entity," then, as something that has being. Part of what makes an entity an entity is its ontologically-grounded characteristics, features, tendencies, capacities, orientations, et cetera, that define what it is.

I take human beings to be a natural kind of something in reality, a particular kind of animal. Humans are related to other animals, but they are also distinct in their own way. I take all living human beings to be persons, in a pretty strong sense of that word, which I can unpack. "Persons" I do not view as just a legal category

---

1   For critical realism in the social sciences, see Smith, Christian. 2010. What is a Person? Rethinking Humanity, Social Life, and Moral Good from the Person Up. Chicago: University of Chicago Press. For more detailed and general accounts, see Niiniluoto, Ilkka. 1999. Critical Scientific Realism. Oxford and New York: Oxford University Press; and Psillos, Stathis. 1999. Scientific Realism: How Science Tracks Truth. London: Routledge. Competitors of critical realism include various forms of positivism, constructivism, and empiricism.

to assign some kind of rights, or some kind of positive assignment of attributes, but a real ontologically existent thing in the universe, a personhood.

If persons are actually a natural kind, they are emergent, in the strong ontological sense, not just in the weaker epistemological sense. They emerge from the activity of human bodies and human capacities, especially neural, but the whole embodied person developing and acting and interacting enables the natural ontological features of personhood to develop and, ideally, flourish. That is my basic orientation.

That means that there, of course, is such a thing as human nature. If we could not identify humans as a particular thing with particular proclivities, capacities, powers and tendencies, then we would be in trouble, it seems to me. I would not even know what we were talking about. That is not to deny that humans, over the very long haul, can change. Maybe features of their nature can develop and change. That does not mean they do not have a nature, at any given point in time.

Aku: *That already puts you, let us say, at loggerheads with quite a lot of what is going on in sociology. You not only start from a strongly realist position, critical realism, but you also assume the existence of persons that are genuinely explanatory.*

Christian: I would say that I am in opposition to mainstream sociology in all of these issues. I am a distinct minority voice of protest. I do not find the accomplishments of sociology so impressive that I feel obliged to be loyal to the dogmas that exist. I would not say I am in loggerheads, in the sense that we were all stuck, but I would say I am attacking it and critiquing it. I think many of its commitments are erroneous.

Aku: *What would be the competitors to your view? What would you describe as the mainline?*

Christian: The mainline would be the ghost of positivism. Nobody is officially a positivist, but the ghost of positivism haunts us all. That would say that the study of the social needs to be modeled very clearly on natural science, in a way that has difficulty making sense of things like persons and value. It is also empiricist, in the Humean sense of you have to be able to directly see it or observe it or experiment on it, or else it is epistemologically not reliable—which I find to be preposterous and unhelpful. Sociology is empiri*cal*, but it is not empiri*cist*.

This kind of positivism leads to an interest in looking for the relationship between variables, between surface events. If A, then B. If X, then more likely Y, sort of thing, which lends itself to multivariate statistics. From a realist point of view, that is mostly dealing on the surface of events. That commits the sin of "actualism": focusing only on what is actual instead of what is real.

As a realist, I am happy to acknowledge that there are things well below and behind and beneath at a level of depth that we cannot directly observe. It seems to me, most natural sciences are in that kind of business already. The ghost of positivism makes us skittish to accept that, however.

One counter to positivism is the hermeneutics or interpretive approach to social science, which I am very friendly towards. I just think it is inadequate. There are certain streams of hermeneutics that are hostile to the idea of sciences in the business of discovering the *causes* of things. As a realist, I think the world operates causally, even the human world. It is just that causes are not all mechanistic and deterministic. It is much more complicated. Beliefs, meanings, desires, feelings, and values—none of which are directly observable, by the way—can be causes too.

Anyway, if we want to understand human social life, we need an account, a realistic account, of the actor or the agent or the person who is the constituent part of whatever the social is. All sociology does this implicitly or covertly anyway: whether it is rational choice theory or some kind of evolutionary psychology or who knows what, it is assumed that some kinds of agents exist. There is always an explicit or *implicit* model of what the human actor is up to. I just want to bring that out into the open, make it more complex, make it more realistic. I think that will be hard to do, but it will give us better social science.

All this is a kind of preamble for my thoughts on human nature. To be short, what I mean by "nature" in human nature is something like the stable characteristic properties, capacities, tendencies,

features, powers, and limitations of any entity by virtue of its ontological character. That's what I would say I mean by nature.

Of course, the discourse on human nature has lots of associations, historically, with theological language. Human nature is sin-
ful, or human nature is perfectible, or whatever. Science does not
want to go there, of course, so that makes science allergic to talk
about human nature. I just think that is silly. We cannot get away
from the question of human nature.

Aku: *From a certain kind of scientific point of view, people are worried about the notion of human nature because of theological conno-
tations. Then, on the other side, again, even in anthropology and in
many ways in social sciences in general, especially through the postmodern thinking, there is widespread criticism of the idea of something having an essence or nature. If there are no natures or essences,
there will be no human nature.*

Christian: I am not completely unsympathetic to such positions in
terms of their moral motivations, their concern not to essentialize
non-essential things. Philosophically or theoretically, on the other
hand, I find their claims to be completely implausible. To say that
reality does not contain entities that have essential natures is just
rubbish.

I think there is a lot in postmodernism that represented a valid
critique of naïve modernity. But the arguments have gone so overboard and so extreme towards so deep social constructivism that
they have got to be reined in by some kind of realism, otherwise
what we end up with is reality as nothing but a bunch of particles
floating together in various combinations for small periods of time,
and that is it.

There is a certain radical reductionism involved in social con-
structionism. It is either super reductionistic in a physicalist sense,
whereas we are nothing but neutrinos and who knows what all the
elementary particles are. Or it is the other way: the social order just
imprints upon us its meaning. The crucial idea that critical realism
brings to the table is the idea of *ontological emergence*. Entities interacting in certain ways or having particular kinds of relations that
bring into existence, at a new ontological level, new entities with

new capacities, powers, the features that cannot be found at the lower level. Everything is upwardly emergent, and downwardly causally efficacious. We can say, "These entities exist in the real world. They actually have causal powers to make things happen in the world."

Now, I know I am doing a lot of talking here—

Aku: *It is your interview [laughter].*

Christian: If we do a genealogy, so to speak, of where the postmodern concern comes from, we realize it is true that talk about the essence of things has been abused a lot in history. If we say women are essentially weaker and more emotional, or belong in a subordinate position by virtue of their essence, that is wrong. Just because an idea like things having essences has been abused does not mean you just throw it out the window. It means you use it more intelligently; you stop abusing it.

Aku: *It seems that we are all trying to find a middle way. We are trying to find a middle way between, let us say, these radically postmodern ideas on the one side. Then, on the other side, let us say, crudely reductionistic or scientistic ways of understanding what the human beings are like. We are all caught in between.*

Christian: The strong version of emergence is resolutely anti-reductionistic. As far as I can tell, this is the only way to resist reductionism. If we did not have emergence, I do not see why everything would not go down to the most elementary particles of reality and mere mathematics. If things are genuinely emergent—that is, if reality is what critical realists call ordered, complex, and stratified, that there are different levels of depths of reality, ontologically—not spatially, but ontologically—then, we have every reason to have different disciplines, and to care about how biology is connected to neurology is connected to consciousness is connected to culture, and so on. All of these things operate in their own ontological levels, in a way that we can connect them but keep them from being reduced to the lowest common denominator.

Aku: *What discipline should we look at when we want to discuss human nature, when we want to understand what persons are like?*

Christian: That is hard because, in the actual development of western higher education, we have all these boundaries and distinct disciplines. It seems to me you have to get anthropologists and psychologists talking with sociologists and philosophers. We should think people who are reflective about different religious traditions should be at the table. I do not want to say theologians in some narrow sense. People have been reflecting on human existence from a "religious" point of view for some millennia, and they would be good to have at the table, at least as conversation partners.

Unfortunately, we have all been trained in our disciplines—at least, in the United States—to just be narrow specialists in what we do, sometimes mere analytical technicians, and not learn each others' discourses and languages and categories. Most American sociologists do not even know anything about critical realism, much less how the brain works. That has to change.

Aku: *One problem in this kind of interdisciplinary or transdisciplinary work is colonialism or imperialism. We try to build bridges between disciplines but sometimes others only want to take others over. Often disciplines like biology, economics, and cognitive science are looking to expand their territory.*

Christian: This brings us back to emergence. If you get the idea of complexity, stratification of reality, and ontological emergence and downward causation, you are able to allow each discipline to do what it does, as a perfectly legitimate enterprise, without allowing it to take over everyone else, while still recognizing there are real linkages between.

After becoming a critical realist, I have become much more science-friendly and ecumenical in approach to science in the sense of most of what is going on, when it is done legitimately, has something to contribute that is really valuable and important.

Aku: *Coming back to the notion of persons, you said that persons are real things, real kinds, and have certain capacities. What would these capacities be?*

Christian: In my book *What is a Person?* I answer this in many hundreds of pages.

Aku: *Yes, I think you give an account of about thirty capacities.*

Christian: Basically, I point out thirty specific capacities. They are mostly examples; it is not the definitive list.[2] The basic idea is that the activity of the human body, human brain, human consciousness, gives rise to all sorts of capacities and powers, for memory, for identity formation, for social bonding, for aesthetic judgment, for creativity, to mastery—all the way at the bottom, from subconscious capacity to be motivated by things we are not even aware of, all the way up to the top to what I call interpersonal communion and love.

All of these capacities are emergent from the body and its functions, especially the brain. Then, personhood, I argue, is not just the sum total of those. Personhood is an *emergent*, at another level of ontology, reality that springs up out of those capacities. To be exact, personhood is primordial, *sui generis*. It is not just a result of these capacities functioning. It is the essence of the living person that actually is also the causal power behind the development of those capacities.

What varies between individual humans is not whether they are persons or that they are 30 percent a person or 90 percent a person. Personhood is always 100 percent. It is either zero or one. Capacities make personhood possible but do not define it. What varies is the existential development or realization or expression of the capacities of personhood. Even if you are sleeping or in a coma, you are still a person, even if most of your capacities are temporarily or permanently shut down.

Aku: *When you talk about human capacities, you want to say that human agency is robustly explanatory, right? Capacities give you a leverage to talk about the causal powers of the agent, to say that the agent, given these capacities, can explain all sorts of things that go on. So the agent is not just the object of various social or psychological forces.*

Christian: My view is a person-centered view. It is not an individualistic view, but it is a person-centered view. It is always about acting persons instead of just the social acting upon the person, like in certain

---

2   This account can be found in Smith, Christian. 2015. To Flourish or Destruct: A Personalist Theory of Human Goods, Motivations, Failure, and Evil. Chicago: University of Chicago Press.

readings of Durkheim, in which persons are these lumps of material that "social facts" push around or form or shape or determine.

Again, if you get back to emergence and downward causation, you see why this does not work. Anything social is the emergent social fact of active human persons. The downward causal force of social life indeed causally influences active human persons. It is this constant interactive upward emergent, downward influence moving dynamic that, ultimately, explains everything in sociology: one has to go back to the acting persons and their capacities, their intentions, their motivations.

Aku: *We have been talking about persons, but you also mentioned another term—"culture." What do you mean by that? How would you characterize the relationship of culture and biology, if there were one?*

Christian: I view biology as an upwardly-moving, very powerful force in life. Human beings have very strong trajectories and limits and abilities, based on our biology. The whole world does, based on chemistry, physics, and biology.

One of the spiritual projects of modernity has been to liberate humans from all constraint: human autonomy. At its extreme, this has meant, for some humans, to try to liberate humans from the constraints and directives of biology. I find this interesting to the extent that it means we invent Tylenol so we are not doomed to have headaches. But the project has gone overboard: it has gotten to the point where I just think it does not take seriously the materiality of the world and the biological facts of reality.

Part of what I'm trying to do is to push back against this unfettered human autonomy and say, "No, a lot of human life is very profoundly governed by biological facts, even human institutional life." We just cannot be and do everything. What I am trying to say is that we need to take biology and its enablements and constraints a lot more seriously in social science than we have so far.

At the same time, the idea of emergence gives us a way to explain how it is that humans, in some sense, do transcend our biology. We develop minds and intentions and emotions and so on that can act back down upon biology and transform biology or limit biology— not absolutely, but to some extent.

Again, the critical realist approach enables me, in principle, to take biology fully seriously, and to learn, really, what it drives, what it governs, everything down to neurotransmitters in the brain and all sorts of things, and how they affect social life and the possibilities of individual and collective life, without assuming any kind of reductionism or determinism.

One emergent capacity is creativity that makes it possible for us to transcend the limits of biology. What human persons possess is a natural, innate—by virtue of their essence—capacity to create new things, what John Searle calls *institutional* facts, and not just brute facts. That is where culture comes from.

I have a pretty narrow view of culture, which, again, goes back to Plato and Aristotle, in which culture is networks of more or less shared human beliefs about what is true, good, and beautiful. Those beliefs, then, get instantiated or worked out in practices and artifacts and institutions, which we also often call cultural. I would make a distinction between "culture," which is the beliefs rooted in persons, and "the cultural," which is how those beliefs are manifest.

Then, of course, there is this dialectic of the beliefs giving rise to these socially shared practices and institutions and artifacts, which, then, reinforce or make plausible, again, the beliefs. The beliefs can change, too.

Aku: *Agustín, of course, has been working in this area of biology and culture for a long time. It seems that—*

Christian: Augustine of Hippo or Fuentes? [*Laughter*]

Aku: *Augustine of Fuentes. Agustín. He has argued that humans not only shape their physical environment but their cultural environment as well. The kind of human metaphysics we have in turn shapes our cultural and physical environment that then feeds back into our biology. It is not just genes driving evolution or just natural selection, but culture creates its own level of selection, let us say evolution in the symbolic realm.*

The goal is to integrate this work with the study of emotion, neuroscience, and psychology. This leads to a broader notion of the mind, let us say, the extended mind that is working through the body, through the endocrine system, different sorts of systems, and all that. It seems to me that we have crossed a kind of peak or threshold, and now we are trying to integrate different approaches. I find this, myself, a very good thing.

Christian: Yes, it is great. Not to constantly be blowing the same horn, but, to me, it vindicates the critical realist sensibility. Comparatively, earlier in my career, there was lots of talk about whether we are going to find the X gene? Are we going to find the religion gene? Are we going to find the happiness gene? As if these genes would work in a one-way direction to determine something.

Of course, what we have since learned is that it is more complex than that. These things interact, just as you described. Again, I am no expert in this. From what I understand, how genetics develop is interactive with environment and experience. Different ones get switched on and off. That makes total sense to me. That forces us to be a lot more complex. Again, it is anti-reductionist and anti-imperialistic.

Aku: *This brings us back to a general question about the continuity between animals and human beings. You said that there is a kind of human uniqueness that you are looking for. You say that human persons are of their own kind. How would you address the issue of human uniqueness?*

Christian: This is an area that I have not yet put much effort into working out. I only have some preliminary placeholder thoughts. I do believe, as a personalist, that there is an immense—some people would say even infinite—difference between the personal and the non-personal. They are just extraordinarily different things.

However, the person is an emergent reality. That from which it emerges is very similar to many other animals, obviously. We share a great deal, biologically, and even in some senses of emergence, with non-human animals. Clearly, humans are closer to certain kinds of animals than others.

My agenda is *not* to say humans and only humans, in the entirety of reality, are the only things that could be personal. Whether there are other animals or people, creatures on other planets, I have no investment in denying or affirming. At the moment, it seems to me that we can say something like other animals have personal-like features and capacities, relative to some other animal. How could humans relate to dogs in certain ways, if there were not at least some person-like features in dogs?

I think there is a difference between saying there are person-like features than saying they are persons, too. Some activists want to protect animals in zoos on the grounds that they have some kind of legal personhood. That does not seem helpful to me.

At the same time, I would say there might be emergent realities that other animals—bats or dolphins—have. They have their own emergent reality that we are pretty clueless about, but it might be amazing—not personal, but something else, equally amazing that we are just dumb about.

Let's see, do I want to say this? On the one hand, in a hierarchy of being, persons are pretty high up there, even though we are really animals. At the same time I argue that persons possess some kind of *dignity*, which means there is a certain value that is different from what a frog might have. That is not to say only persons are valuable, and the rest of the world is not valuable. It is not to justify an attitude, "Well, let's exploit the hell out of nature and use it only for human wellbeing." It does not entail that kind of moral or ethical conclusion at all.

Aku: *Could you expand on human dignity issue that you mentioned? Normally, in books about sociology, you seldom see people dealing with these kinds of issues.*

Christian: Explicitly, perhaps. But all of sociology is finally driven by these moral passions, although explicitly they are often ignored. This goes back to positivism and empiricism. Modernity, generally, has made this radical separation between the "is" and the "ought." It is a misreading of Hume.[3]

Critical realism, basically, is interested in breaking down the strict separation of is and ought, and follows a fair amount of smart philosophy these days, which says ought statements and is statements are really not entirely separable from each other.

....

3   Philosopher David Hume provided various arguments against the claim that we can derive normative conclusions from factual statements alone.

From an Aristotelian point of view, if you make the claim "It is the case that things ought to move toward their natural telos of flourishing in whatever they are," is that an is statement or an ought statement? Well, it is both. You are just saying this is the way reality is. It also says here is what things ought to do.

That is to say, if you strip reality of any *teleological* orientation, then oughts suddenly become problematic. You end up with some kind of Kantian ethics that comes from somewhere else and has nothing to do with nature.[4] If you have a view of reality that entails at least some dimension of a natural *telos*, there is no clear difference between the ought and the is.[5] I am not saying that comets are pursuing their telos of essentially burning out, but at least in the human world there is a naturally-grounded teleological good of human nature. This good consists of what it takes to flourish and what it looks like to flourish as a human being.

Very little of contemporary sociology cares about Aristotle, or thinks in Aristotelian terms. As such, it has very poor accounts of how to put together the ought and the is. Why should we all be devoted to justice and equality and liberation and peace, or human rights, when we are working with a science and an understanding of how the world works that cannot even explain where these come from?

Critical realism pushes us in the direction of naturalistic, rather than the anti-naturalistic morality. What is right and wrong, and good and bad, and just and unjust is related to the way things actually are, the way nature is.

Aku: *Philosophers would call that a form of moral realism.*

Christian: Yes, moral realism, exactly. Moral facts exist as part of reality. We do not (necessarily) get them from some divine realm, which has nothing to do with nature. Nor can we reduce morality

---

4   Partly responding to David Hume's criticisms, philosopher Immanuel Kant argued that ethical norms cannot be derived from natural facts or goals. Instead, the fundamental moral norm, the categorical imperative, is to be inferred from pure reason alone.

5   "Telos" comes from Greek and refers to goals or purposes. Similarly, "teleology" refers to purposiveness or goal-directedness.

to individual, subjective emotions, which is what a lot of popular morality has come down to. I "feel" that this is wrong. I cannot give you a rational explanation; it is just how I feel.

Aku: *Coming back to dignity, you would then say that human dignity is based on these capacities and actual personhood?*

Christian: I say dignity is a natural property of personhood. It is an ineliminable, inextinguishable, emergent aspect of what it means to be a person. It is not based on the capacities, per se, because otherwise, if you lost the capacities, you would no longer have personhood.

It is just part of what it means to be a person, that you have a certain inestimable value that demands certain moral responses from other people in the world, of love, respect, and justice. Yes, dignity is just a natural fact. Now, people say, "Well, where does that come from?" It's an emergent thing. Why is it that *anything* operates the way it does? It is just the way reality is. I do not know if you know Russ Shafer-Landau's book *Moral Realism*. Basically, he says, "Why do I have to explain this? It's just the way it is."

Aku: *Usually, that is called a brute-fact account of moral realism. Simply put, it means that moral facts are not identical or reducible to any other kinds of facts, but are brute facts.*

Moral psychologists tell us that some kind of moral realism seems to be a default position for human beings that have not been, let us say, deeply informed by the contemporary, Western tradition.[6] If you go outside of our tradition, most people assume the existence of some kinds of moral facts and moral truths about things that are wrong and right and good and bad.

Actually, I also wanted to ask you about freedom. Traditionally, when people have talked about human nature, one big theme has been freedom and the nature of human freedom. Again, from your point of view, if we take this critical realist personalism, as you call it, it would seem that there are some constraints to human freedom.

....

6   See, e.g., Haidt, Jonathan. 2012. The Righteous Mind: Why Good People Are Divided by Politics and Religion. New York: Pantheon.

Christian: Tightly bounded human freedom, yes. As everything does, this depends on what you mean by freedom. I want to vindicate a certain traditional humanistic view of freedom as mattering, without it becoming unfettered volunteerism, or this modern liberal freedom according to which to be free is to be able to do anything you want without any external constraints, or some craziness like that.

I have not worked this all the way out, but from an Aristotelian and maybe even arguably a certain version of a reading of St. Paul, a human person could be entirely free even when he or she chooses to do something without having a choice to do otherwise.

I am sure philosophers have got this all categorized and figured out. Even in such cases, the agent can still be involved as an agent, in the doing of the thing, willfully, even if they did not have any other choice. This goes back to St. Augustine, I guess *[laughter]*. I do not have this all worked out so, I want avoid the extremes. It seems to me there are some complex plays in the middle that are reasonable.

Aku: *The problem is that, from a kind of modern point of view, the paradigm got mixed up. Before, modernity people used to think about freedom in terms of being able to choose the good, or the valuable, or something like that. From that point of view, there is no problem in relating choices, decisions, and causes. We can be perfectly free even if we do not have a choice, provided that the only option available is indeed good.*

In that sense, Thomas Aquinas or St. Augustine could easily have said that, even if there is just one option, but that is the Good option, you are as free as you can be. Opposed to this, from a modern point of view, the relationship between freedom and causes becomes a problem. In order to be free, there must be no predetermining causes at work in your decisions.

Christian: Which is not freedom. It is random arbitrariness.

Aku: *That is right. With the premoderns, realism was already in the play, in the game. The idea was that you orient yourself towards these good and true and beautiful things. They are the ones that draw you. You are free when you follow them. If you remove the realist assumption from the equation, and then you put in the modern idea of what causality is, then freedom basically becomes an issue of choosing between options. The more things you have to choose from, the more you are free.*

Christian: In sociology, this gets played out in the most interminably unresolved arguments about agency versus structure. That is how it is talked about. Agency entails, in the mainstream sociology, this idea that the unfettered individual can do whatever they want, or exert all these causal forces on the world. What sociology is mostly in the business of is showing how individuals are incredibly constrained, if not determined by the social forces, institutions, and cultures around them.

I am not in this schizophrenic project myself. But many sociologists are in the business of freeing individuals from that which they are in the business of showing you are imprisoned to. They do not want to give up agency, but they are constantly showing the power of structure. It is bizarre. The whole thing is misframed, misguided, it seems to me.

Aku: *That seems to be a problem for the many postmodern thinkers. On the one hand, the subject is eroding. They are losing the grip on the subject. At the same time, they want put the subject on a higher and higher pedestal.*

Christian: Yes, unlimited self-creation. I do not understand what is the thing that is supposed to be acting in that model? They have to smuggle in all sorts of stuff in the back door that is inconsistent with their core convictions.

Aku: *Yes. From a realist point of view, one could say that something like truth and rationality and even morality, in this realist sense, have to be brought in through some door or window. If you do not bring it through the front door, you will bring it through the back. It sneaks in the back.*

Christian: Of course, that is just the nature of reality. At some point, reality will start pushing back. You can only deny it so much. I used to be much more friendly towards postmodernism in the 1990s. I hit the wall on that and realized, if you really are serious about this, it takes you over a cliff in which there is no bottom. That is what drove me to critical realism. I think critical realism is able to affirm many of the good critiques that were part of postmodernism, without being insane about it, like a lot of postmodernism is.

Suggested Readings

Archer, Margaret. 2000. Being Human: The Problem of Agency. Cambridge: Cambridge University Press.

Archer, Margaret, Roy Bhaskar, Andrew Collier, Tony Lawson, and Alan Norrie, eds. 1998. Critical Realism: Essential Readings. London: Routledge.

Danermark, Berth, Mats Ekstrom, Liselotte Jakobsen, and Jan Karlsson. 2002. Explaining Society: Critical Realism in the Social Sciences. London: Routledge.

Smith, Christian. 2015. To Flourish or Destruct: A Personalist Theory of Human Goods, Motivations, Failure, and Evil. Chicago: University of Chicago Press.

Smith, Christian. 2010. What is a Person? Rethinking Humanity, Social Life, and Moral Good from the Person Up. Chicago: University of Chicago Press.

Smith, Christian. 2003. Moral, Believing Animals: Human Personhood and Culture. New York: Oxford University Press.

Interviewee: Dean Zimmerman

Bio. Dean Zimmerman has a PhD from Brown University. Zimmerman specializes in metaphysics and the philosophy of religion. He is a professor of philosophy at Rutgers University, New Brunswick, New Jersey. He is director of the Rutgers Center for the Philosophy of Religion; founder of Metaphysical Mayhem, a biennial summer workshop for graduate students; and co-organizer, with Michael Rota, of the St. Thomas Summer Seminars in Philosophy of Religion and Philosophical Theology. His articles include "Presentism and the Space-Time Manifold" in *The Oxford Handbook of Time* (2011) and "From Property Dualism to Substance Dualism" in *Proceedings of the Aristotelian Society*, Supplementary Vol. 84 (2010). Zimmerman is editor or co-editor of a dozen books, including nine volumes of the ongoing *Oxford Studies in Metaphysics*. He is currently writing a book on the philosophy of religion for the series Princeton Foundations of Philosophy.

Slogan. *"Persons seem to be thoroughly embedded within the physical world, and they should be natural products of it. I suppose wherever there is a brain, there is a soul, and brains naturally give rise to souls."*

Aku: *Would you be able to offer any kind of definition of human nature?*

Dean: Well, my first thought about what "human nature" means is that it refers to a set of interesting, intrinsic, essential properties that are peculiar to or definitive of persons, human persons if human persons are a special kind. Defining "human nature" would be like looking for the essence of, say, a natural kind. If you ask me what is the nature of water, I would say, well, we did not know for a long time. For a long time, we thought water was an infinitely divisible, homogeneous kind of substance—that every portion of water was composed of smaller portions of the same kind, ad infinitum. Then we discovered that it was not homogeneous, that it was made out of these two other elements and has a certain structure.

What is the nature of the panther, or what is the nature of water? What is the nature of human beings? I take all of these to be heavily metaphysically loaded questions.

Aku: *Yes, the question is what the essential properties of that kind are. One of the things that we have noticed so far is that this very question is the question to which philosophers and theologians answer pretty much the same way, and the scientists answer a completely different way. Thus, when theologians and philosophers talk about human nature, they talk about it in a very different way than scientists.*

Theologians and philosophers usually understand human nature as having some set of essential properties. They look for something that is essential to humans, whereas when the scientists, especially biologists and anthropologists, talk about human nature, what they usually mean is a set of typical capacities of humans as animals, something like intuitive ways of thinking about human persons, psychological capacities, biological capacities, things like that.

Then the question about whether we have human nature or not is a question about whether there are, let us say, innate or hardwired traits. Whereas from the philosophical point of view, that is not what the question is about.

Dean: These are quite different questions, yes.

Aku: *The question is not whether there are innate things, it is that the essential properties might be innate or not.*

Dean: Well, in a way I cannot see how the general essential properties of a natural kind could fail a test for innateness, because if the test for innateness is whether, in normal circumstances, every member of this class will come naturally to display these characteristics in virtue of the way it is intrinsically—if that is the test for innateness—then your essential properties will turn out to be innate, because every member of the class will have them. But lots and lots of innate properties, or things that would turn out to be innate by the other, more scientific definition of innateness, will not turn out to be essential, because they can be blocked from developing. You can stop them from developing if you have a mismatched environment, an environment that stunts a thing's natural growth.

Aku: *The problem with the scientific debates is that the notion of innateness is pretty slippery, and it has been criticized. The core of it is that there are some capacities that have been selected for by natural selection to perform a certain task, and develop in a rigid way.*

If it is the case that the capacities that we have are a product of various causes, natural selection just being one of them, a not very distinctive one, then it turns out that we do not really have innate capacities, even if we might have universal capacities.

Dean: I would have thought that the notion of innateness that would be useful within the human sciences would not require an evolutionary explanation for every trait that is truly innate, but rather the test for innateness would be something like: every member of the species, if not damaged, would naturally develop this aspect of itself in normal conditions. That test for innateness would not care whether a trait was kludged together from adaptive traits. It could be completely non-adaptive and just accidentally acquired. Still, that feature, that aspect of the human species, would count as innate.

Aku: *Yes. This is one of the arguments that some anti-nativist or anti-innate people have given, that the innateness notion itself actually runs together several different issues. What you are describing is more like innate in the sense of typical development or developmental canalization.*

Dean: Yes.

Aku: *But that says nothing about the biological causality.*

Dean: Right. Innateness is a more general notion, and you can divide it up. Using a rough-and-ready, relatively non-technical notion of innateness, we can say that a subset of the features that are innate in that sense are ones that we have for good reason, because of selective pressures, and because they are adaptive. But others are not like that.

It is a very philosophical notion of innateness that I first think of, and that I have views about. About the other, more biologically-based kind of innateness, I have only half-baked opinions—ideas that I pick up from linguists and cognitive scientists. For instance, I hear that there are all kinds of innate language acquisition features, but I leave it to the scientists to figure out what is innate and what isn't in this sense.

Aku: *What you are saying is that the causal origins of psychological capacities and their development is pretty much a scientific issue, so let us jus—*

Dean: Yeah, let them figure it out. And it's a really interesting question, because the blank slate picture is just not on the table anymore.

Aku: *Yes, that is definitely out. There is a lot here, but I want to come back to the philosophical question. You used the notion "person." Do you want to explain what you mean by that?*

Dean: By person, I mean a thing that can think and has—well, basically, that is it. A thing that can think.

Aku: *[Chuckle] A thinking thing?*

Dean: What I assume is that persons could come in very different kinds. I am with John Locke on this, where he says, "Of course, we're immaterial souls, but were consciousness superadded to a physical object, then it would be a thinker, and therefore a person." There is nothing incoherent in supposing that consciousness is superadded to a particle, or an aggregate of matter, or what have you.

Again, although it is not quite as clearly a scientific question, it is still at least a contingent matter, what kind of thing I am—what is this particular thinker? I take it that I am not unique, that there is a bunch of thinkers similar to me in kind. Let us call this kind "human person." Now what are its features? What are its essential properties?

These various philosophical theories about the nature of persons are competing answers to that question. Animalism says I am a biological organism. The thinker in question is this organism. You also have the brain theory. I think if I were a materialist, I would probably be a brain guy. I would say, "I'm the brain. I go where the brain goes."

Aku: *Would you mind explaining what the difference is between animalism and the brain theory?*

Dean: Animalism is the thesis that—well, you can work out the essential boundaries, spatial and temporal, of organisms by looking at a whole bunch of examples of organisms, from vegetable to animal. You have simple ones, slugs, and then you have lizards and birds and fish and so on.

We have a good idea of where the boundaries are of these things, because they are clearly enough separated from their environment, and they have a tendency to keep themselves in shape and retain their structure.

Aku: *They have an identity over time.*

Dean: Yes. There is a way of dividing up the world into organisms and non-organisms. Now, whatever I am, I cannot deny that there is something here, wearing my clothes, which is of the same type as one of those organisms. Its boundaries should be determined in the same way that we determine the boundaries of these other kinds of animals, whether they are sentient or not. Animalism then is the view that I, the thinking thing in question, am one of those, and in particular one with this kind of genetic makeup.

Aku: *This particular Homo sapiens is what the thinking thing is. Let me just stop you a second. The basic question is: I am a thinking thing; what kind of a thing am I?*

Dean: Exactly. That is the kind of question I, as a metaphysician, would be asking when I say, "What is human nature?"

There are animals, then, and we can figure out where their boundaries are. I could be one of those. There are also organs, which are parts of animals—lungs, kidneys, brains. For those, too, we can distinguish their beginnings and their endings. They, too, have a typical structure and natural functions. When they die, they lose that structure, and stop working. Their endings are pretty sharp. It takes a little while for an organ die. A lot of the cells are still alive in your kidney, if it is removed and just left there, but it will not be too long before there is no kidney anymore.

One possibility is that there is one organ in the body that is special. That is the thing that I am. I come into existence when that organ comes into existence, and I go out of existence when it goes out of existence. I get moved to another organism when it gets moved to another organism.

That seems like a pretty good view. After all, we discover that all of our thinking ability depends upon the functioning of that organ. You can keep the head of a dog alive—horribly. It is alert, and you think, "Oh, shit! that could happen to me." And if that could happen to me, then I am not an organism. I am smaller than an organism.

Aku: *Yeah, you are part of an organism, the brain.*

Dean: I am part of an organism, because in theory, you could pare me right down to just the brain. Then, in theory, you might say it is just one hemisphere, because that is an organ too, or part of an organ. It has a definite size and shape and lifespan. It is distinguished from the other hemisphere.

Aku: *Yeah, but then you could say things that look quite obvious, that I have hands, for instance. If I am the brain, I am acting through these hands, but these are not really my hands, are they?*

Dean: Well, they are not anybody else's. *[Chuckle]* They are yours in the sense that they are intimately connected with you and only you. They are things that you can use without using anything else to move them.

If you were a brain in a vat controlling a body somewhere, or if you were the people lying in the trailer in *Avatar*, certainly there would be one body that was your body out there swinging through the trees and whatnot. Its hands would be your hands in a very intimate sort of way. You feel what is going on in them directly. That seems good enough to me for it to be true that I have hands.

Aku: *Even if I were a brain in a vat, and I could control a body like that, that would qualify as having hands. Similarly, if I kissed someone, it was actually me who was kissing, even if I am just a brain.*

Dean: Right.

Aku: *Okay, I get that.*

Dean: This is important because another view on the spectrum is going to be that I am a soul. If the brain view can perfectly coherently say that I have hands and you see me when you see the surface of this organism, then the soul person should be able to say the same thing if they are intimately connected to this brain and body.

Aku: *Right. What would the so-called soul view then be?*

Dean: The version I like best just says that the soul is a thinking thing. It is not made out of matter, and that is the thinker and the perceiver and the experiencer and so on. Obviously, it is intimately associated with this brain, and it somehow uses this brain to think.

Then there are further questions. Is it dependent for its existence on the brain? Does the brain give rise to it? This is William Hasker's emergent dualism.[7] Persons seem to be thoroughly embedded

----

7   For more, see Hasker, William. 1999. The Emergent Self. Ithaca, NY: Cornell University Press.

within the physical world, and they should be natural products of it. I suppose wherever there is a brain, there is a soul, and brains naturally give rise to souls.

Aku: *Where does human nature come from? Let us say that we adopt the soul view. According to some traditional soul views, souls are special creations, that God made them, and that they are future eternal. They are not past eternal. They are created at one point, and then they do not perish. They just keep existing forever.*

This is not the view that you are describing here. You are saying that the person, the thinking thing, is somehow a natural product.

Dean: Yes, it is natural somehow. My view about qualia[8] is relevant here, because I take it that experiential properties involve—

Aku: *Seemings, feelings.*

Dean: —seemings, feelings, appearances that are distinct from all the physical properties that are exemplified in the world by inanimate physical objects and also then by brains. They are this further kind of property, and if you have a new property, often you have a new subject.

Aku: *For the property.*

Dean: Yes. If by causing two protons to collide, you can generate something that has a mass that no proton or electron or neutron has, you would not suppose that, "Oh, well, I guess protons can have this other kind of mass." You would say, "No, by causing this collision we caused something new to have this new kind of property." With a radically new property comes a radically new kind of bearer of that property. Souls could be the natural product of brains if brains are producing things that have qualitative experience, and qualitative experience is a new kind of property.

Aku: *In your written work, you basically proceed as follows. You begin by arguing for what is normally called property dualism claiming that*

....

8 Qualitative states of consciousness, such as what it is like to see red or to have a pain in one's neck.

there are these weird first-person properties. Then, from that you go on to argue that—

Dean: There is indeed a non-physical subject for them.

Aku: *I find it quite plausible as well, that there are such first-person properties. If you buy into that, it seems rather natural to think that there has to be something that is a bit different from a material thing that has these properties.*

Dean: Yes, that is the avenue. Then of course there are theological reasons to believe in souls, I think. These bolster one another in my own mind, but I do not expect everybody—not even everyone who is part of the Christian theological traditions that I identify with—to accept the idea that immaterial souls are supported by Scripture and tradition. But I do. I think so. That, plus these other philosophical considerations about qualia, makes the view very appealing to me, and I think it is probably true.

It should be a contingent matter, which kind of thinking thing I am. Whether I am a soul or an organism or a brain, I could have turned out to be a different sort of thing: somebody who felt very like me, subjectively, could discover that, oh, they are some other kind of physical object. Now, I am not absolutely sure this is a radically contingent matter. There might be some deep reason why brains could not be thinkers, or why extended animal bodies could not be thinkers, but I am not sure what that reason would be. I do not want to rule that out.

The kind of extreme dualism I like says brains generate consciousness. A new subject has to be there. That subject is not a material thing, but it has the properties of being aware, being conscious and so on. It uses the brain to think in some sense. It has powers of some kind that can affect the brain. You are aware of using these powers when you are thinking or trying to do something.

Anyway, the question for this sort of view, the question "What is human nature?" understood philosophically, and assuming this dualistic picture of what persons are, is the question "What are the essential properties of these new subjects?" Are they essentially tied to particular brains? Could God hold them in existence miraculously without the brain that generated them? I hope so.

Furthermore, what is the range of kinds of brains that they could be connected with? Some people, like Alvin Plantinga, will say, "I could have been an alligator. This soul could have been hooked up to an alligator brain. It wouldn't have been able to do very much in those circumstances, but there is no difference in kind between—"

Aku: *A soul guy could say that you are the alligator, but it is still you, whereas if you are an animalist or a brain guy—*

Dean: —then, no way could that be you. It has to be a *Homo sapiens* organism or brain, otherwise it is not you. Again, the answer to the question whether I could have been an alligator is not something I can read off of the soul view. It is similar to the question "Could I have had different parents?" People go different ways on that. It is not obvious that your origins are essential to you in every respect.

Aku: *I think two typical views on this end of the spectrum have been presented by, first of all, Richard Swinburne and William Hasker.[9] Is there any difference between your view and their view?*

Dean: No. Well, there might be a difference between me and Swinburne—I'm not sure how Hasker goes on this, I forget. But I really do not like the view that Swinburne explicitly affirms: that I am a composite thing made of a body and a soul, that my soul has my mental properties and my body has my physical properties.

If my mental properties are things like deciding to move my arm, thinking about Vienna, feeling hungry, if those are my mental properties and my soul has those, and then there is this other thing, which just has the soul as a part…well, that other thing is only thinking about Vienna or feeling hungry because *something else* is thinking about Vienna and feeling hungry. It does those things in virtue of the soul doing those things.

Aku: *Then we have two things thinking.*

Dean: Yes.

....
9 See Hasker, William. 1999. The Emergent Self. Ithaca, NY: Cornell University Press; Swinburne, Richard. 2013. Mind, Brain and Free Will. London: Oxford Universty Press.

Aku: *Which one are you?*

Dean: Exactly. My gut reaction is, "Well, I couldn't"—and this is just a Chisholmian datum or motto or something[10]—"I couldn't be thinking in virtue of somebody else thinking. Nobody else could be doing my thinking for me."

Aku: *Right. Thinking is essentially something that you do yourself. If someone is doing it for you, you are not really thinking, you are not active.*

Dean: Exactly. Swinburne says, "I am a composite thing. My soul has my mental properties. My body has my physical properties." That is his view.

I guess what he thinks is that when you survive the destruction of your body, you are pared down to just the one part in the same way that if a car loses its tires, it is pared down to one of its former—something that used to be just a part of it is now the whole of it. Apparently, that would be the picture on his view.

There is also another kind of dualism, Thomistic dualism. The difference between that kind of dualism and the dualism I just described is that when body and soul are united, the soul is not bearing all the mental properties. Rather, the composite has the mental properties. The soul is somehow crucial to this thing's being able to think, but it is also crucial to its being able to grow and so on. However, the soul could exist without the body, and if it did exist without the body, it could miraculously be enabled to think by itself.

This would be analogous to an animalist view—well, really, it would be analogous to a view which we have not discussed so far, which is a view that says, "I have the size and shape of an organism, but I am not an organism, because I could be pared down to something that isn't an organism, say, a brain, in which case, the organism would cease to exist. I would continue to exist. I would be constituted by something that was a proper part of me in the past."

The Thomistic dualist, I take it, is just like that, except that the part in question is not the brain, it is the soul. The reason I do not

....

10 Dean is referring here to Robert Chisholm's view according to which thinking is a primary activity, that is, one cannot think in virtue of something else's thinking for you.

like that view is that I do not understand this notion of the soul as a substantial form.[11] I cannot wrap my mind around it.

Aku: *There seems to be two ways of reading that. One way would be somewhat materialistic, saying that the form is just a structure of the material thing. Then the problem is, well, how could that structure exist without the thing, without structuring something. That would be the big problem. But then if you say that the structure is a kind of thing in itself, then the question is, "Well, why is it then not just a kind of proper thing?" It is a thing that is not really a thing.*

Dean: Right. It is those kinds of worries that keep me over in the more sharply dualistic camp.

Aku: *How would you respond to the basic counter arguments that are presented against sharp dualist views, first of all, the interaction problem—how the soul interacts with the physical things if it is not physical itself—and identifying souls, getting mixed up, and things like that?*

Dean: Yeah. Well, to the question, "How does it come about that my soul interacts with my brain and not yours?"... I do not have any problem supposing my soul is located, in some sense, in my head. Your soul is in there. And each soul is hooked up with the nearest brain.

This does not preclude my being a simple substance. Maybe a soul can be located wherever it needs to be, but not by having different parts in different places. It could be multiply located, or it could be indefinitely located within a region, with no precise place where it is. There are various possibilities here.

I am not totally tied to the idea of the soul as a simple substance, but I do not see any reason to suppose that the soul has parts, either—other than distinct kinds of powers, dispositions. But different powers does not require distinct parts. You can have a particle that attracts particles in virtue of its charge, and resists forces in virtue of its mass. Different aspects of the one thing, but it could be simple, partless.

A qualitative experience could be one kind of property of a soul. An ability to keep some part of the brain in a state, to keep it in the

---

11 According to Thomas Aquinas, a substantial form is a form that could exist without informing some matter. In Aristotle's view on form and matter, this would be impossible.

same state for a little while, that might be another property of a soul, a kind of basic power that a soul has. If I am a soul inside of this head, a soul can apparently do that. A soul does not know how it is directly affecting the brain, in the same way that I do not know how I am moving my arm. There is all this stuff happening, and I make it happen when I directly will to move my arm. I might be just directly doing something to the brain when I use it to think. Which brain? The one that I am in, the one that I am inside of.

As for the further questions about how interaction happens, I have only a defensive move, which is to say, "Well, you're already a property dualist, aren't you?" If you say yes, then I say, "Well, you've already got this huge problem about how it is that neurons that are discrete from one another, firing in this sort of way, can generate a smooth scene that looks like this, or let's say a smooth patch of brain or whatever."

Aku: *Is this what is usually called the unity of consciousness argument?*

Dean: Well, I would want to say these sorts of things not just about experiences of color, but also about smells, tastes, and all different kinds of phenomenal experience. And then I will ask, "What are the laws connecting neural firing with this experience, and with this other experience?" They will be crazy complex.

Aku: *Yes. This is what Swinburne says.*

Dean: Right. And Robert Adams says it, too. The laws will be crazy complex. They will be like that whether you have souls or not. In fact, introducing souls might give you resources to simplify the laws, and this is where Robin Collins comes in and says, "Well, souls might have further properties besides just the ones that are evident to you. They may do something like vibrating, something on the order of oscillating or something."[12] This allows him to suppose that there are mathematizable laws connecting brain activity with various states of a soul, which when combined give you phenomenal feelings of different kinds, something like that.

Or to go back a little, the particular argument I was going for with the smooth array of visual qualia and the discrete cause in the fir-

---

12 See, e.g., Collins, Robin. 2012. Naturalism. *In* The Routledge Companion to Theism. Charles Taliaferro, Victoria Harrison, and Stewart Goetz, eds. New York: Routledge.

ing of neurons is Wilfred Sellars' grain argument. He says the brain events are granular. There are discrete separate neurons that are firing. Phenomenal spreads of color are homogeneous and smooth, so there is a kind of mismatch between any plausible property of a brain that could be identified with the experience of smooth color and the property of sensing a smooth color.

I do not know how great that argument is, because the appearance of smoothness may be illusory. Maybe it is made out of little experiences, and we cannot tell one from another, but they actually are different. When you look at the old comic books, you see different colors, but when you look closely, you see four colors, really, and they are pixelated. I do not know how good Sellars' grain argument is, really.

Aku: *Another topic that we usually talk about a little bit at least is freedom. It seems that a lot of people have the gut feeling that to be a person has something to do with freedom. What would you say about free will and its relation to the view that you just described, the dualistic view?*

Dean: If there is a deep connection between genuine freedom and being a person, it is not one that is obvious to me. I do not see why I could not be under the illusion that I am acting freely all the time, although I am never actually free. I just do not. Whether I am a compatibilist or an incompatibilist, I do not see any essential connection between being free and being a person.

Aku: *Would you describe yourself as a libertarian or a compatibilist?*

Dean: Libertarian. I am absolutely, definitely a libertarian, but again, it strikes me as something I hope is true, that I am free. But it could turn out to be that I am totally determined. There are all kinds of cases where you come to worry that you were not really free when you chose to do something, that it was already settled, even though it felt free at the time. That is a worry that I think could arise for everything that I have ever done.

Aku: *Does dualism feature in some way in your defense of libertarianism? Could you be a libertarian and be a non-dualist? There are people, of course, who think along those lines. Could it turn out that after we study the brain long enough we find out that there is nothing,*

as it were, interfering what is going on in the brain, and then we could
infer that dualism is false and we're not free?

Dean: Yes. Or you could infer at least we are not free. Maybe the
dualist is right, but the soul is not affecting the brain. Some think
that there is a deep connection between libertarianism and dualism: if the libertarian is right, you better believe in souls because a
brain could not be the kind of thing that would exercise free will.
I'm tempted by that argument, but not really sure how great it is.

Aku: *Another question that we have touched upon but have not touched*
on directly has to do with empirical evidence and empirical sciences.
To what extent, when we are thinking about these issues, are empirical
questions relevant? Because a lot of the scientists are going to push the
argument and say that "These are empirical issues, whether we have free
will, whether we are souls or brains; these are all things that, when we do
enough science, we will just find out." But it seems that to some extent
these issues are more conceptual or let us say metaphysical.

Dean: I do want say that empirical scientific study of the brain and
the organism as a whole is relevant to the question "What kind of
thing am I?" If you could discover that there was no causal input to
the system which is my brain, other than prior physical states of the
brain and impinging physical forces, then either epiphenomenalism
is true or dualism is false. I would probably lean towards the latter,
then. That seems to me to go quite a ways towards accepting the
relevance of the empirical examination of human beings upon the
question whether dualism is true.

Aku: *One thing that I still have in mind has to do with the rela-*
tionship of consciousness and dualism and human nature to, let
us say, animal nature. If dualism is true, what about non-human
animals? Do they have souls or do they have different sorts of con-
sciousness, or what is going on with them?

Dean: I am with William Hasker on this.[13] We are intimately bound
up with this natural world. We are the products of evolution; we are

----

13 Hasker, William. 1974. Souls of Beasts and Men. Religious Studies
10(3):265-277.

related to these guys—the rest of the animal kingdom. If souls naturally arise in us when consciousness is generated, then when consciousness is generated in those kinds of brains, there are subjects for them as well.

Given that you are a property dualist, you are thinking that conscious properties are real and there are fundamental laws about them. There is a fact about when something has them or does not have them. Maybe ants just do not have them, but maybe slugs do. I don't know. Maybe when you get to things like lizards or something, it is a sort of a flickering thing, where consciousness is there sometimes, sometimes it is not—and sometimes there is a soul, sometimes there is not.

Suggested Readings

Baker, Mark, and Stewart Goetz, eds. The Soul Hypothesis. London: Continuum.

Hasker, William. 1999. The Emergent Self. Ithaca, NY: Cornell University Press.

Olson, Eric. 2007. What Are We? New York: Oxford University Press.

Swinburne, Richard. 1997. The Evolution of the Soul. Rev. edition. Oxford: Clarendon Press.

Zimmerman, Dean. 2012. Personal Identity and the Survival of Death. In The Oxford Handbook of Philosophy of Death. Ben Bradley, Fred Feldman, and Jens Johansson, eds. Pp. 97-153. Oxford: Oxford University Press

Interviewee: Carl Gillett

Bio. Carl Gillett is a professor of philosophy at Northern Illinois University. His research areas are the philosophy of mind/ psychology, the philosophy of science, and metaphysics, and he also has interests in the philosophy of neuroscience and philosophy of religion. He has published in all of these areas in a variety of journals including *Anal-*

ysis, *The Journal of Philosophy*, *Faith and Philosophy* and *Nous*, and he is the co-founder of the new *Society for the Metaphysics of Science*. Gillett just completed a book project on reduction and emergence in science, forthcoming from Cambridge University Press, and has recently embarked on another long-term project focused on the foundations of neuroscience and its implications for human nature.

Slogan. *"We are expansive, thinking brains that experience themselves as bodies or minds."*

Aku: *So, Carl, what is the connection between human nature and what you are up to?*

Carl: I have recently become interested in how to engage the issue of what we are from an empirical rather than a priori angle. I have been looking at the implications of the so-called "Neuroscience Revolution" for views about human nature. Thanks to work I did in a fellowship at the Notre Dame Institute for Advanced Study, I am now firmly convinced that advances in the neurosciences point to a new, empirically supported picture of what we are—one that accommodates much of what we assume about ourselves but with a shocking twist about our substance. It turns out that the neurosciences confirm that we think, remember, hope, etc., that we control and experience our bodies, that we act in the world, apparently freely, but all of this evidence also supports our being identical to the kind of "thinking" or "expansive" brain that I contend the Neuroscience Revolution shows has these properties. So I endorse the "Brain view," that we are identical to thinking brains, as an answer to what I call the "Foundational Question" of human nature. That is, the question of which deeper kind of individual are we. To understand the view, we have to talk about what has gone on in the neurosciences, but it is perhaps best to start with the state of the present debates about the Question.

Aku: *What exactly is the issue?*

Carl: The Foundational Question is just this: What kind of deeper individual are we, are you, am I?[14] Philosophers offer all kinds of answers to that question over the millennia, right? One of the older answers was that you are an immaterial soul. Another, neo-Lockean answer is that you are a psychological system. The latter is the big, dominant position amongst philosophers, which virtually no one else in wider intellectual debates outside philosophy seems to endorse.

Aku: *[Laughter]*

Carl: The position that is dominant in wider debates at the moment is the claim that you are identical to an animal in a *Homo sapiens* organism. Philosophers aptly call this view "Animalism." The view that we are an animal is so widely and deeply accepted that it is rarely articulated or defended. In contrast, the position that I am interested in, and that is being pushed by neuroscientists tentatively, is that you are identical to a brain. Notice, that Animalism and the Brain view are incompatible, since you cannot both be identical to an animal and a brain. For example, brains are a certain size and animals are a different size. If you are a brain, you are not an animal.

Aku: *You are a part of an animal, right?*

Carl: Right, you are this amazingly special part that the neurosciences have shown to have all these complex psychological properties. That is my favored view about what you are and it contrasts with other answers to the Foundational Question. The neo-Lockean psychological theorists in philosophy normally take you to be something associated with either an animal or sometimes a brain, but the Neo-Lockean does not take you to be identical to either. The defenders of the Soul view have got still another answer, that you are an immaterial mind. But which kind of individual are you? That has been one of the things philosophers have toyed with and fought about for a very long time—and the answer to the Foundational

14 For a clear introduction to the problem, and current answers in philosophy, see Olson, Eric T. 2006. The Bodily Criterion of Personal Identity. *In* Identity and Modality. F. MacBride, ed. London: Oxford University Press.

Question is an important one with wide ranging political, legal, and moral implications. Just consider issues about the beginning and ending of life: the different theories of what you are give different answers about when and why one of our kind comes into, or goes out of, existence. What could be more important?

Aku: *The idea that we are psychological systems seems to be, as you said, rather popular among philosophers. Why do you think this is the case?*

Carl: Answering that question allows us to touch on the very different approaches to what we are. It is actually quite important to see that the wider debates and positions about human nature, say in the sciences and the public discussions building on them, are really methodologically very different in their approach than the philosophical debates—hence the different answers favored in the two areas. The philosophical debates are idiosyncratic in being committed to what is called the "Method of Cases."

The Method of Cases is this approach that philosophers have been using off and on for a very long time, but in recent work it has been dominating really from the '60s. The way it works is this: You take imagined cases, often impossible, or very fantastical. Then you ask yourself would you judge the thing in the case to be one of our kind, or not?

For example, philosophers consider cases where the transporter from *Star Trek* malfunctions and makes two bodies just like yours. Or imagine taking the hemispheres of your brain and transplanting them into two new bodies. Or consider two *Homo sapiens* animals that are so called "Siamese Twins," but who share one cerebrum which is actually a case we have never come across in actuality. All of these cases may be impossible, but in each of them you ask: Is that (a duplicate of your body, transplanted brain hemisphere, conjoined twin, etc.) one of our kind? Is it me? Then you use your judgments about these imagined cases to assess the competing theories about what we are, i.e. that you are a soul, mind, animal, etc. If you find a case where, for instance, we judge something that is not an animal to be one of our kind, then Animalism, the view that we are *Homo sapiens* animals, is false. If you find a case where we intuitively say there is one of our kind, but there is not a psychological system, the Neo-Lockean psychological position is taken to be false.[15] Okay?

This has been the dominant philosophical methodology and I have always been concerned about it. Basically, the whole approach is totally a priori because it is based around our intuitive judgments about imagined cases and we know our intuitions about many other topics have long since been shown to be mistaken. Now, of course, when you also go to people working in other areas as a philosopher and you try to sell the idea that we can work out what we are by just reflecting on imagined, often impossible, examples of transplanted brains, or *Star Trek* transporters, it is very hard to convince people, whether scientists or others, that this philosophical work is getting to the deeper fact of human nature.

Outside philosophy, at least in anthropology and biology, people think we already have an a posteriori, empirical answer to the Foundational Question. People in wider debates think the matter has been empirically settled, rather than by reflection on transplanted brains or other impossible thought experiments. They think it has been settled by evolution. As far as I can tell, the received view in much of intellectual life is that we are identical to *Homo sapiens* animals. The argument goes something like this. In the nineteenth century, everyone thought we were a special kind of thing, a thing descended from things directly created by God. We are either that kind of thing and unevolved, or we are animals and evolved.

Aku: *Only two basic options there.*

Carl: Then Darwin came along and the sciences subsequently showed that we are plausibly evolved. Therefore, goes the commonly accepted argument, we must be animals. So everyone outside philosophy, and perhaps theology, thinks the debate over the Foundational Question of human nature is finished—we are animals. Then, what people fight about with regard to human nature is, well, what *kind* of animal are we? For example, the nature versus nurture debate is a

....

15 The idea that we are identical to various psychological states, such as memories, was famously defended by English philosopher John Locke (1632-1704).

dispute over what kind of animal we are. To what degree is the kind of animal that we are determined by genetics? Neurophysiology? To what degree is it determined by culture, learning?

My view is that the scientific debates are on the right track in thinking that empirical evidence is relevant to answering the Foundational Question of human nature but have been too hasty in endorsing Animalism. One of the methodological points I am arguing is that the empirically driven approach looks far more plausible than the widespread philosophical commitment to the Method of Cases, which is based on the idea that our *intuitive conceptions* of ourselves reflect the reality about what we are. But it has often been the case that our intuitive conceptions of various subject matters have been utterly mistaken. Furthermore, in this case in particular there are special reasons to worry. I mean, the success of our conceptions about our kind is not one that really suggests optimism. For a very long time, we did not think that different races or cultures were of our kind. For a very long time, we did not think various kinds of disabled people were of our kind.

Aku: *So you say you want to oppose Animalism and the neo-Lockean psychological view. Furthermore, we have empirical reasons to do so, right?*

Carl: I think the Neuroscience Revolution is especially interesting in this regard because I contend that in cognitive neuroscience we now find hypotheses all over the place about personal level, or what I term "rich" psychological properties such as episodic remembering, attending, experiencing, fearing, etc. Now, that interpretation of cognitive neuroscience is a contentious philosophical position I wish to defend in its own right, so let me explain this new position about the foundations of neuroscience. And, after some build-up, I can then explain why it supports a new approach to the Foundational Question of human nature and a new answer to it.

Crucially, I think one of the big changes wrought by the Neuroscience Revolution in the last few decades is that we now find work in the neurosciences about our rich psychological properties and we have a scientifically supported answer about which individual has such properties.

Aku: *The new neuroscientific work seems to challenge older views according to which mind is up here and the brain stuff is somewhere else down below. The psychological properties are at the cognitive science level, whereas neuroscience just looks at what goes on in the cells. What I hear you saying here is that the psychological stuff goes on at the brain level too, right?*

Carl: Right. I want to argue that we have seen a huge change in the neurosciences that philosophers have not yet fully appreciated. We can give a couple of different kinds of argument to push that conclusion: the first kind is sociological and points at various scientific practices; the second kind is a rigorous ontological argument that shows the recent sociological changes are justified.

To start, just look at scientific practices and at the sociology of academic departments. For example, consider Endel Tulving, who is the father of work on episodic remembering and has been researching it for many decades. Some time ago, people like Tulving used to call remembering a "psychological" property. Now Tulving explicitly calls it a "neurocognitive" property. Similarly, at the start of his career Tulving called himself a "psychologist" and now he calls himself a "cognitive neuroscientist." If you look at psychology departments, they have now often reorganized themselves to have all kinds of programs on "Memory and Brain" or such like. There is this manifest merging between what we thought was the psychological and what we thought was neural in all sorts of ways.

Now, such sociological phenomena alone should not convince us—a cynic could suggest certain scientists have just "rebranded" as a funding grab. Such stuff happens. But I am arguing that we can give a second, rigorous type of ontological argument that justifies these changes for reasons deeper than funding or the sociology of the academy.

This second type of argument looks at the evidence provided by explanatory successful accounts in cognitive neuroscience and explores their implications using certain ontological frameworks. Basically, first, I assume what is called the "causal theory of properties" that takes a property to play a certain causal role—thus any individual that has the property must play that role. Second, I assume that parts and wholes in the sciences do not causally interact. Using these assumptions we can now offer an argument about which kind of individual (organism, brain, brain area, neural population, neuron, etc.) cannot, and can, have a property like episodic remembering, given what the neuroscience tells us about it.

Let us just stick to the two main candidates in animals and brains. Various scientific accounts of episodic remembering, for example, take it to be a property that is produced by visual organs like eyes, that produces other rich psychological episodes in the same individual, and that produces muscle stimulations. On one side, I argue we can see that an animal cannot play this role, since eyes and muscles are parts of animals, but in the sciences it is assumed parts and whole cannot causally interact so the animal cannot play the causal role of being causally affected by eyes and causing changes in muscles. On the other hand, what we know of our physiology suggests the brain can play the causal role of episodically remembering—so the brain is the most plausible candidate for the individual that instantiates the property of episodic remembering. I call this type of reasoning the "Argument from Scientific Roles" and it can be applied to any of the rich psychological properties studied by cognitive neuroscience and not just episodically remembering. The conclusion of the Argument is that the brain instantiates the properties of remembering, experiencing (whether perceptually, introspectively, proprioceptively) fearing, thinking, etc.

Notice that the conclusion of this second type of argument provides a justification for the practices and sociological changes I noted in the first argument—we have a sociological merging of the psychological and neural because our scientific findings show that the brain is the individual with rich psychology. Unsurprisingly, the new science is called "cognitive neuroscience" since it studies the cognitive or psychological properties of a paradigmatically neural entity in the brain. So, of course, we can now see the justification for why working scientists like Tulving and others now constantly ascribe properties like episodic remembering, attending, fearing, to brains and call them "neurocognitive" properties.

The latter is the new position I am defending about the foundations of neuroscience. This position is also being implicitly and explicitly pushed by many working neuroscientists and it is what I call "Expansive materialism" because it is based around the *expansion* of our understanding of the properties of brains to include rich psychology. (Hence I term such brains "expansive," too.) It is materialist because it takes something material, in a brain, to have psychology. Expansive materialism takes the Neuroscience Revolution, amongst other changes, to have established that the cognitive level is the highest neurobiological level and that the level of the brain is the level of rich psychology.

I therefore take the Neuroscience Revolution to have shaken up what we should take to be the best view about the foundations of neuroscience. And Expansive materialism challenges both the two older views, inspired by earlier scientific developments, that presently dominate the foundations of neuroscience.

In the '60s and '70s, everyone became what I term a "Separatist materialist."

Aku: *What is that?*

Carl: Inspired by the rise of cognitive science, Separatist materialists like the philosopher Jerry Fodor said science was going to embrace rich psychology, like belief, desire, hope, and fear.[16] We were going to have a science of psychology, rich psychology. But Fodor and others crucially claimed psychology was going to be at the level of individuals *above* the brain. It was supposed to be thoroughly materialistic. There are psychological properties which are composed by lower level properties, but the picture is separatist, because it takes these psychological properties to be had by a separate level of individuals above the brain.

Aku: *This is a way to save the psychology from neuroscience?*

Carl: Well, it was more the idea that cognitive science was dealing with psychological properties, and Separatist materialism putatively reflects the fact of the matter on the ground in the sciences at this time. It was supposed to reflect what cognitive science was doing.

....

16 For more, see, e.g., Fodor, Jerry. 1979. Representations: Essays on the Foundations of Cognitive Science. Brighton, U.K.: Harvester Press and Cambridge, MA: MIT Press.

In contrast, another turn in the sciences threw up the second dominant view. In the '80s and '90s, cellular and molecular neuroscience burst onto the scene. This suggested to philosophers like Patricia and Paul Churchland that we would not find rich (or as they term them "folk") psychological predicates in future science *at all*—just as we still do not find them in molecular and cellular neuroscience.[17] Their idea was really to *eliminate* rich psychology from the sciences and hence they are dubbed "Eliminative materialists." The contention was that there is no rich psychology at all and we just have the molecular or neuronal levels and that is it. Okay?

Given the Argument from Scientific Roles, both of these older views are mistaken. Eliminative materialism is wrong. We have not eliminated rich psychological properties from the sciences, for we are now up to our necks in rich psychological properties in cognitive neuroscience. On the other hand, Separatist materialism is also wrong: We do have rich psychology in the sciences, but it is not at a level of individuals above the brain—rich psychology is had by brains. So, I contend, Expansive materialism provides a better picture of where the recent developments of the Neuroscience Revolution have left us.

Aku: *How are these issues in the foundation of neurosciences related to human nature?*

Carl: Here is a thesis, what I call the "Thinker Thesis," with which most of us agree: You are identical to the individual in your chair that instantiates the property of episodic memory, hoping, fearing, thinking, etc. But the Thesis implies that if you find the individual in the chair with rich psychology, then we find *you*—and can hence resolve what kind of individual you are and the Foundational Question of human nature.

But we have just seen what the neurosciences have shown us, so the Argument from Scientific Roles implies that the individual in your chair remembering, or thinking your thoughts, and so on, is a brain. Therefore, you are identical to a brain.

....

17 Paul and Patricia Churchland defend a view commonly known as eliminative materialism. In this view, there are no mental states or properties. See, e.g., Churchland, Paul. 1984. Matter and Consciousness. Cambridge, MA: MIT Press.

Given the Thinker Thesis, the Expansive materialist understanding of the neuroscientists' findings almost immediately leads you to the Brain View as an answer to the Foundational Question. I am a brain—albeit a thinking, remembering, experiencing brain. And that is an implication that neuroscientists themselves are beginning to come to. Michael Gazzaniga, Jaak Panksepp, and other neuroscientists have begun to press the claim that what we are is this thinking brain.

Aku: *What I hear you saying here in terms of human nature is that the issue of what human beings are is not just an issue of introspection. It is not something that we can access on the basis of our intuitions, or that we have some innate knowledge or introspective knowledge that somehow trumps everything else. The nature of human nature is at least to some extent an empirical issue.*

Carl: On one side, you cannot resolve the Foundational Question of what you are in an a priori fashion simply using introspection and your intuitive judgments about your lived experience—hopefully we can discuss later some detailed arguments to support that claim further.

On the other side, you also cannot resolve the Foundational Question about what you are *solely* using evolutionary biology, or evolutionary accounts of anything. Why? Firstly, we should note that brains are also products of evolution. So, the argument from evolution does allow us to plausibly reject the view that we are products of direct divine creation because we are evolved—but that only consequently licences the conclusion that you are *either* an animal *or* a brain.

Secondly, you are the individual with rich psychology so we were always going to need a science of psychology, and not just evolutionary biology, to answer the Foundational Question. But we now have that science and the cognitive neuroscience now makes it plausible that the individual with rich psychology is the brain—so the evolved kind of individual that you are is plausibly a brain.

Aku: *Let me stop you there. Your view is that we are thinking, or "expansive," brains. Let us say we adopt this view. What about our other questions about human nature? What about selves or freedom? If we* *accept that we are brains, these material organs, can the self really exist, can we really be free?*

Carl: Well, what about the self? Where does the self go under this view? In the media, one of the main things that neuroscientific findings are often associated with is actually "Nihilism" and hence a rejection of the self. You have people like Thomas Metzinger pressing the idea that neuroscience shows that the self, and we, are illusions.[18] But there is this other strand in the neurosciences that we have been talking about, which focuses on work on rich psychology, which I contend actually supports a very different, non-Nihilist, positive answer about the existence of selves.

To see the point, you have to be careful what you mean by "self." There are a number of different notions of self. Let us just distinguish two. First, let us call one the "self-S." Let us take that to be a substance or individual that instantiates rich psychology. Let us take "self-R" to be a self-representational system—and lots of scientists use "self" to mean sense or experience of self in this way.

Now, there are different strands to the Nihilist's argument. I hope we can discuss another shortly, but what they often seem to point out is that we now have really interesting scientific work on our self-representational systems. For example, our experiences of ourselves, whether in introspection or our experience of our bodies, our "proprioceptive" experiences, are systems of self-representation. Then the Nihilists often seem to think that various sceptical conclusions follow from these accounts of our self-representation as representations—often implying self-R is an "illusion" and hence implying there is no "self."

But under Expansive materialism, and the Brain view it entails, the individual brain is what instantiates rich psychology including self-representational experience and systems, so the brain looks like a substance that should be counted to be a self-S. Sure, the brain has lots of self-representational systems, which lead us to conclude we are bodies or minds. But such self-representational properties are again instances of the rich psychological properties that work in the

18 See, e.g., Metzinger, Thomas. 2010. *The Ego Tunnel: The Science of the Mind and the Myth of the Self.* New York: Basic Books.

neurosciences and implies they are had by the brain, which is a very plausible candidate to be a self-S, that is, a substantive self.

Aku: *What about human freedom? The same Eliminativist or Nihilist logic that is applied to selves can also be applied to freedom, right? Think about the way in which neuroscientists look at how we make decisions. It is obvious that there are certain neurological things going on in decision-making. After explaining those, can we jump to the conclusion that there are no such things as decisions, or free will?*

Carl: Freedom is a really difficult philosophical issue and I have no settled views about the overall problem. Luckily, however, all views of free-will presuppose that if you act freely, then it is you who act and that you are determinative and make things happen. Now, I think the Nihilist and actually some of the people engaging in attacking freedom from the neurosciences are really attacking the assumptions either that you even exist or, at the least, that you are determinative.

One strand of these critiques uses a very common scientific reductionist argument that goes something like this: Scientific explanations show certain wholes are made of certain parts. But once we explain a whole in this way, then we can explain everything using the parts alone—so we should conclude that wholes are nothing but parts, that there are no wholes, or at the least that parts are the only determinative entities. The critics now think we can apply this in the neurosciences, since they think the neurosciences have finally begun to show that the individual human being and its thoughts, memories, and fears are wholes composed of neurons and their properties or relations as parts. So, applying the general scientific reductionist argument about parts and wholes, if we can explain the individual's fears, thoughts, and remembrances at the level of the neurons that are its parts, we should conclude that there is no higher-level whole that exists or acts, instead there is nothing but neurons—hence free-will does not exist because key preconditions for its existence can now be seen to be absent.

But I contend that the problem is that the simple scientific reductionist argument is flawed—and emergentists across the sciences have outlined the basic problem with the argument that I highlight. Importantly, such emergentist responses have been pressed in the neurosciences by writers like Walter Freeman and Gazzaniga.[19]

The simple reductionist argument assumes that whenever we have parts and wholes we can explain everything at higher and lower levels using the parts alone. But the scientific emergentist, pointing to real cases like electrons in superconductors, or neurons in neural populations, is that there appear to be situations where what the *components* do, the powers and behaviors the *parts* have, is determined by the composed things, i.e. *wholes*, you find them in. So it appears that sometimes we do need to posit wholes to explain features of their parts—so the scientific reductionist is mistaken that merely showing something is a whole, i.e. that it has parts, suffices to show this whole cannot be determinative as well as its parts. That is the basic worry, though establishing the critique holds up takes a lot more work—I wrote a book to do that work!

Ultimately, I think we can show the reductionist argument is flawed and, perhaps more importantly, that the fight between scientific reductionist and emergentist is, as one would hope, a completely empirical question.

For example, do neurons behave differently in certain composed individuals, i.e. you, that is a brain, than outside the composed individual? That looks like an empirical question: whether the composed thing, like a brain, is determining that its parts, like neurons, have those new powers, but it also looks like *open* empirical question going well beyond whether neurons are parts of brains and hence you. Emergentist writers in the neurosciences like Freeman appear to be pressing this picture that would allow that composed things could be determinative.

So long as the truth of that picture is open, then it looks as if it is still an open possibility that wholes like brains, and hence you, could be actors and hence that they could be free actors.

Aku: *For many people, including myself, the worry is that on the one hand, we have this common sense view of ourselves as actors, being at least to some extent free. I have these rich psychological properties to*

....

19 See, e.g., Gazzaniga, Michael. 2011. Who's in Charge?: Free Will and the Science of the Brain. 1st edition. New York: Ecco.

my life. I can introspect and I find freedom, self, and agency. Again, the Nihilist and Eliminativist argumentation goes against this common sense picture, claiming that there is no room for any of that, because of science. The sciences say that such things cannot really exist.

Carl: Good, I hope I have begun to illustrate how the opposing Expansive materialist picture suggests the sciences paint an anti-Eliminativist and anti-Nihilist view showing that a substantive self exists, that we exist, that we have memories, hopes, etcetera, that we may act freely, including in making free choices and actions. The only shocking part of Expansive materialism is that it shows that we are just the thing no one intuitively thinks we are—a brain!

Your mentioning introspection is therefore very appropriate, since it is crucial for a proponent of the Brain view like myself to engage the issue of lived experience and our intuitive judgements about it—but also what the sciences are beginning to illuminate about it, too. Overall, I once again want to thread the needle between the Nihilist or Eliminativist on one side who denies there is an individual that experiences, and the people on the other side who think that lived experience on its own illuminates something about the Foundational Question about human nature.

Perhaps the main reason people think the Brain view is completely nonsensical, or plain crazy, is their lived experience. And they are quite right that the nature of our experience points to other kinds of individuals as what we are, so it is quite a plausible inference to go from our introspective or proprioceptive experience to the conclusion that we are a mind or animal, respectively.

For example, you have a proprioceptive experience of your arms and legs. Scientific work highlights how you experience your arms and legs as *owned* by you, *yours*, or just *you*. If your arms and legs are you, then you are an animal because you are five feet, six feet tall. After all a brain is not five, six feet tall, so you are not a brain—what could be more obvious? You can see why most people have this visceral and deep rejection of the Brain view, because their lived experience, the thing most central to our lives, most palpable to them, gives them an obvious reason to think that they are animals, not brains.

On the other hand, you can focus on your inner mental or psychological experience. If you focus on such introspective experience of, say, your inner dialogue, then the sciences have again highlighted how these experiences represent the inner dialogue as *owned* by you, *yours*, or just *you*. So, in this case, you naturally think, "Gosh, I'm having a dialogue. It's mine. It feels like me. It is me." Then you are naturally led intuitively into the Neo-Lockean psychological view that you are something psychological like this inner dialogue that is experienced as you.

Interestingly, depending which experience you focus upon, we can intuitively go towards either of the views philosophers favor: If we think about our psychological experience, we easily see ourselves as psychological systems, but if we focus on our experience of ownership of our bodies we find the Animalist view plausible. So we can see how intuitive judgment is really driven by the nature of lived experience, which is hence driving philosophical debates.

Now I agree that for most people, including myself, their lived experience and its nature really drive them to a different place than the Brain view. But the question is "Should we trust our lived experience in this matter?" Here is the problem: The neurosciences have given us lots of insight into our bodily and psychological experiences and that provides us with very good reasons not to trust our lived experience as a guide to what we are. (Though such experience is a great guide to the state of your body or mind, the question we are discussing is whether experience is reliable about the kind of individual you are.)

Let us just think about bodily experience. We now know that people can have the ownership aspect of their experience turned off. We have people with various kinds of brain lesion that experience their limbs, but do not experience them as theirs, or owned. So we know the ownership aspect is just one more aspect of a certain kind of constructed representation that is your experience. More importantly, our scientific evidence shows which individual plausibly has proprioceptive experience. Running the Argument from Scientific Roles for such experience, we conclude that brains instantiate the property of experiencing a certain body. So, using the Thinker Thesis, we use proprioceptive experience to show you are a brain—and hence to conclude that our intuitive judgments based on lived experience that we are an animal are mistaken. Our intuitive judgments are unreliable on the issue of what we are. Similar reasoning can be applied to introspective experience to support the same conclusion.

Again, this is not to say that all of our intuitive judgements are unreliable. I am really good at judging under the right conditions about what beliefs and desires I have. I am really, really good under most conditions about judging where my arms and legs are, right? [Chuckles] How many fingers am I holding up? I am fantastically good at knowing that without looking by using my proprioceptive experience. Crucially, I am not denying the reliability of such judgments. I am only denying the reliability of our lived experience about the abstract question of what deeper kind of individual we are. For the reasons I have begun to outline with you, I am convinced that recent scientific evidence now shows that using our intuitive judgments and lived experiences to form conclusions about human nature, about what we are, is horribly unreliable. So we have a strong case that we should not use the Method of Cases to investigate what we are.

Aku: *Many people, especially in the humanities, associate the brain-talk of neuroscientists with all sorts of imperialistic programs to take over the humanities and social sciences. We can fire the social scientists and philosophers now that we have neurosciences that finally offer us properly scientific explanations of what we are and why we do what we do. Are you only throwing more wood on this fire? If we are brains, then, surely, only the neurosciences are necessary to tell us about human nature? Similarly, if we were animals, the biologists would answer all our questions.*

So the debate about human nature would, in a way, be a power struggle between academic disciplines, a struggle of who gets to define what we are and explain why we do what we do.

Carl: Good questions again. It is the middle position that I think we once more need to appreciate. The Nihilists think it is just all neurons. Sure, if that is the case, then the only person that maybe we should pay is the guy who studies neurons. However, the Expansive materialist view I take to offer the best account of contemporary neuroscience is neither Reductionist nor Eliminativist and it explicitly rejects Nihilism.

One might initially think that the Brain view of what we are supports neuroscientific imperialism—the neurosciences are the only disciplines that will articulate our natures. Actually, I think appreciating the Brain view has exactly the *reverse* conclusion because the Brain view has a flip side. It is not just that you are identical to a brain, but that this brain is identical to a human being that is you. Identity is a symmetrical relation.

But I contend that it is overwhelmingly plausible that the humanities and social sciences have provided all kinds of insights about our properties and our capabilities—that is, all kinds of truths about the nature of human beings. If that is true, that means that the humanities, social sciences, have illuminated all kinds of insights about brains because the Brain view implies brains are such human beings.

The bottom line of the Brain view, properly understood, is not neuroscientific imperialism. It is actually a methodological pluralism about the variety of disciplines needed to understand human brains and hence human beings. The social sciences and the humanities have clearly got an important continuing part to play in illuminating our natures and hence the natures of the brains that humans are. Under the Expansive materialist picture, we need methodological pluralism rather than imperialism. And I should also point out that the neurosciences are beginning to reach out across disciplines to bring in social scientists and humanists and to do interdisciplinary research. Lots of work on social neuroscience is interdisciplinary in just this way, reaching out beyond the exploration of neurons.

Suggested Readings

Freeman, Walter. 2001. How Brains Make Up their Minds. New York: Columbia University Press.

Gazzaniga, Michael S. 2006. The Ethical Brain. New York: HarperCollins.

McMahan, Jeff. 2003. The Ethics of Killing: Problems at the Margins of Life. Oxford: Oxford University Press.

Metzinger, Thomas. 2004. Being No One: The Self Model of Subjectivity. Cambridge, MA: MIT Press.

Metzinger, Thomas. 2010. The Ego Tunnel: The Science of the Mind and the Myth of the Self. New York: Basic Books.

Olson, Eric. 2007. What Are We? A Study in Personal Ontology. Oxford: Oxford University Press.

Panksepp, Jaak. 2004. Affective Neuroscience: The Foundations of Human and Animal Emotions. Oxford: Oxford University Press.

Panksepp, Jaak, and Lucy Biven. 2012. The Archaeology of Mind: Origins of Human Emotions. New York: W.W. Norton.

Interviewee: Lynne Rudder Baker

Bio. Dr. Baker is an American philosopher and author, formerly a Distinguished Professor at the University of Massachusetts Amherst. Currently, she is Professor Emerita. A native of Atlanta, she got her PhD in 1972 from Vanderbilt University. She was a fellow of the National Humanities Center (1983–1984) and the Woodrow Wilson International Center for Scholars (1988–1989). She joined the faculty of UMass Amherst in 1989. She is the author of several books, notably *Saving Belief: A Critique of Physicalism* (1987), *Explaining Attitudes: A Practical Approach to the Mind* (1995), *Persons and Bodies: A Constitution View* (2000), *The Metaphysics of Everyday Life: An Essay in Practical Realism* (2007), and *Naturalism and the First-Person Perspective* (2013). Along with several other scholars, Baker delivered the 2001 Gifford Lectures in Natural Theology at the University of Glasgow, published as *The Nature and Limits of Human Understanding* (ed. Anthony Sanford, T & T Clark, 2003).

Slogan. *"Our essence is to have a first-person perspective—the rudimentary stage that we're born with, and the robust stage as we learn a language. Having a first-person perspective is essentially what distinguishes us from all other beings."*

Agustín: *What would your definition and/or description of human nature or natures be?*

Lynne: I think that our essence is to have a first-person perspective, which I take to be a dispositional property that has two stages. The first stage is a rudimentary stage that we're born with, and then as we learn a language we develop a robust stage. I think that this— having a first-person perspective essentially—is what distinguishes us, I think, from all other beings.

Agustín: *You talked about this first-person perspective, so how do you classify then the human person, and this relation to the body and the environment in humans relative to other beings?*

Lynne: Okay, well, I think we have two kinds of essential properties, but the real essence of us, I think, is to have a first-person perspective. In particular, a robust first-person perspective, but I'll come back to that. In terms of bodies, I think we're constituted by bodies. I think we are embodied substances. I think we are necessarily embodied, but we do not necessarily have the bodies that we happen to have right now. That is, I think we're constituted by bodies, but not identical to the bodies that constitute us.

For example, I think biotechnology gives us a take on this. As we know now, we have brain-thought interfaces. We have all kinds of prosthetic, robotic parts that can substitute for what we have naturally, and we can just wonder how many of those changes would mean that we're no longer organisms? We may no longer be constituted by organisms. We may be constituted by all this other apparatus. This other apparatus, like organisms, is not what we fundamentally are. We fundamentally have a first-person perspective, and for most of us, a robust first-person perspective.

Agustín: *Do you think then this robust first-person perspective, as a context in which to understand human nature, places humans as unique relative to the rest of the world?*

Lynne: Yes, only the robust stage though, because I think that what ties us to the animal kingdom is not only that we're born with human bodies, with organic bodies, but also that non-human animals have first-person perspectives; some do, like cows, and dogs, and cats, but they have them only contingently. They are essentially of the species they are, so they're essentially dogs, or cows, or something. We're essentially not human organisms. We are essentially persons.

Agustín: *Do you think there's a way to define person such that—I mean you're using this robust first-person perspective. Is there a way to connect that, as you've just done right now, but I want to push you a little bit on it, to connect that to the broader theory of mind literature, or anything like that, or do you see this as more complex and embodied itself?*

Lynne: Yes, of course, it's theory of mind because I think it means we have first-personal persistence conditions—

Agustín: *Right.*

Lynne: —and that, likewise, makes us unique among natural beings.

Agustín: *Yeah, so I guess to clarify this, there's the big argument about how much theory of mind is spread across the animal kingdom, and—*

Lynne: Right.

Agustín: *—is it something like Michael Tomasello[20] argues, "It's not just theory of mind, but it's shared intentionality of some great form"?*

Lynne: Sure, absolutely. Absolutely, yes. I think we're essentially social, and I think we evolve from animals that are essentially social. Then our language was—when the animals got to be humanoid, human-like animals, they developed language, and language with the resources that language now has, I think, made such a difference in our causal powers that we language-users are a different kind of thing from an animal.

Agustín: *Yeah, what do you think about human agency? Do you think that human agency, or as some philosophers, and even theologians, would argue, "Free will is the indicator, or the marker, of this human nature"?*

....

20 See Tomasello, Michael. 2014. A Natural History of Human Thinking. Cambridge, MA: Harvard University Press.

Lynne: Well, I'm a compatibilist; that is, I don't believe in libertarian free will. I do not. I think I make decisions, and I think I act on my decisions. I think I'm accountable for my decisions, and that's all a part of my first-person perspective. I do not think that these decisions come out of the blue. I think they're all conditioned, or even if I do something just that seems random, it may even be a random decision.

I may flip a coin, or something, to decide something, but nonetheless, my decisions are my decisions, and that's what makes me an agent. I'm not saying anything about determinism; I think determinism is probably false, but I do not believe in libertarianism, that these decisions just pop out of nowhere.

Agustín: *[Laughter] You've argued that the first-person perspective challenges naturalism in some particularly potentially deep senses. How do you think this plays out into the very discussion that we're having here? This perspective of naturalism versus the first-person challenge.*

Lynne: I think a naturalistic perspective is a non-personal perspective, and I think if I'm right, the world that we live in is essentially personal. That is, it essentially has—we have these essential properties, and we are ontologically basic entities. These basic entities have first-person—as I say, first-person persistence conditions. Say more. Ask me again, or another question.

Agustín: *Yeah, so in this same vein then, there's some that would argue there are kinds of naturalism that would not go as far as this first-person perspective, right? They would try to argue for more uniformity across the board.*

Lynne: They would, but I wouldn't. That is, I think we are distinct from animals. I think we are—our causal powers are different, and what we're accountable for is different. In fact, I don't even think animals are accountable for anything, but we ask for reasons. We get reasons. I think language is really the big difference between the robust first-person perspective and the rudimentary first-person perspective that we share with animals.

Agustín: *Yeah, so—*

Lynne: The rudimentary first-person perspective is the perspective from which we have consciousness and intentionality. I think animals have consciousness and intentionality, and I think that the animal kingdom is a continuum. I think the animal kingdom is seamless, but I think when it got to human organism, human animals who developed a language, it's a social idea because language depends on social being.

Human persons, I suspect, came into existence when these human organisms, or humanoid organisms, developed a language that had the complexity, the resources that our language has for thinking, conceiving of ourselves in the first-person. Not just acting intentionally, not just being conscious of friend or foe, but to know that, gee, if I were to see a friend, I'd go kiss them or something.

Agustín: *[Laughter] Do you think then that the role of human culture, which, of course, language is a central component—do you think that that has acted in a feedback co-creative loop with the ways in which humans experience a human nature today?*

Lynne: I think that's a good way to put it, yes. In fact, I think that—well, and it's well put. I think Wittgenstein says unfortunately in one place, something like, "The limits of my language are the limits of my world."

Agustín: *[Laughter]*

Lynne: I'm not sure I'd go that far, but language opens up the world to us. Our conventions and our social activities open up the world to us, and that's the way we live in the world.

Agustín: *Do you think then this opening up through language and culture, this human experience in the world, is really the way in which self-consciousness manifests itself?*

Lynne: Yes, that's one way. Yes, as I say, I think we're—I think that we have—essentially we have first-person perspective, but we're born with only a rudimentary first-person perspective. As we learn a language, we learn to think. We just learned the world in a new way. Here's a story from my niece, who is two years old. Her parents had a birthday party for her and invited all of her cousins. One of her cousins was named Donald. She found Donald in her bedroom taking all the toys out of her toy box playing with them, and she said, "Dammit, Donald, mine!" That is a manifestation of the robust first-person perspective which baby toddlers get around the age of two.

Agustín: *Yeah.*

Lynne: In fact, what I thought was so funny about that story was that her parents were appalled. Where did she learn "dammit"? *[Laughter]* Whereas, I thought, wow, that's a perfect example of the onset of a first-person perspective.

Agustín: *This brings up—and a couple of other things you've already said bring it up as well. What do you think the role in relationship of morality is then to this take on human natures?*

Lynne: I don't have any ethical theories. I really don't know what to think about ethical theories, many of them.

I think we're accountable, and a condition for accountability is that we know what we are doing, that is, a robust first-person perspective. Earlier I said just first-person perspective, but it's the *robust* first-person perspective that allowed my niece to say, "Dammit, Donald, mine!" Also, it's a robust first-person perspective that allows us—or is a necessary condition for our being accountable.

Agustín: *Right.*

Lynne: If you can't realize that you're doing something under a proper description, I'd say you're not accountable. That's as far as I've gone.

Agustín: *What do you think about someone like Frans de Waal[21] who argues there's deep roots of morality in other species? Apes, for example, or dolphins and whales, things like that? Do you think that we're talking—maybe he's referring to a different thing than the kind of human morality that you're discussing that emerges from this robust first-person perspective?*

....

21 See de Waal, Frans. 2010. The Age of Empathy: Nature's Lessons for a Kinder Society. New York: Broadway Books.

Lynne: No, I don't think that. I think that they could—I don't know actually enough about animal morality, but I do think that animals can—I do think they have rudimentary first-person perspectives which gives them a certain semi-moral view on the world. They can't ask for reasons. They can't give you excuses or justifications, but they can be trained by their peers, or their superiors, to behave in certain ways, and that's what I think. I think that is a root of morality.

Agustín: *Yeah, I agree. I think this idea of social tradition is very important, and it resonates with the way you've been talking about language, because in humans the social tradition can create an infrastructure that's worlds away from that of many other animals to develop these kinds of ideas of ethics and morality.*

Lynne: Just think of things like international courts, or terrorism acts, or art, government. I mean just all the things that are characteristically human involve a robust first-person perspective.

Agustín: *Well, what do you think about, then, this role of malleability and plasticity in human nature? Is there an enormous amount of variation in the way in which individuals participate, and embody, and perceive of this robust first-person perspective?*

Lynne: I think, in terms of malleability, that we're pretty malleable. I think that especially once you start thinking of the biotechnology advances that have gone on. I have no idea what the limits of our malleability are, but I think we could be induced to behave in rather different ways from the ways we do.

Agustín: *Do you think this biotechnology, the adding of artificial created components to human limbs, to human sight, hearing, maybe even the brain eventually—does that have the potential to change the way in which this robust first-person perspective is experienced, or develops, or do you think it could just be part and parcel of its expansion?*

Lynne: I think it would be part and parcel, but that's because I think of a first-person perspective as a dispositional property with just endless dispositions you could be taught to have, or learn to have, or be given a drug to have, or something. Anyway, but I think the first-person perspective is a non-qualitative dispositional property which enables you to do, and think, various different kinds of thoughts, and do various different kinds of things almost without limit.

Agustín: *What would you say, or where do you think this puts you in dialogue with peoples of different faith practices who try to identify human natures in some sort of theological context? Do you think these are compatible, incompatible?*

Lynne: I think that my view is compatible with a number of people of different faith practices. I'm compatible. Actually, in the last chapter of my most recent book *Naturalism and the First-Person Perspective*[22], it's called near-naturalism. Near-naturalism is quite naturalistic up to a point, but it's one thing. It's personal, not non-personal. Another thing is, I leave open the question of theism, and that's gotten some guff about that. I mean I'm not making any claims one way or another about theism, and that might put a lot of people off.

Agustín: *[Laughter]*

Lynne: I, myself, am a Christian, so I'm not going to make any claims. I mean I don't care. It's too bad if they're put off.

Agustín: *Yeah, I know.*

Lynne: I'm not at odds with the atheistic view. I mean personally I'm not, and I don't think my view is at odds with it either. I think it is really truly—it's truly open from my view.

Agustín: *A recent book by Thomas Nagel, Mind and Cosmos*[23]—

Lynne: Yes.

....

22 Baker, Lynne Rudder. 2013. Naturalism and the First-Person Perspective. New York: Oxford University Press.

23 See Nagel, Thomas. 2012. Mind and Cosmos: Why the Materialist Neo-Darwinian Conception of Nature Is Almost Certainly False. Oxford: Oxford University Press.

Agustín: *—got attacked on all sides.*

Lynne: Yes.

Agustín: *In some ways, he might have been trying at something there, but had a atheistic teleological component, so I'm—*

Lynne: Right. Well, he's got his own burdens there. I mean it seems to me tough to be atheistically theological.

Agustín: *[Laughter]*

Lynne: I do believe in teleology, but I don't think it. And my view stands on its own quite apart from views about teleology and God.

Agustín: *Do you think that there's a bit of fear not just in the philosophical realm, but in the public realm to leave these things open, or do you think people want someone to follow on one side or another?*

Lynne: I think they want you to follow on the atheist side. I think the Zeitgeist is very secular.

Agustín: *Yeah, yeah. Do you think that there's a benefit in both the philosophical academic context, but also maybe in a broader public context to give this discourse on human nature serious consideration? That is, to really invest some time in thinking about what people have to say about it?*

Lynne: Yeah, sure. I think—I've been thinking about it for, I don't know, fifteen or twenty years. I mean I just got hooked on it.

Agustín: *It is a very interesting area of inquiry.*

Lynne: Right. What I started out in—my dissertation was on time. I went from time to indexicals and now, and from now to indexical propositional attitudes to what does it mean? What's the bearer of the propositional attitudes? I don't think it's a brain. I don't think it's a mind. I don't think it's any part of us. I think it's the whole person. That's why I think—that's why I'm a non-reductionist. I think that persons are basic entities, so that we are the—we are basic bearers of properties without any qualification.

Agustín: *Excellent. That is a perfect summary of your perspective... it's fantastic. I really appreciate it that last summary because I think* *it does a nice job in clarifying how this speaks in a different way than some of these Reductivists, or other perspectives.*

Lynne: It's certainly not reductionistic, but it also is not explicitly religious either.

Agustín: *Yeah.*

Lynne: As I say, I think it stands on its own.

Agustín: *Absolutely. You make an argument for constitutionalism.... Why might that be preferable to animalism or substance dualism?*

Lynne: I consider that a huge virtue of my view that it avoids both animalism and substance dualism. We are connected to the animal kingdom, but we are not just animals. We're not just another—just human animals. We are essentially different because, I think, of our robust first-person perspectives.

Substance dualism is a nonstarter for me because I cannot understand what an immaterial mind, or soul, would be. So I'm very happy not to have such things.

Agustín: *Yeah. Well, what do you think the attraction then is of substance dualism? I agree with you, but it remains a powerful draw for many people.*

Lynne: I know. I think the attraction might be even a religious attraction a lot of times. In fact, I think a lot of times, but even if it's not religious, it wants to highlight our uniqueness. Well, I don't think that's the best way to highlight our uniqueness. I think we should highlight our uniqueness by thinking about robust first-person perspective's language, culture, conventions, the way we do things.

Agustín: *We've mentioned this already a little bit in the conversation, but you use this dichotomy of animalism and substance dualism as two separate ends. Really, those are the areas where many people congregate, but constitutionalism, or your version of robust first-person perspective, offers—it's not really an alternative on the same continuum is it?*

Lynne: Oh, perhaps not, but it seems to me it is because it's more than animalism and less than substance dualism.

Agustín: *[Laughter]*

Lynne: I don't start with either animalism or substance dualism and to get to constitutionalism. As I say, I started in philosophy of mind—well, first metaphysics, then philosophy of mind, and then back to metaphysics and persons.

Agustín: *That seems like quite a journey. [Laughter]*

Lynne: Yeah, it's been a wonderful one.

Agustín: *[Laughter] I guess I want to ask one more question on this thread.*

Lynne: Okay.

Agustín: *Do you think that the particular philosophical orientation one has, let's say constitutionalism or animalism or substance dualism, heavily influences the way you think about how morality is engaged with, or emergent from, human nature?*

Lynne: It might. I don't know. I don't really know how, say, animalists can really be animalists, but I guess they can, or a substance dualist. As I say, I can't understand what a mind or a soul immaterial—an immaterial particular in the natural world—could be. I definitely am not a Nihilist about morality, or anything else. I don't have any theories, but it doesn't seem to me that you really need a theory. Maybe this is part of Wittgenstein again.

Agustín: *Yeah. [Laughter]*

Lynne: It doesn't seem to me you really need a theory. You want to live a good life. You want to be moral. You want to be kind. You want to forgive your enemies, all that stuff. You want those things, and you endorse all those things, but there's nothing like systematic anything. It's not systematic. I don't think life is systematic.

Suggested Readings

Baker, Lynne Rudder. 2015. Human Persons as Social Entities. Journal of Social Ontology 1(1):77-87.

Baker, Lynne Rudder. 2014. Swinburne on Substance Dualism. European Journal for Philosophy of Religion 6(1):5-15.

Baker, Lynne Rudder. 2013. Technology and the Future of Persons. The Monist 96(1):37-53.

Baker, Lynne Rudder. 2012. From Consciousness to Self-Consciousness. Grazer Philosophische Studien (84):19-38.

Baker, Lynne Rudder. 2011. Christian Materialism in a Scientific Age. International Journal for Philosophy of Religion 69(1):1-12.

Baker, Lynne Rudder. 2008. A Metaphysics of Ordinary Things and Why We Need It. Philosophy 83:5-24.

Baker, Lynne Rudder. 2008. Big-Tent Metaphysics. Abstracta: Revista de Filosofia, 1:8-15. Special issue on Eric Olson's The Human Animal.

Baker, Lynne Rudder. 2008. Response to Eric Olson. Abstracta: Revista de Filosofia, 1:43-45. Special issue on Eric Olson's The Human Animal.

Baker, Lynne Rudder. 2008. Persons: Natural, Yet Ontologically Unique. Encyclopaideia: rivista di fonemenologia, pedagogia, formazione, 23:17-30. Proceedings of a workshop entitled "Are Persons More Than Social Objects?" held at San Raffaele University, Milan, May, 2007.

CHAPTER 5

Human Nature, Religion, and Theology

Interviewee: Wesley Wildman

Bio. Dr. Wildman is professor of philosophy, theology, and ethics in Boston University's School of Theology and the director of the multidisciplinary Religion & Science PhD program in the Graduate School. He is the co-director and co-founder of the Institute for Biocultural Study of Religion and the journal *Religion, Brain and Behavior*. Wildman's academic work has focused on interpreting religious ideas and building theories of religious beliefs, behaviors, and experiences that acknowledge value in longstanding traditions while attempting to remain intellectually viable in light of the biological, cognitive, evolutionary, physical, and social sciences. He is the author of many books, including *Science and Religious Anthropology: A Spiritually Evocative Naturalist Interpretation of Human Life* (Aldershot, UK: Ashgate, 2009), *Religious Philosophy as Multidisciplinary Comparative Inquiry: Envisioning a Future for the Philosophy of Religion* (Albany, NY: State University of New York Press, 2010), and *Religious and Spiritual Experiences* (Cambridge, UK: Cambridge University Press, 2011).

Slogan. *"The human species as a whole is marked by the tendency to create meaning."*

Agustín Fuentes and Aku Visala, *Conversations on Human Nature*, pp. 233-299. © 2016 Left Coast Press, Inc. All rights reserved.

Aku: *Let us start with the most basic and general question: what does "human nature" mean? How would you answer that question?*

Wesley: I prefer not to define an inherently vague concept, so I would steer clear of answering the question. Conceptual analysis should be fitted to the nature of the thing being analyzed. You want vagueness in the conceptual analysis to match the vagueness of the object. For example, I would not define a chair. Chairs cannot be given a closed-form definition. The very idea is vague: some are for sitting, some aren't; some have legs, some don't; and so on. If this is true of chairs, it is true a thousand-fold of human nature.

I will talk about features of human beings, though. For instance, I will say that human beings are products of an evolutionary process in this particular ecosystem. And I'll say that this way of developing has made us inherently spiritual beings—not accidentally, but inevitably and necessarily spiritual. Every human person, with all of our individual differences, has some tendency toward spiritual questions, quests for meaning, sensitivity to value. Those are the sorts of features that I attach to the idea of spirituality. People with very muted interest in this area often still have a tendency in that direction. Some people have extremely intense interests in that direction. I think intensity of spiritual or religious interest probably has a bell-curve type of distribution across our species.

The human species as a whole is marked by the tendency to create meaning. I take spirituality and meaning construction to be a collaborative project between "meaning-affordances" or "value possibilities" in the environment, and the creative capacities and interests of the human person. Now that is not a definition of the essence of human nature. That is the definition of a characteristic, an important characteristic related to spirituality. It's not necessarily the most important characteristic, but it is a characteristic vital for understanding human nature.

Aku: *In your book* Science and Religious Anthropology, *you use the term "homo religiosus" to describe this characteristic.*

Wesley: Right. The central argument I'm trying to make there is that human beings are homo religious not accidentally or circumstantially but necessarily and essentially. In that book, I treat human beings as products of an evolutionary process in a particular ecosystem, as value-sensitive explorers, and as social creatures. All of that conditions the ways we are *homo religiosus*. There's no fancy phrase for those biocultural conditions, but they are vital components of human nature.

Aku: *You already began to answer my next question, which is this: What disciplines should we look at, when we want to know something about human nature? Of course biology is the one that you already mentioned, but what about others?*

Wesley: Everything that could possibly be relevant.1 I wrote about this in *Religious Philosophy as Multidisciplinary Comparative Inquiry*. The topics of study determine the relevant disciplines, so anyone who has got anything to say about human beings, human behavior, human biology, human relationships to other species, human relationships to the past—all of them are relevant.

Aku: *That is a pretty broad take on it.*

Wesley: Yes, but what can you do? We humans are fascinated by ourselves and that fascination shows up in a host of disciplines. Consequently, I have tried to learn a bit about history, biology, ecology, philosophy, theology, biological anthropology, archeology, psychology, and down the list. I have tried to learn as much as I can about human individual and group life, and that is what informs my work as a philosophical and theological interpreter of the human condition. From my point of view, there's not a lot of choice in the matter. It's just what we have to do to be responsive to the relevant information.

Aku: *It is really difficult to operate in this area, because there are so many different kinds of approaches. What kind of problems have you encountered in trying to straddle all these different disciplines? Any areas of conflict, or consonance?*

----

1   For a more detailed account, see Wildman, W. J. 2010. Religious Philosophy as Multidisciplinary Comparative Inquiry. Albany, NY: State University of New York Press.

Wesley: I have experienced less difficulty, fewer instances of incommensurable disciplinary perspectives, than I expected. The sort of difficulty we run into routinely—you would see this in your own work, as well—is the blinkered character of pretty much all disciplines. We are not great at bridging from the categories of our home discipline across to the categories of some other disciplinary insights. But I think that is simply due to lack of practice. We have not really tried to figure out, say, how the larger scale emergent features of human sociality, which we study in sociology and political economy, fit with biological realities of human life. But there is no insurmountable or intrinsic problem with doing this. An evolutionary framework pretty much guarantees continuity across disciplines in principle, so it's just a matter of digging into the details to see how to put the various disciplinary perspectives together.

The gap between biology and culture to which I just alluded can be bridged in certain cases, with enough patience, and enough openness to other disciplinary insights. It just takes a bit of imagination and patience. There are quite a few people, I have found, who are able to move backwards and forwards, between the biological and cultural levels. That has pleasantly surprised me. Also, I have found many researchers quite interested and open to spiritual questions, seeing that as part of the big picture of human life—and more interested when those questions are framed as bio-cultural aspects of an evolutionarily conditioned species. They find themselves less averse to religion when it is framed in these terms, and so they are more able to participate in research efforts related to religion and spirituality.

Aku: *You used the term "spiritual" again, and you gave a kind of blanket definition, including quite a lot of things. Could you elaborate on that a little bit? What do you mean when you say "spiritual aspect"?*

Wesley: It is another one of these vague container categories. Again, it is not something that I would venture to define, except operationally, for the sake of a particular research study—or for the sake of a particular argument, if I happened to be writing philosophy at the time. Operationalizing a definition of X is one thing. Saying what X means in the abstract, quite another. For example, one of my research studies operationalizes spirituality as a complex construct with more than twenty sub-dimensions or aspects which cluster into a few major dimensions. I wouldn't say that's a definition but it is a highly productive lens through which to look at phenomena that people are often willing to call spiritual.

One point about spirituality is that it is not just an individual thing; it is a social thing. You cannot ignore sociality when thinking about spirituality. Another is that the ways cognition and the human brain work condition the way spirituality gets expressed. So you cannot ignore cognitive neurosciences or empirical psychology of religion. A third thing is that spiritual quests are a part of human life: we seem to be in the business of looking for answers, or constructing meaning. Those "spiritual quests" open up a diachronic aspect to spirituality, which necessarily then involves things like traditions that encode wisdom, and practices that people use to cultivate certain types of habits or virtues.

Sitting behind all of these features of spirituality is a pattern of evolutionary development where all of this got started in our species. That evolutionary history is murky, and it's difficult to look back there, trying to figure out what happened. At some point, though, human beings awoke to the intense axiological or valuational depths of reality. At one point we did not know many value possibilities were available, and then we figured it out. That, I think, is the period in which spirituality was born in our species.

Aku: *What do you mean exactly when you talk about axiological depth? Is it something that we discover, or do we make it when we observe?*

Wesley: It's both. This is a constraint-without-determination type of situation. There are structures and flow dynamics in the world that have a value potential. For instance, if you behave in this particular way, these other things will probably happen; or this thing is always going to be more beautiful than this thing, under certain circumstances. These are not deterministic rules; they are constraints that express relationships among value possibilities. Those value possibilities are engaged by beings with the right kind of sensory and cognitive capacities, human beings among them. Human beings explore an axiological landscape replete with value possibilities, and we realize some values and not others when we construct our own spiritual, valuational pathways through it.

There are low energy pathways in this landscape, the ones that stay close to the valley floors, and reflect the most common patterns of meaning-making and spiritual engagement. There are also adventurous people who say, "Let's try the new, the different, the strange. Even though most people won't appreciate it, we'll learn how to cultivate appreciation for it." They are the adventurers who scale the side of the valley walls in search of intense valuational possibilities to realize. In this way, concrete values and meanings are a collaborative achievement between individual, imaginative construction and given axiological potentials. So there is an objective aspect and a subjective aspect to the axiological depths of reality.

Aku: *Let me come back to an earlier topic, on disciplines again, and ask you whether you think that there are certain disciplines, looking at human nature, that are now, let us say, spearheading the discussion. Are there some areas now where the action is?*

Wesley: As I have poked around, I have found several areas like that. Certain areas have dropped out, theology being one. Theological anthropology is massively out of date, so it has become a non-player. Lots of other areas have become crucial. Anything supporting the bio-cultural linkages in the study of human life is important. Everything from cognitive neurosciences through to biological anthropology and on to sociology have really large, vibrant literatures that are extremely promising for understanding the religious and spiritual tendencies of our species. I would not say any one of them is leading the way.

Philosophical approaches to anthropology have also fallen by the wayside. They used to help to lead the way, but now they are almost inert. They merely respond, most of the time, and they rarely offer anything to outsiders, to non-philosophers. The semi-platonic assertion I was just making, about value-potential structures, is a contribution that philosophers should be making to the study of human nature, but it is uncommon. Most philosophers are just sitting back passively, and working off of the insights furnished by, say, cognitive sciences.

Aku: *You also said that theology has fallen to the wayside. Do you have a diagnosis as to why that is?*

Wesley: Too many theologians have not exerted themselves to learn what they need to learn from the sciences of cognition and culture. Just think of Augustine or Thomas within the Christian tradition, or Maimonides in the Jewish tradition; these were cutting-edge thinkers who were masters of the sciences of their time. But most contemporary theologians have wound up resorting to very useful, but tired, categories such as sin to talk about the human condition; then use those words as if they had a stable meaning, and do not need to be rearticulated for our time, in relation to the various other insights we now possess into human behavior. That is what I mean by inertness. Theology has not been agile enough to rearticulate its fundamental pathways in relation to the rapidly changing understanding of human nature created by the sciences of cognition and culture. As theologians, we have not followed in the footsteps of Augustine and Thomas, Maimonides, and Sankara, and all the rest of our luminous-genius forebears. I take the fundamental theological categories themselves to contain priceless insights, but those insights are profoundly obscured when the anthropology in which they are expressed is 1,500 years out of date.

Aku: *I would like to come back to the issue of biology and culture. How would you describe the relationship of biology and culture? Putting the question another way, how would you think about the role of culture in shaping human nature?*

Wesley: Well, this is essentially, I think, an empirical question. You need to approach the biological and the cultural spheres with a kind of openness, and allow what you see in both domains to speak freely. It is very important to avoid pre-conditions on inquiries in this area. If you begin thinking that biological determinism is true, that is all you will ever see. If you think everything is cultural construction, then that is all you'll see. We see so many examples of intellectuals who have fallen prey to the temptation to focus exclusively on one side or the other of the biology-culture relationship. Openness of inquiry about biological and cultural aspects of human life is important if we are going to produce well-rounded interpretations of the human condition.

Once you are out there, open to the possibility of bio-cultural interaction, you see an amazing story of constraint without determination, along the lines I was talking about before. You have constraints from DNA, which are very difficult to articulate, because of developmental and epigenetic effects. You also have constraints from cultural traditions that affect the way children are raised, and the way this incredibly plastic brain that little babies have gets shaped in particular directions. Even with all of the fluidity of individuals and cultures in relation to those constraints, somehow we still wind up with cultural universals.

Every type of human culture has economic exchange. They all have child-rearing techniques that are more or less comparable. They all have hierarchy systems, and deference, even in mostly egalitarian cultures. They all have particular ways of handling justice and punishing unfairness. Everyone has to know how to handle sex. This recurrence of cultural universals shows that, even within the fluidity of individual development under biological and cultural constraints, we wind up reproducing in cognition and culture something like that incipient axiological landscape I was trying to describe before. The cultural universals just keep showing up.

That is what bio-cultural means: recurring structures, but flexibly explored and articulated by cultures at one level, and by individuals at another. You cannot study that without combining insights from sociology, cultural anthropology, psychology, and evolutionary biology. Only by coordinating insights across domains of knowledge can we get at the significance of individual variations and the cultural variations in relation to cognitive and cultural universals.

You cannot get locked into looking at the variations and the individual differences, because then you will lose track of the structural features that do appear universally. And *vice versa*. This is a complicated answer to your question, but to me the bio-cultural approaches open up one of the most fascinating areas of the study of human life: the give and take between structures and individual variations.

Aku: *On that note, would you say that there is something uniquely, or distinctly human? Is there something special about us that would distinguish us from non-human animals, or our late ancestors?*

Wesley: Yes, it is our axiological sensitivity, what theologians and philosophers call self-transcendence, and what I am inclined to call an intensification of the ordinary sensory system, so as to become open to axiological affordances in the environment. We seem to be really good at that. There does seem to be some degree of that ability in other primates. The historical record of hominid species suggests that Neanderthals had something like that, too, judging from burial practices at any rate. They were a more solitary species, it looks like, and we are more social, but they probably possessed some degree of axiological awareness.

There has been a host of precursor homo species exploring the axiological landscape in these incipient preliminary ways. Then 40,000 or 50,000 years ago, in a great transition, modern human beings had some kind of breakthrough that stabilized across our species within a matter of mere thousands of years. Sexual selection effects are the key to this rapid spread and stabilization of intense axiological awareness, I suspect. People who were able to feel the axiological world were much more attractive as mates. Their genes started dominating the pool. This transformation of our species spread over the globe, and we have the Great Leap Forward, as Jared Diamond calls it. Whenever and however it occurred, something big certainly seems to have happened. At that time, we find new technologies, new hunting techniques, and explosion of art, different burial practices. There were rare, earlier instances of these things, as we might expect, but everything is different after these cognitive and cultural features of human life become dominant in our species.

Aku: *What kind of capacities would we need, in order to have this explosion?*

Wesley: Well, described philosophically, what you need is sensitivity to valuational possibilities, the ability to sense axiological fields of potential that can be engaged and realized in creative ways. What that means metaphysically requires a lot of discussion. What it means neurologically is also important. I reckon this transformation required a capacity for interconnectivity of diverse parts of the brain—a cortical rather than a sub-cortical capacity that allows us to become capable of moments of intense experience, where everything seems interconnected. Those intense experiences may predate religion, and they are at least co-primordial with the rise of anything we might want to call religion in our species. The capacity for them seems really important for modern humans, especially in and after whatever passes for the Great Leap Forward.

These moments of lucid awareness feel extraordinarily meaningful. You are in an intense experience when everything from the practical affairs of your life, to the people you love, to the thing you work on professionally, to aspirations for your future all seem co-present in the mind. It is an astonishing state, but it appears to be reasonably common among human beings. I would say that intense experiences are the basis for a wide variety of other experiences that are more specific in character, from aesthetic experiences to socially expressed ecstasy, and I'd include certain types of religious experience as well.

Aku: *One of the things that has been talked about in the literature is more developed theory of mind, and the possibility of higher levels, fifth, sixth level theory of mind. This seems related to this issue of connectivity, and being able to represent several different levels of connectivity between people, and the ideas of people, and their reference in the world.*

Wesley: Terrence Deacon talks about levels in order to describe the emergence of consciousness, and before that, in his work, the emergence of language.[2] The capacity for complex system-based reference, which is a kind of symbolic reference, is another way of talking about the connectivity required to support new levels of consciousness. The transformation of reference, to make it symbolic, is a neurologically

---

2   See, e.g., Deacon, Terrence W. 2009. The Symbolic Species. New York: W. W. Norton & Co.

demanding activity, and our species didn't always have the capacity to do it. Some people will say language is the key to the transformation of our species in the direction of neurological hyper-connectivity, the capacity for intense experiences, and the emergence of exquisite axiological sensitivity. I think it is actually the other way around: the capacity for symbolic representation co-evolves with this capacity, or is one of the first things to happen after it, or something similar.

Aku: *Yes, it seems to be quite intuitive that one needs to get some sort of symbolism going, before one can get language going. There needs to be some precursor for language, and it seems quite natural to think that it is something to do with this kind of fluidity of symbolic thinking.*

Wesley: Yes, cross-cutting ideas where you have domains of experience, relatively unrelated to one another, co-present in the mind, would be important for the evolution of a capacity for symbolic thinking. This certainly lies at the root of metaphorical thinking. But even that does not really explain *systems* of symbols, which is what you need for language. I would not know where to go with that stuff. It is still very early days in trying to figure out how the emergence of language fits with the emergence of axiological sensitivity and the emergence of systemic symbolic reference.

Aku: *We already talked about language, but how about morality? How are morality and human nature linked?*

Wesley: I take morality just to be one aspect of axiological engagement with the landscape of value affordances I have tried to describe. There is a range of possible ways of constructing moral life, so there is space for creative expression. It is a constraint-without-determination situation, again, with structural features of value possibility interacting with the creative individual and cultural realization of concrete values.

For instance, if you try to run your civilization with unlimited love and infinite compassion for everyone, it won't last long. You will not have the guts required to fight off marauders who just want your territory and your resources, when they come. If you try running it with in-group compassion limited by in-group hierarchical authority combined with intense suspicion toward outsiders and free-riders, you might have a better chance at long-term survival. So that's probably a structure in the axiological landscape that we had to navigate, and there are going to be "sweet-spot" resolutions of the problems we face as we try to navigate the axiological landscape in that respect.

Even with that structure and its sweet-spot equilibrium in morality and social structure, we still have options. If we don't like our hyper-competitive society, we can adopt counter-cultural values such as unlimited altruistic love and create pacifist communities who endorse the same values. In doing this, we might free-ride on the wider society to some extent. But we might also get away with it, especially if our distinctive values enjoy the support of an economically self-sustaining community.

I think human morality has settled down in this sweet spot between too little and too much compassion, and this in turn has given our sensitivity to in-group/out-group boundaries profound moral significance. I know there are arguments against this, but I think Jonathan Haidt does a pretty good job of articulating where that sweet spot is, with five or six domains of moral intuition, all roughly equally strongly functional in the default social worlds of human life: harm and care, justice and fairness, in-group/out-group vigilance, hierarchy and deference, purity and sanctity, bullying coercion and freedom.[3] At least those six appear in small-scale human cultures, in small towns in America or anywhere else, to be roughly equally active. I think that really is the default moral way of human life.

Again, though, that itself is just a constraint. You still determine moral traditions in relation to that, and none of that can define what the good is, normatively. Accounts like Haidt's still just describe the landscape, the tendencies, the structural constraints. To get normative good, you still need to make a decision and implement it. The creation of moral norms is usually a team sport, not an individual activity. It is traditions that enshrined these decisions. Those traditions unfold over millennia, they adapt and they slowly mutate, and they become more and sometimes less nuanced. They have

----

3   See Haidt, J. 2012. The Righteous Mind: Why Good People Are Divided by Politics and Religion. New York: Pantheon.

commentarial layers, with commentaries on commentaries. When I say "team sport," I am talking about a multi-millennial exploration of this landscape of axiological affordances, in respect of its moral significance for human life.

I think the naturalistic fallacy is a real issue here. I do not think there is any such thing as a straightforward natural theology, or natural morality, where you read morals off nature, as if God or the Mandate of Heaven or Karma had put them there, and all you needed was the capacity to notice them. No, I think Nietzsche is closer to the mark. We actually have to assert moral norms, and there is no sufficient natural ground for them. The fact that we are responsible for creating our moral norms makes us feel a bit queasy. Realizing that other people are different than us, morally, can bring on this feeling in a potent way: we feel queasy because we realize we are actually making our own decisions about norms. We are guided by traditions, and constrained by the axiological landscape and personal temperament, of course, but our normative moral orientations are still in our own creative hands. Nietzsche may have had that right, but he also seemed unaware of the social constraints on human beings, or uninterested in them. He is far too individualistic in his articulation of those things.

I take philosophical awareness to be crucial for avoiding the problems associated with naturalistic fallacy, from jumping from "is" to "ought." Philosophy is also important for reminding us that normative moral discourse cannot be avoided. Anyone who wants to say there are no norms in life, or that normative disciplines are useless, is just not paying attention. It is just as bad a reductionism as the theological or philosophical reductionism holding that we can do our ethical work in the abstract, finding clear and distinct ideas without guidance from any actual exposure to experience. There is no room for reductionism on either side.

Aku: *What about religion? Which side would you find yourself on the debates about religion being a byproduct, or an adaptation? You will probably say that it is a complex issue, and some aspects might be adaptations.*

Wesley: Yes, of course I would say that. You can identify some things that look adaptive, and you can identify some things that look exacted, that is, subsequently adaptive, having not previously or originally been adaptive. Some things look like functional byproducts, as well, that might never have been exposed to selection pressures. Everyone in religious studies knows religion is complex. If people studying this question knew more religious studies, they would hesitate to allow their account of the evolutionary origins of religion to be reduced to a simple story of adaptation or exaptation, or so I argue. That is my religious studies training speaking.

If you are a philosopher, you have been infected by the distinct quality of normative discourse. If you are a theologian, you have been infected by the distinctive quality of the conditioned character, or dependence-on-something, of every part of nature. If you are a religious studies person, you have been permanently impacted by the complexity of religious phenomena. I have all three types of training, and so I bring all three of those demands to any adequate explanation of the evolutionary origins of religion. Most accounts of the evolutionary origins struggle to pass all three tests. Most of them tend to be, I think, oversimplified.

Most people now who write about religion being an adaptation due to individual health effects write like Durkheim never existed, as if the sociology of religion never existed.[4] Likewise, it is amazing to me that experts can talk about religion as adapted solely because it enhances cooperation, as if existential issues or meaning and life purpose were unimportant. I have rarely been satisfied with accounts of the evolutionary origins of religion because of such reductionistic oversimplifications.

Aku: *My own experience of these matters is not from a very long period of time, but it seems to me there has been a change, in the last ten years. People are getting much more flexible about these things, whereas*

....

4   Emile Durkheim (1858-1917) was a French sociologist. According to Durkheim, religions serve a crucial social function by making the group itself the implicit target of religious worship and commitment. Thus, practicing religion is what ultimately binds a human group together.

*if you read the stuff from late nineties, early two thousands, you usual-
ly see this kind of clear opposition. One group of people saying, "Well,
it's an adaptation, and this is what it's for." Then you have another
group of people saying, "No, no. It's not an adaptation. It is an outcome
of cognitive mechanisms adapted for something else."*

Wesley: You are dead right about where the consensus is, but I am
actually complaining not only about the older work, but also about
this more recent emerging consensus. I still do not see the type of
sensitivity to the complexity of religion, as it has emerged in religious
studies, the home of the people who are experts on how complex
religion is. I still do not see it in the hybrid accounts that are really
forming the consensus view. It is headed in the right direction, but—

Aku: *It is still not there.*

Wesley: Yes. We have not gotten religious studies people sufficiently
involved. The people who are in the "scientific study of religion" are
coming more from biological anthropology, or evolutionary studies.
They are still not sufficiently closely connected to religious studies.

Aku: *One problem is that most scientists and psychologists still come to
the table by saying, "Well, we've got the causal explanations. You've got
the data." The religious studies people and the sociologists come in and
say, "Well, your biological stuff is just irrelevant. You're just explaining
something, like having two legs and a nose. We are interested in the actual—the way that people actually think and live."*

Wesley: That is a good summary.

Aku: *In your book* Science and Religious Anthropology, *you claim
that something called "religious naturalism" would be a good host for
this kind of pluralistic and multidisciplinary discussion. Could you
elaborate a bit on what you mean by religious naturalism? Why do
you think that it is an approach or a general framework that would be
good to adopt?*

Wesley: There are lots of different definitions of naturalism out
there, so this is contested territory. Similarly, there are more than
a healthy herd full of definitions of religious naturalism. Through

teaching a graduate seminar on varieties of religious naturalism, I have learned that there is some need to take responsibility for the fact that you have to cut off certain options when you offer a definition.

Aku: *The problem with the term "naturalism" in contemporary philosophy is that basically everybody wants to be a naturalist—*

Wesley: Right.

Aku: *—so most people, whatever they come up with, they just call that naturalism.*

Wesley: Right.

Aku: *You have to look at what they actually say before you can figure out what they are talking about. Then it is anybody's guess what "naturalism" means.*

Wesley: In order to operationalize the term in a useful way, for a philosophic argument, I need to define it. Again, operationally, not essentially. I have a theological bias when I approach this question. I am interested in the questions that most affect theology, and theology as impacted by the cognitive science of religion. My attention is drawn fairly quickly to disembodied entities, minds that do not have bodies, such as bodhisattvas, ancestors, gods, angels, demons, genies, things that are spirits, things that are important in a host of different types of popular religiosity, but are not acceptable in virtually any form of naturalism.

We have to avoid the circularity associated with saying that naturalism is anti-supernaturalism, which amounts to saying that naturalism is anti-anti-naturalism. For the sake of an operationalized definition, I say naturalism rules out the possibility of disembodied intentionality, awareness, and agency. The only time you get intentionality, awareness, or agency is if you have a body—intentionality, awareness, and urgency are emergent features of a complex bodily system. I am ruling out certain types of ontological dualism there, obviously. I am ruling out certain understandings of God, as well. It's a fairly aggressive criterion, but it's also clear, non-circular, and very useful for engaging theology. It's also very useful for engaging religious studies, cognitive science, and cultural anthropology, and other things.

Aku: *Yes, this is the naturalism part in religious naturalism.*

Wesley: Correct.

Aku: *Then what is the religious part?*

Wesley: Religious naturalism, for me, is going to involve recognizing that what I have called before in this interview the *axiological depth structures and dynamics of nature* are part of our biocultural heritage as a species. Our axiological sensitivity is a vital part of the sort of creatures we are.

When we engage those axiological possibilities and creatively realize some values rather than others, we are actually exploring the spiritual world, the spiritual realm, for want of a better word. It is not about encountering supernatural agents; it is about exploring the axiological depth structures of life. For me, therefore, religion and spirituality are very broadly construed. Religiosity and spirituality are things that everyone does. In my broad sense, religion and spirituality are not limited to organized religions, so-called. People who think that religion necessarily has to do with God can count as religious in my sense, despite their possible disagreement with me about disembodied intentionality, awareness, and agency. People wanting nothing to do with organized traditions can count as religious, too, despite their disagreement with me about the importance of acknowledging the social dimensions of human spirituality.

One of the effects of the *homo religiosus* argument in *Science and Religious Anthropology* is to articulate religious naturalism in a way that liberates religion and spirituality from the exclusive control of religious traditions. Religious traditions are just one type of religiosity, and it is a very impressive and powerful type. It's not the only kind, and I think Paul Tillich's genius as a theological thinker was his ability to show non-religious people that their intensive acts of exploring the axiological world, what he would call the ground of being, were authentically religious or spiritual.[5]

....

5   Paul Tillich was a German born-academic philosopher and theologian who had a significant influence on twentieth century American and European theology.

I am thoroughly Tillichian at that point. For me, religious naturalism has a lot more to do with the axiological landscape of valuational possibilities than with organized religious traditions. Organized religious traditions are one, probably unavoidable, and certainly hyper-powerful type of socially organized spiritual quest. They are in there, in the mix.

Aku: *Your approach is a bit different than, say, the cognitive science of religion that starts from the idea that religion is about supernatural agents, like gods and spirits.*

Wesley: I feel as though when we ditch culturally postulated supernatural agents, disembodied agents, we only toss out a part of religion. Most people in religious studies are going to criticize cognitive science of religion for defining religion in terms of supernatural agents. I don't define religion that way. Supernatural agents are symbolic ways of engaging this complex axiological landscape, and that engagement can be existentially authentic even when there are in fact no such supernatural agents. My way of approaching things is wide open to the academic study of religion, in its host of different approaches.

Religious naturalism can connect with a whole range of philosophical and theological perspectives, including people who want to pursue normative, not just descriptive questions. It effortlessly connects with the cognitive science of religion, to bio-cultural approaches to religion, and to the practical challenges of human life. It connects to moral theory. If you want to say there really are supernatural agents, and you want to know the status of those agents, then, in this religious-naturalist hosting environment, they are understood to be symbolic forms of describing potentially authentic engagements with this other thing, the axiological landscape of possibilities. If that is not enough for you to feel as though you can participate in the conversation, then you are not going to feel welcome in a discussion hosted by religious naturalism, and you will have to go somewhere else.

Aku: *Yes, I think I get that. I can imagine a person coming into the interdisciplinary discussion, and thinking that there is something behind our ideas of supernatural agents—that there is the ancestor, or the god* *on the metaphysical side of things. But even that person has some sort of a story to tell about the concrete interaction. Then that is something that you can take up, and talk about.*

Wesley: Exactly. Believing in an ancestor has consequences. We can talk about those consequences. We can analyze them, and there is a basis for consensus of interpretation there. This is true even if we disagree on whether or not there is an ontological ancestor corresponding to this symbolic way we have of engaging axiological possibilities related to ancestors. Most people who believe in supernatural agents are happy enough with that as a basis for conversation. What they rightly protest is the form of eliminative reductionism that will not even allow that beliefs in supernatural agents are efficacious or potentially authentic.

The fact that religious naturalism can acknowledge a normatively positive role for belief in supernatural agents, even while rejecting their ontological standing, is what marks the difference between it and a Richard Dawkins-style outlook, where there is no sympathy at all for a normatively positive role for belief in or engagement with culturally postulated supernatural agents.

Suggested Readings

Haidt, Jonathan. 2012. The Righteous Mind: Why Good People Are Divided by Politics and Religion. New York: Vintage Books.

Tillich, Paul. 1957. Systematic Theology, vol. 2. Chicago: University of Chicago Press.

Wildman, Wesley J. 2009. Science and Religious Anthropology: A Spiritually Evocative Naturalist Interpretation of Human Life. Aldershot, UK: Ashgate.

Wildman, Wesley J. 2010. Religious Philosophy as Multidisciplinary Comparative Inquiry: Envisioning a Future for the Philosophy of Religion. Albany, NY: State University of New York Press.

Wildman, Wesley J. 2011. Religious and Spiritual Experiences. Cambridge, U.K.: Cambridge University Press.

Wildman, Wesley J. 2014. Religious Naturalism. What It Can Be, and What It Need Not Be. Philosophy, Theology and the Sciences 1(1):36-58.

Interviewee: Lluis Oviedo

Bio. Dr. Oviedo is a full professor for theological anthropology at the Pontifical University Antonianum of Rome and Fundamental Theology at the Theological Institute of Murcia (Spain). He holds a Doctorate in Theology with a specialization in Fundamental Theology from the Gregorian University of Rome, where he taught from 2003 to 2010. Oviedo currently leads a project titled "Interdisciplinary and Empirical Theology" at the Antonianum University, which focuses on the dialogue of theology with the human and social sciences, and is a team member of the project on Human Specificity, funded by the Templeton Foundation. He has previously served as the editor of the periodical *Antonianum* (1997-2004), and is currently the editor of the *Bulletin of the European Society for the Study of Science and Theology* (*ESSSAT News & Reviews*). He participates regularly in international conferences such as the Annual Meeting of the Society for the Scientific Study of Religion (SSSR) and the European Conference on Science and Theology (ECST), and in the research group on Creditions, based in Graz (Austria).

Slogan. "*You cannot pretend that faith remains untouched by the impact of scientific knowledge and scientific representation of the world, of nature, of human reality. I am convinced that science today provides a framework in which traditional philosophical and theological views can be reformulated and updated.*"

Aku: *The first question I usually ask is how would you define the term "human nature"?*

Lluis: That is a difficult question. Perhaps it is not even fair to come up with a definition in the case of humans. Humans in the Christian tradition are said to be persons, and as such, they transcend any objective condition, they go beyond what could be objectified or defined. I would rather approach human nature via humans as being subjects that are able to interact at a very conscious level. In this sense, humans are free subjects that—the tradition says have a spiritual dimension—are able to transcend the natural or the physical order and go beyond, being open to transcendence.

Aku: *Yes. In doing all these interviews, we have noticed that even at the get-go, when we are trying to come up with an idea of what we are talking about when we are talking about human nature, there are already considerable differences because of background assumptions. What you are saying is that when you look at human nature from a theological point of view, theology comes in very early on in how to understand humanity.*

Lluis: Yes. We could say that there is bias, a theological bias. I think that no one can avoid being biased in one way or another when dealing with human nature. Human nature is an argument in which everybody is self-involved.

Aku: *[Laughter]. Yes.*

Lluis: You cannot avoid projecting your own grand categories or forms or frameworks. I doubt that there could be a completely objective approach that could entail unity among the different parties or that could reach a unifying overarching theory—a super theory—able to avoid the pitfalls of particular biases or particular frameworks.

Aku: *What you seem to be saying is that there is no privileged point of view to human nature or we should not expect to find one single definition or view that would somehow encompass all the disciplines that are interested in human nature.*

Lluis: It is impossible.

Aku: *Yes, but what could we do to make the interdisciplinary exchange better? How can we talk to each other better on human nature?*

Lluis: My point is that although we cannot reach this total theory on human beings, it does not mean that we should not engage in this interdisciplinary exercise or that we should indulge in just cultivating our own approach and theory and avoid exchange or interference with other views. I think that because human nature is so complex, so mysterious, so difficult to deal with, the more perspectives we are able to gather and to put together the richer a view we get.

I am convinced that this complexity requires a multidisciplinary perspective. Theology, per se, would be unable to account for many aspects of human nature that in the Christian tradition have been prominent. Christian anthropology deals with issues like freedom, spirituality, sociality, capacity to love, and virtues and so on without accounting for other scientific and philosophical traditions. Now these new approaches will enrich the Christian understanding.

Aku: *What is the panoply of disciplines that we should be looking at when we want to study human nature?*

Lluis: It is huge. I would say that perhaps there are some concentric circles. Even economics are important: some approaches in rational choice theory have been applied. Cultural studies and cultural anthropology, ethnography, for example, are important.

Currently, perhaps the biggest challenges come from the evolutionary biology applied to human nature, evolutionary psychology, or human ethology. There are different names, but all driven by similar axiomatics or the same method and approach. Then there is neurology or neuroscience that represents the cognitive sciences.

Neuroscience represents a great challenge, especially because many of these scientists pretend to discover what traditionally was called human mystery, the mystery of human nature. If we complete the map of neurological connections in our brains or if we manage to represent in an accurate way the evolutionary mechanisms presiding the adaptation of human brains and so on, we would be able to discover, to reveal the mystery of human nature. After that, no mystery, no enigma.

Aku: *A lot of people who were working on the Human Genome Project also thought that when they would finally come up with the map of the whole genome, then the mysteries would be solved. It did not turn out that way. We will see whether this quest of unraveling the mystery of the brain will suffer the same fate.*

Lluis: Indeed, genetics will be connected to evolutionary biology. Then another field that I should include would be paleoanthropology that nowadays is closely linked with primatology. There are no more clear boundaries between these areas, and they are all pursuing the same goal of better understanding through these analyses of human development, evolution, and neurological development of the human mind.

Aku: *One of the main questions in this area is the relationship between biology and culture. What is the role of culture, do you think, on shaping human nature? Is human nature a given and then culture builds on top of that, or is culture itself something that forms and informs human nature?*

Lluis: That is a big challenge, not only for Christian anthropology, but also for every scientific approach to human nature. The problem is that human beings are very complex, and we cannot isolate human nature from other humans and from society and from cultural frameworks. The human mind does not work in isolation from the cultural environment as various models of extended and distributed cognition in the last twenty years have claimed.[6]

A big challenge now is how to integrate all these aspects of culture, brains, and society and so on into our knowledge of human beings. We cannot disentangle human minds, genetics, and culture. We cannot just study neural networks, for instance, and disregard cultural aspects of humans.

Aku: *Would you say that there is something distinctly or uniquely human? This idea of human distinctiveness or human uniqueness has traditionally been one way of understanding human nature, saying that human nature is whatever is uniquely human or makes humans distinct.*

Lluis: Yes, that is the big question. My feeling is that much depends of the extent of the word "unique." I remember in a research seminary organized in our university a prominent German neurologist compared human brains with our hominin ancestors and other primates.

---

6   For extended cognition, see Menary, Richard, ed. 2010. The Extended Mind. Cambridge MA: MIT Press.

He was not happy with the qualification of uniqueness because their evolution might have gone quite differently. I know that primatologists like Frans de Waal are also very uncomfortable with this idea of uniqueness.

What about Christian anthropology? I think we need still to hold onto the claim that human beings are unique or have a unique kind of relationship with the Divine, a unique relationship, certainly not exclusive. The relationship is unique in the sense of a special way to relate to each other and to the Divine or to transcend. I am convinced that our hominin ancestors shared many aspects with our nature, so it would be beside the point trying to say, "Well, they're not *Homo sapiens*, so they are not in any way unique or special." The level of evolution and development that reaches the human species renders them unique in the sense of special and different to some extent, relative to other species.

Then the question is the nature of this difference. Is it qualitative or just quantitative in terms of having more neural connections or having a better neural network or more cognitive processing power?

Aku: *It seems that sometimes this is just a terminological dispute, that you end up disagreeing about what constitutes uniqueness, how to define the term "uniqueness." Of course everybody acknowledges in a very blatant way that in some ways we are not unique. There are a lot of things about us that we share with other species.*

Then again, at what point of the continuum do we start talking about uniqueness or distinctiveness or something like that? It is easy to go either way. It is easy to say that there are aspects of us that are completely unique, have no precedence, or go the other way and say, "Well, there's nothing about us that's special in a strong way." These are really easy options.

Lluis: Anyway, for me, perhaps the most specific if not unique trait of human nature is consciousness. I do not want to say that we are the only species having consciousness, but the level of consciousness we reach renders us special or different. Again, I am convinced that there is continuity between humans and other primates who have some forms of consciousness. Nevertheless, other species are not at the level of consciousness that humans have reached.

Aku: *Sometimes people also say that freedom—or our capacity of freedom—is what makes us unique, that we have free will. Would you characterize human beings as having a certain kind of freedom or distinctive freedom with respect to other species?*

Lluis: Yes, yes, yes. I am pretty sure that with respect to our ancestors the level of freedom we have reached regarding biological instincts is unique.

The other point of comparison is potentially intelligent machines. The level of freedom we have is bound with consciousness and self-reflection and the capacity to consider different ways of acting. A complex enough machine with good software and access to information about different ways of acting would still operate too mechanically, or too rationally perhaps.

I am convinced that human freedom does not work in this way, as simply processing the available information in the right way. I think that human freedom is much more than just following the instincts of survival and reproductive success in a way that improves our lot or provides the better outcome.

At the same time, I must acknowledge that our freedom is bounded in many ways. Sometimes I explain to my students when I deal with this topic that perhaps what ensures us humans a certain level of freedom is the fact that there are so many different variables determining our freedom: biological, environmental, developmental, neurological, genetic—everything.

Usually when you have to deal with more than six variables, you cannot determine the outcome, from a statistical, mathematic point of view. There are even more variables influencing human decisions, human courses of action.

This is not the same as with other living things or with hypothetical robots that would be endowed with some very developed software. That is different. I think that freedom belongs to the mystery of the human condition, like consciousness. At this level, theology is unavoidable.

Aku: *Some transhumanists have argued that we can use our agency and the freedom we have to actually shape our nature. What do you think of this? Even if we can shape our nature, should we do it?*

Lluis: Well, again, we have to distinguish between a strong and a weak version of transhumanism or posthumanism. If we take a weak understanding of transhumanism, it would be content with what could be called enhancement of human nature both in physical terms and in cognitive terms. The strong version is about much more than just enhancement. It is about changing the condition of human nature, rendering us superhumans.

I am very skeptical about such a condition ever being reached. Nevertheless, I think some forms of enhancement that nowadays are being practiced—some replacement of organs or so on—can at least improve the human condition. We can delay the effects of aging. That is okay.

The problem for me is that when you try to enhance the cognitive dimension, you cannot avoid unexpected and very probably damaging consequences in other dimensions. There seems to be a trade-off here: you can get one enhancement but a problematic condition might develop somewhere else.

Aku: *You gain something, you lose something else.*

Lluis: Yes, yes. I feel that due to the complexity of the human being, you cannot enhance everything. You enhance an aspect but at the cost of other aspects. I am not convinced that the gain would be a net gain or a shared gain, a complete achievement to radically improve human nature.

I think there is still too much of science fiction in all of this and not too enough empirical—experimental—results that could ensure us about the prospects of posthumanism or transhumanism. I know that this is the direction to which many scientists and our scientifically driven culture aspire. It might be a dystopia, like Huxley's Happy World?

Aku: *Brave New World.*

Lluis: *Brave New World.* It seems that these subjects that have been very enhanced, very developed, they are nevertheless not so happy.

Aku: *Yes, yes. What about morality? Morality seems to be, again, one of the things that people associate with human nature. Sometimes people even identify a certain kind of morality as being distinctively or* *uniquely human. How would you describe the relationship between morality and human nature?*

Lluis: Yeah. I think, again, that humans are special in being able to conceive moral codes. However, after all the scientific study, interdisciplinary engagement with biology and anthropology, I am not sure if morality is naturally driven, something natural, or transcendental in Kantian terms.

Indeed, if you take the point of view of biology, you could discover some basic rules of behavior, like pursuing one's own survival chances or improving survival chances or pursuing reproductive success or even how altruistic drives could be understood inside a shared naturalistic biological framework. If you take the cultural stance—I mean the anthropological-cultural stance or ethnographical stance—and you compare several different cultures, you could find some common structures, what we could say a kind of universal moral grammar.

But such a grammar might end up being rather minimal or formal, just some principles. The content of morality changes radically between cultures. You visit cultures in which it is perfectly legitimate to abandon your children or to kill the children when they are female. After that you are not sure that morality could be universal or just biological in some sense.

I am more and more convinced that culture is a product of humanity and more still of enculturated humanity so that we would never have morality by just attending to our biological condition. We have to take into account the fact of sociality and culture. My fear is that this could be somehow relativistic. I am in this sense closer to Charles Taylor—not in interpreting it as relativistic, but in the sense that we have to account for many models of morality. Alasdair MacIntyre has somewhat the same idea.

Competing models does not mean that all the models are the same or have the same value. At the end, these competing cultural models of morality and the competition should point to those models that are more convenient, plausible in the long term for the human beings. In this sense, morality is very, very human-specific. It is not just biological drives but biological drives feed back into moral values.

Aku: *How would you identify certain common ground or common points of discussion on human nature between different disciplines, like theology, philosophy, and the sciences? Where would the most interesting stuff be now, the common areas?*

Lluis: I think nowadays the main worry for all—for theologians, philosophers, and scientists—or, by the same token, psychologists, sociologists, anthropologists, and so on— is how to ensure or reach a full life or the fullness of life, as Charles Taylor describes.

Aku: *The traditional philosophical and theological term would be happiness, but what we would nowadays call more like human flourishing.*

Lluis: Yes, yes, yes. Anyway, I am not sure that to reach this goal you can disentangle anthropological discussion from economics, politics, the studies of culture—I mean, literature, arts, and so on. This goal is shared by all the disciplines that converge on the human condition. How can the human condition evolve to overcome the pain, suffering, disasters we have been going through in the last century? How could we be better human beings? I think this is the common ground for everybody.

Even for a neurologist who could be described as one far from normative or teleological ideas, I perceive some sense of the purpose their own research should serve as, in some way, an amelioration or enhancement of the human condition. I do not think it makes sense to pursue a research program that does not help to improve the human condition in some way.

Aku: *Again, coming back to this issue of interdisciplinarity, a lot of scientists would probably say that we just need science to find out what human nature is. Why should the scientists listen to anybody else? Vice versa. Sometimes you have it the other way. Some people in cultural studies, perhaps in anthropology as well, some philosophers, even theologians, they say, "Well why should we listen to the sciences? Why should we listen to psychology or biology?" What would you say to both sides?*

Lluis: That is a big question for me, because I have been trying to engage in the dialogue between science, theology, and humanities for many years now. Well, I think scientists need philosophy and theology for many reasons.

I find that many scientific approaches to social and human phenomena are limited in the sense that they are unable to interpret their results. In order to do this, you need good hermeneutics, and good hermeneutics presupposes the humanities. By the same token, if you are studying—from a scientific point of view—religious phenomena, a perfectly legitimate enterprise that often could bear good fruits, you need to have some theological knowledge. Otherwise you commit pitfalls that are sometimes ridiculous.

On the other side of the question, philosophers and theologians should pay attention to scientific developments: there are many results that should be taken into account. I think you cannot avoid the impact of what is called scientific culture on your beliefs, on your religious doctrines, and so on. You cannot pretend that faith remains untouched by the impact of scientific knowledge, scientific representation of the world, of nature, of human reality.

In a more positive way, I am convinced that science today provides a framework in which traditional philosophical and theological views can be reformulated and updated. Theology needs to be reformulated or updated, no longer following Aristotelian categories or Kantian transcendental or Hegelian idealistic models, but following or trying to adapt to our scientific framework.

I must say that the scientific framework often closes doors that were open since old times in the Christian tradition. At the same time, scientific inspiration opens rear doors or new windows that allow you to appreciate new panoramas or new landscapes that formerly were neglected. Even more, science helps to solve some enigmas, I would say, or some—how you say it in English?—a *rätsel* in German.

Aku: *Puzzles?*

Lluis: Yes, like the one about the presence of evil in the world. Spanish evolutionary biologist Francisco Ayala[7] says that science can offer big gifts, big presents to theology. That is true.

At the same time, I think that the relationship between science and theology helps humanities and, by the same token, helps science to be a little bit more humble and theology to be more humble.

....
7   See Ayala's interview in Chapter 2.

I am frustrated with views about theology that are idealistic, proud. Many are convinced that theology is a superscience that has no limits or boundaries: science has to deal with penultimate things, while theology has to deal with ultimate things. We would enjoy a privilege that science does not enjoy. Engagements with the sciences and humanities can help both to be more humble and recognize their own limits.

This opens a way of reflection about scientific practices, limits of science, in which ethical questions and so humanity, sociology, and even theology should be present, too. The illusion that science is a self-referential and self-closed system able to provide its own remedies, self-correcting system, self-leveling system, is no longer convincing.

Aku: *In terms of human nature, you see the role of theology as reminding scientists and others that there is something mysterious or something transcendental about humans—human nature—that is difficult to pin down, that there is something that goes beyond.*

Lluis: Well, my experience in dealing with scientists points in two directions. On the one hand, you find nice scientists, even light-hearted materialists and reductionists, who recognize the limits of their respective disciplines, who through this recognition accept inputs coming from other views—from humanities, from theology—and who are really committed to openness to avoid the pitfalls in scientific study. Then there are these other kind of scientists who are completely closed to any kind of dialogue, transcendence, and who are convinced that the limits of science are just the temporal limits.

Aku: *Is there some particular area related to human nature that you are working on now?*

Lluis: Yes, for many years I have been quite committed to the scientific study of religious cognition and behavior. I am convinced that religious experience is perhaps the—if not the only one, one of the most complex experiences in human nature involving more aspects and has deep consequences in how humans behave and live and understand themselves.

I think that it is extremely important to engage in an open dialogue with these legitimate attempts to describe religion, religious mind, and behavior in order to vindicate the human-specific traits and to indicate that these aspects are related to the human capacity to transcend their everyday conditions and to point to dimensions that go beyond the scientific domain.

The only thing I complain about is that there are too few theologians committed to this field of research. It is very hard to recruit students, PhD candidates who would put their strength and effort in pursuing these interdisciplinary studies.

In international conferences, I feel often rather isolated. I am the only one discussing—for example, in the Society for the Scientific Study of Religion, with a group of biology of religious behavior. Theological input is needed but it is a pity that I am almost the only theologian contributing to the ongoing discussion.

The problem often is that for many of my colleagues, it seems that the purpose of all this research is to "tame religion." Religion brings a lot of trouble to an advanced society. It is a hindrance for human progress and so on. If we through research manage to better know the deep dynamics of religion, we could perhaps tame or render religion less troublesome, something like that.

This kind of goal is present in scholars who have gone through bad experiences with religion and/or are otherwise committed to some antireligious agenda. At the same time, you have to remind them that you could pursue this taming of religion for the benefit of humanity, to avoid the worst effects of religious fanaticism and bigotry.

You have to remind them that it would be a pity if religious experience would be extinct and would be unable to provide to new generations who have the right to live the same or similar deep, joyful, plentiful experiences that you can live only through religious faith, religious practice, religious celebration or services and so on. It would really be a pity if religious experience gets lost because we try to avoid through elimination strategies the worst aspects of religion.

Anyway, there is some kind of apologetic dimension in all this, but apologetic in the sense of apologetic for Christians or for religious believers. On the other side, they defend their own apologetic program for atheism.

I respect this and it is interesting to engage in the discussion. It seems that when you are engaging with these scholars concerning the scientific study of religion, you are just displacing the old debate between theism and atheism to the scientific study of religion.

Aku: *So what you are saying is that in our current situation, in our Western culture and scientific culture, the debate between theism and atheism, religion and non-religion, is actually being partly, at least, conducted in the context of this scientific discussion.*

Lluis: Yes, exactly. You can see that some of the New Atheists, like Dawkins and Dennett, are using the arguments taken from this research. It is simply the age-old game all over again played with different cards.

These people are nourishing the expectation that science will slowly but surely provide all the answers we need. We need not care about religion any longer. As long as society progresses and we get better standards in economics and welfare and scientific knowledge, better education and so on, we will no longer need religion. Even the philosophical issues about life's purpose and finitude and human condition will be dropped.

Aku: *If I understand you correctly, you are worried that these, let us say, transcendental aspects of human nature are being dropped out because of a strong focus on scientific questions. These aspects that have been traditionally dealt with in philosophy, even some forms of psychology and theology, are now being eclipsed.*

Lluis: Yes, that is the question. I think those scientists who take the burden of discussing religion or trying to debunk religious beliefs are nevertheless important and valuable. This is because the huge majority of scientists do not care at all about religion or they are just indifferent or have no interest at all on what religion could mean. They just consider that science will provide them everything they need. This, for me, is the dark side of our current scientific culture.

Suggested Readings

Tallis, Raymond. 2011. Aping Mankind: Neuromania, Darwinitis and the Misrepresentation of Humanity. Durham, UK: Acumen.

Welker, Michael, ed. 2014. The Depth of the Human Person: A Multidisciplinary Approach. Grand Rapids, MI: Eerdmans.

Tomasello, Michael. 2014. A Natural History of Human Thinking. Cambridge, MA: Harvard University Press.

Donald, Merlin. 2001. A Mind So Rare: The Evolution of Human Consciousness. New York: W.W. Norton & Co.

Hefner, Philip. 1993. The Human Factor: Evolution, Culture and Religion. Minneapolis: Fortress Press.

Murphy, Nancey. Bodies and Souls, or Spirited Bodies? Cambridge, UK: Cambridge University Press.

Schwarz, Hans. 2013. The Human Being: A Theological Anthropology. Grand Rapids, MI: Eerdmans.

Interviewee: J. Wentzel van Huyssteen

Bio. Until recently, J. Wentzel van Huyssteen was Princeton Theological Seminary's James I. McCord Professor of Theology and Science. Ordained in the Dutch Reformed Church of South Africa and a native of that country, he holds an MA in philosophy from the University of Stellenbosch in South Africa and a PhD in philosophical theology from the Free University of Amsterdam. His areas of academic interest include theology and science, and religion and scientific epistemology. Van Huyssteen teaches courses on the role of worldviews in theological reflection, theology and the problem of rationality, theology and cosmology, and theology and evolution. He serves on the editorial boards of the *American Journal of Theology and Philosophy*, the *Nederduits Gereformeerde Teologiese Tydskrif*, and the *Journal of Theology and Science*, and is co-editor of the *Science and Religion Series* (Ashgate Press). He delivered the Gifford Lectures in 2004, titled "Alone in the World? Science and Theology on Human Uniqueness."

Slogan. "*What it means to have a religious disposition is deeply embedded in the questions of morality, embodiment of music, language, and everything else that makes us who we are.*"

Agustín: *Basically, I want to have an informal conversation on human nature, because I find that what is published is not always how people personally talk and think. The first question is—the one I start with is the most difficult and yet the most obvious. That is, how would you describe or define a human nature?*

Wentzel: Well, maybe I should start by telling you what I have found extremely problematic. Am I close enough?

Agustín: *Yes.*

Wentzel: What I have found as a theologian and philosopher, and also been extremely frustrated with, is the narrow and the top-down character of theological and ethical approaches. Which is, in a sense, so cerebral and so constructive and completely disembodied. In my book *Alone in the World* (2006), I trace the long history of what it means to be created in the image of God. This is just another way of asking "What does it mean to be human?" and how theological answers to this question have become very narrow, justified by certain ways of looking at the Bible and Revelation. All of that I found tremendously unsatisfactory.

In terms of a methodology I want to start from the bottom up, and I can only get that through an interdisciplinary conversation, looking at what anthropology and archeology say about where we are from and how we became what we are. For the past two or three years I have also worked on the role of embodiment, which may be a very natural, normal thing for you to think about as an anthropologist, but in theology, only feminist theologians talk about embodiment and sexuality and things like that.

It became very clear to me that we have to look for the nature of humanity from the Darwinian process. What does it mean to be aware, what does it mean to be conscious, why do we all have a moral sense, do we have a religious sense? All these capacities come through the bodies we have, and in that sense it is really a bottom up process for me.

Finally, just to get it out there, in talking about human nature from a really broad interdisciplinary, theological viewpoint, I would like to see how certain significant propensities or trends that we associate with being human arise via evolution. By the way, I'm a little more cautious now in talking about human uniqueness.

Agustín: [Laughs]

Wentzel: I know I circumscribed it in the book too, but I would rather talk about human nature or human species specificity, or whatever you want.

Agustín: Malcolm Jeeves talks about human distinctiveness as opposed to human uniqueness.[8] What do you think of that?

Wentzel: Yes, distinctiveness might be good. I think that certain embodied features and propensities make up human distinctiveness. It is fascinating to me how neuroscience, cognitive science, and neuropsychology are fleshing this out now. Even primatology, as you know.

For me, to think about human nature is to think about what is distinctively human, the evolution of morality, the evolution of the religious sense, language, music, and very specifically also the evolution of sexuality.

So it is clear to me that being human has a very strong genetic and physiological component. I'm fascinated by some of the work that some geneticists are doing about human advanced regions. Some are at Yale and Katherine Pollard at Berkeley.[9] I think these voices together with anthropological voices and philosophical voices all point to the same direction.

Religion itself has this physical and genetic component as well. We do not, it seems, construct religion out of thin air, as some cognitive scientists claim: there might be something deeper to the fact that we do ask these ultimate questions. The question of what it means to have a religious disposition, I think, is deeply imbedded in the questions of morality, embodiment of music, language, and everything else that makes us who we are.

....

8   See, e.g., Jeeves, Malcolm, ed. 2011. Rethinking Human Nature: A Multidisciplinary Approach. Grand Rapids, MI: Eerdmans.

9   See, e.g., Pollard, Katherine S. 2012. The Genetics of Humanness. Evolutionary Anthropology 21(5):184.

This is where I go against the history of my subject, which has so narrowed its idea of the image of God. I think all of that can be fleshed out through evolutionary history. In this case, to be distinctively human or have a human nature would have a very strong focus on moral dimension of humanity.

A related question is whether we can distinguish between a moral sense and the way we construct moral codes. I think we do that. I think the one is kind of an evolutionary given, most probably. The other one is not.

It is very difficult for religious people, especially if you're Christian or Jewish or Muslim, to think of moral codes as something that we construct retrospectively. When we look at what it means to be human, we should look at what various sciences say about the moral dimension and the religious disposition of human beings.

Agustín: *I see we are going have some wonderful conversations on embodiment, because that is also a great interest of mine. All this is very nice: you just answered about half the questions I had!*

Wentzel: *[Laughs]* I'm sorry. It's just they're so interrelated.

Agustín: *That is pretty much my point, I think. What you just ended with does also raise the question—and this is a very interesting sticking point between theologians and others—What do you think about the presence or absence and role of free will in being human?*

Wentzel: Yes, that is a very, very sticky question. I would like to think that—well I do believe we have free will. Of course, within human physiological and psychological constraints, but I don't think there are theological or religious reasons to suppose that we are determined to do what we do. The kind of religious believer that I am, I could never go back to any kind of deterministic idea of God like fate. We're determined to be this. We determined to do that.

Whatever you say about genetics, I do not think our genes embedded in culture determine our actions. I think we are constrained by the bodies and the psychology we have. Nevertheless, on a conscious level and a level of self-awareness we do have at least a certain spectrum of clear choices that we can make for and against good things and bad things, for and against evil or personal decisions. That's a very quick superficial answer.

Agustín: *It's sort of a conversation starter more than anything. That also leads then to another question. Where do you see culture, which people refer to and almost never define? Is culture internal to human nature or do you see a distinction between those things?*

Wentzel: I think you could make an argument that there is always interplay of nature and culture, but I think you could also distinguish them—again it all depends on whose definition of culture you take on board. I do believe that there is a certain "massivity" of things about culture. The cultures we construct, that we are born into and grown out of, at least some humans then innovate further from.

Say for instance, you are a spectacular musician or painter. Obviously it doesn't come from nowhere and it doesn't go anywhere except in a contingent sense through the cultural life that we breathe and take in. You are formed by a tradition and you can then paint in this tradition or become a musician in that tradition. In that sense there's always a starting point, but I think that the starting point doesn't determine the way we are going eventually. There's freedom in how we construct culture but also politically and otherwise.

Our human nature, our ability to be moral, sexual, religious beings shapes the cultures we have. But the deep traditions and paradigms of our cultures tell us where we come from.

If you ask me what I think culture is, I would like to think that culture is creativity. I first of all think of art, and the whole spectrum from architecture through music and the whole broad spectrum. For me, that is what defines the culture of a time in all its diversity. I think that is, of course, deeply connected or interwoven with the kinds of psyches and bodies that we have. What is left behind when we leave or stop painting or stop building is of course the starting point of the next generation. There's a layer of culture that we're born into and that we grow out of, but it is always related to the kind of beings that we are.

Which of course—you would know much more about this—is completely dependent on what the context is, where we are. Whether something took place in the Upper-Paleolithic or the Neolithic makes a huge difference. Why did this and that happen in the twelfth century in Europe but not anywhere else? There are all kinds of cultural questions that link to the early history of culture too.

Agustín: *In that context then, another interdisciplinary question emerges. One of the common properties or propensities of humans is to have some sort of religious faith. How do you see the role of faith in thinking about human nature?*

Wentzel: That is the million-dollar question. If I try to answer in a more phenomenological way instead of theological, I would say that the history of our species seems to point to a natural religiosity. This is not to say that all cultures at all times have had some kind of religion. It is certainly true that humans have always wondered about what comes next, about a future and about the dissatisfaction with death, the mystery of death.

I think there is a sense in which religions, right down to forms of prehistoric religions or others, are all about sensing a different world or constructing a different world and trying to find a world that's better and living out of that. Do you know Harvey Whitehouse?

Agustín: *I know his work but I don't know him.*

Wentzel: Harvey's a good friend of mine, and he has done some very interesting classifications in terms of the different stages of religious cultures that overlap, that even if they're different that they are historically in some sense indistinguishable.[10] I think what fascinates me of our time is the phenomenon of—well, it's not just a modern phenomenon, but the whole idea of the form of atheism, agnostics, and how interesting that is, and how much of a metaphysical position that is.

What I find interesting about faith is that it's so very difficult to not imply a metaphysical position when you talk about it, even if you're a sworn atheist. Two good friends of mine at the American Academy for Religion are a good example: both very minimalist

----

10 See, e.g., Whitehouse, Harvey. 2000. Modes of Religiosity: A Cognitive Theory of Religious Transmission. Walnut Creek: AltaMira Press; and Whitehouse, Harvey. 2000. Arguments and Icons: Divergent Modes of Religiosity. New York: Oxford University Press.

and naturalist in their theologies and anti-supernatural, but the positions flesh out in such a way that they really become metaphysical positions. There is still a faith in both cases, even if not a faith in a God or gods, but in some sense of an ultimate reality.

I think the evolution of religion can be understood in two senses. First, there is the fact that we have these ultimate questions and what cognitive science and neuroscience say about it. Then there is the cultural history of various religions from the beginning through to monotheism and beyond now. I find it fascinating that there is directionality here. I won't say purpose or direction but growth, in some cases, towards monotheism.

The final thing I would say is that faith in a specifically contemporary religious sense is very difficult to define. Why we feel the need to commit to faith? What is the role of habit and what is the role of conviction that there is really something beyond?

In the interest of "full disclosure," as my students always say, I admit that I'm very much a minimalist, but I am a believer and I am a religious person. I sometimes see significant problems: I'm very critical, or agnostic I should say, about some of the traditional big Christian doctrines like the Trinity. I don't believe in some of the doctrines like original sin. I think they are doctrines that have been created over centuries that need to be reconstructed and rethought in the light of what science and theology are telling us.

There are some doctrines that point to a deeper dimension that I think is very important and true. Even there I would say minimal—kind of an apophatic.[11] When talking about faith, I want to move away from language and not necessarily say I'm a mystic, but I have these minimalist inclinations. I'm not saying there's nothing there, but I'm saying that what is there is very difficult to grasp in concepts.

....

11 An apophatic approach to theology insists that ordinary predicates do not apply to God in any meaningful sense and emphasizes the infinite difference between God and the world. We should not, therefore, say that God is omnipotent or omniscient but instead say that God is not restricted by any creaturely limits to power, knowledge, etc. Some apophatic theologians of more mystical leanings would say that even these claims of denying God all creaturely properties are literally false claims.

Agustín: *I think that's a wonderful way to put it. It comes back, in one sense, to your phenomenology and the concepts of embodiment. We embody particular, not just cognitive, but experiential, phenomenological facets of human nature that play out in ritual or in dancing. There's mounting evidence that this is a beneficial way to look at it, especially for interdisciplinary discourse, because a lot of us can come to the table to talk about that. The problem is that we're semantically hamstrung. We really have a dearth of concepts and even words to effectively describe that.*

Wentzel: That is really fascinating. I see a kind of tension in myself: Intellectually I'm very minimalist and I like to streamline things down and avoid complex, exotic baroque doctrines. When I'm in the ritualistic setting, I identify easily with the more mystical moments like the baptism or the Lord's Supper, these kinds of ancient rituals, without thinking about them in any literal sense. They just appeal to you. Words are not always sufficient there.

Agustín: *Given what we've discussed about human nature and these perspectives, there's a big debate now about the role of plasticity and malleability in being human and how that might be related to a human nature. Do you have any thoughts on that?*

Wentzel: It all depends what you mean. I mean, neuroscientists and cognitive scientists are also talking about plasticity a lot and mean different things by that. Some of them mean that, in terms of the way we attach ourselves to other people, to others through attachment and attunement theory of mind and all those things, that there is a tremendous plasticity of the brain, that the brain is never settled or fixed. Even on an adult level or an older level, you could still, through relationships, whether it's romantic or platonic, develop and set new neural pathways that can accommodate that. That's one way to think of plasticity. I think you mean something else. Are you wondering if human nature can be easily or at all changed?

Agustín: *I actually mean both of those things: I think about neural and behavioral plasticity and plasticity of the body itself. But I also worry about fixity, that fixed human nature may be over emphasized.*

Wentzel: I would actually agree with that. I have a sense that there's almost no limit to how we can create, improve, and shape ourselves, if we're aware of the possibilities. A person can really radically change—not so much in terms of personality, but at least in terms of behavior and development over time. That's often what we mean by growing to be more mature. There's certain plasticity there.

Nevertheless, I don't think that such change can happen in all cases. Maybe there are genetic reasons or cultural reasons for why certain people or individuals are much more rigidly constrained and find it almost impossible to break out. Some are determined to like this kind of music instead of that, to read a book about this but not about that, to raise their children in this way and not in that way.

I think there is another way in which behavioral plasticity is actually not so common. Those of us who come from other countries know that some people have the kind of mentality, emotional and intellectual, to really adapt easily to new cultures and settle down. I'm a bit like that myself. I was happy here from the first day, and did not necessarily want to go back to where I came from. Not everybody is like this. Others are much more emotionally tied to well-known behavioral patterns, well-known cultural histories. This kind of plasticity is also difficult.

Suggested Readings

van Huyssteen, J. Wentzel, ed. with Niels Henrik Gregersen. 1998. Rethinking Theology and Science: Six Models for the Current Dialogue. Grand Rapids MI: Eerdmans.

van Huyssteen, J. Wentzel. 1999. The Shaping of Rationality: Toward Interdisciplinarity in Theology and Science. Grand Rapids, MI: Eerdmans.

van Huyssteen, J. Wentzel. 2006. Alone in the World? Human Uniqueness in Science and Theology. The Gifford Lectures. Grand Rapids, MI: Eerdmans.

van Huyssteen, J. Wentzel. 2014. The Historical Self: Memory and Religion at Çatalhöyük. In Vital Matters: Religion and Change at Çatalhöyük. Ian Hodder, ed. Cambridge, UK: Cambridge University Press.

van Huyssteen, J. Wentzel. 2014. From Empathy to Embodied Faith? Interdisciplinary Perspectives on the Evolution of Religion. *In* Evolution, Religion, and Cognitive Science: Critical and Constructive Essays, Fraser Watts and Leon Turner, eds. Oxford: Oxford University Press.

Interviewee: Celia Deane-Drummond

Bio. Dr. Deane-Drummond is a professor of theology at the University of Notre Dame. Trained in natural sciences, plant physiology, and systematic theology at the University of Cambridge, University of British Columbia, and University of Manchester, Dr. Deane-Drummond's work focuses on the intersection of theology and ethics with the biological sciences, in particular genetics, ecology, anthropology, and ethology. Dr. Deane-Drummond has served as the editor for the journal *Ecotheology* (2000-2006), is the Chair of the European Forum for the Study of Religion and Environment (EFSRE) since 2011, is currently joint editor of the new journal *Philosophy, Theology and the Sciences*, and has collaborated extensively with the Catholic Fund for Overseas Development (CAFOD) focusing on climate change and environmental justice. Her publications include *Creation through Wisdom* (2000); *Genetics and Christian Ethics* (2006); *Ecotheology* (2008); *Christ and Evolution* (2009); *Creaturely Theology* (joint ed.) (2009); *Religion and Ecology in the Public Sphere* (joint ed.) (2011), *Animals as Religious Subjects* (joint ed.) 2013; *The Wisdom of the Liminal* (2014) and *ReImaging the Divine Image* (2014).

Slogan. *"I think there is something about being human that makes human beings different from other animals, but at the same time, there are parts of our nature, which we share with animals."*

Agustín: *I start with what is probably the vaguest of the questions on purpose. That is, if you were discussing with a colleague, with a student, with a member of your family, the concept of human nature,* *how would you approach it? What would you tell them if they asked you, "What is it"?*

Celia: This is something I have thought about for some time. Some people would want to deny that there is anything such as human nature, but I would disagree with that. I think there is something about being human that makes human beings different from other animals, but at the same time, there are parts of our nature, which we share with animals. The way I have been thinking about it is to go through what might be called a traditional understanding of image-bearing and what that is and how, maybe, that needs to be turned around in the light of what we know about our own evolutionary history and other animals.[12]

What exactly I would say about human nature would depend on the audience. If I were talking to my young children, I would want them to think about specific responsibilities that humans have as well as humanity's specific characteristics, but not in a way that is demeaning towards other creatures. This is what I am after really: I am after something, which is rounded. I am a biologist as well, so I am always conscious of the human place in the greater ecological scheme of things.

There are ways of thinking about our ecology theologically, as well, in terms of understanding ourselves as *creatures,* as part of the Creation. This is really important to me. As I see it, there is a kinship between humans and other creatures. That is part of what it means to be human. In other words, it is our place in the web, as it were, of creatures, where we find ourselves and our, if you like, *performance* in that web of creatures that marks us out.

Theologically, humans have been understood to be images of God, that is, divine image bearers. In the tradition, image bearing has been associated with what we might call *ontological* characteristics, that is, characteristics of *being* as well as having certain definitive capacities, like reason and language. Then nineteenth-century theologians started talking about particular functions, about functional characteristics

....
12 See, Deane-Drummond, Celia. 2014. The Wisdom of the Liminal: Evolution and Other Animals in Human Becoming. Grand Rapids, MI: Eerdmans; and Deane-Drummond, Celia. 2014, Re-Imgaging the Divine Image: Humans and Other Animals. Kitchener, Ontario: Pandora Press.

in terms of how humans act, that have to do with our dominion over other creatures. Now that, to me, is somewhat problematic because what you do is also related to how you are. You cannot really split being and act quite like that. I prefer to see image bearing as a kind of performance, but not one that is oppressive, but one that is more in kinship relationship with other creatures.

Agustín: *So your template or core for this broader context of human nature seems almost to have both etiological and an evolutionary component simultaneously.*

Celia: Yes, yes. I would say that there is an etiological component in terms of how we act and the futures that we create, but there is also a sense of our history. I feel like I am walking on this tightrope of wanting both/and, rather than either/or. I do not want to separate out human minds from other animal minds, as it were, or to say that we have something so distinctive in our mind that somehow makes us radically different in a way that leaves no room for any connection.

At the same time, there is definitely something distinctive about humans, but distinctiveness as such is also true of other species and other animals. In other words, you cannot just lump them all together and say, you know, only humans are distinct in relation to other animals. Every animal has its own distinctive characteristics. This is something I feel quite strongly about. Even primatologists, like Frans de Waal, for example, talk about the tower of morality where we are on the top of the tower, but that still puts us in a hierarchical position, since the measure of "advancement" on a scale is human beings.

I prefer to see, following Marc Bekoff, who has influenced me a lot, that each creature, each species, each nature, as it were, has its distinctive and wonderful characteristics, and we are, as it were, in that pattern of having those distinct but also equally wonderful characteristics.[13] We do not need to be worried or ashamed of that distinctiveness. We can name it and work with that and then see, maybe, our place in the scheme of things.

----

13 Bekoff, Marc, and Jessica Pierce. 2009. Wild Justice: The Moral Lives of Animals. Chicago: University of Chicago Press.

Agustín: *Do you think that there is a benefit to characterizing human distinctiveness, that many would even push all the way to a uniqueness, while simultaneously not denying the distinctiveness of other creatures? That is to say, is human distinctiveness somehow different in kind from of the distinctiveness of other animals?*

Celia: I suppose this is where my understanding of psychology and science come in: I know that humans are capable of far greater levels of intention, for example, in terms of theory of mind, than is possible for any other animal. Therefore, they have much more sophisticated ability to abstract and symbolize and create their own worlds in a way and have philosophical discussions about human nature. *[Laughter]* I mean, you cannot even begin to think of chimpanzees having this conversation. Therefore, it would be foolish to me to think that there were not something very different about humans and their own cultures.

Boundaries between species are fuzzy, but I would say that there is something unique about human nature. In a sense, maybe that is why humans are said to have been made "in the image of God" in a way that other animals are not. That brings in the religious dimension. Humans can be self-consciously and visibly religious; if religion is there with other animals, it is not visible.

In the case of animals, "religion" would be present more as, I would say, a *passive* response to God rather than something that is self-consciously taken in and articulated in a way that builds up institutions. I am a great believer in trying to stress the level playing field between humans and other creatures, because I think the difference between God and other creatures is far greater than the difference between humans and other creatures. Therefore, to some extent, I want to stop seeing humans and other animals forming a kind of hierarchy, emphasizing our distinctiveness in a way that is oppressive.

At the same time, I also do not want to deny that we have these special capabilities that do not seem to be there in other animals. It may be that there are limits within our capabilities, like wisdom, for example, that have certain, evolved characteristics. In other words, there is some sort of template. Whether that template is in direct evolution and continuity with what we find in our own mental capacities, I have no idea. I think it is very hard to prove one way or another.

In other words, just because we see some developmental patterns towards wisdom, for example, it does not necessarily mean that such developments are hard-wired. There is so much plasticity in our biology and in the expression of our genes that even posing the question about hard wiring might be a mistake.

I am a little bit cautious about some of the language that people use in that area as well. I find it all extremely fascinating to try and tackle. What is it about humans that is different? What does it mean to think about this theologically? Of course, in the tradition, the temptation has been always to stress the human so much that everything else is eventually forgotten. I have been working on that with a few other theologians in the last few years to try and correct that. As I said, it could lead to a distorted picture of what I would call theological anthropology.

Agustín: *In theological anthropology, philosophy, and even psychology lately, this exact question has reared its head with maybe a slightly higher frequency in the context of free will and human agency. Some are even correlating this with theory of mind and—*

Celia: Oh, yes. I mean, this is also extremely interesting and something that I have talked to Frans de Waal, about how far other primates also have this sense of freedom, of theory of mind. He told me that they do not use the term "free will." They use the term "agency." I would say that noticing something or observing something as acting in a certain way does not necessarily tell us whether we have free agency or not. There have to be some quite complicated experiments set up so that you can work out whether they really do know whether someone else is, or another creature is thinking something or working out whether they are aware of that or not.

I would say that there is in some animals what might be called a *second level of intention* in terms of agency. When it comes to higher levels, the third, fourth, fifth level of intention, even the sixth level, which Robin Dunbar talks about in terms of Shakespeare's writing, that is a unique human capacity.[14] I think free will is related to higher levels of intention because if we know that oth-

14   See Robin Dunbar in Chapter 2.

er people are thinking about something, it gives us the momentum to know how to act. In a sense, I would suppose, I would say that free will and levels of intention are somehow interconnected.

Now, we are not quite sure how they are related, though. I have not thought about that enough yet, so I am only speculating. Someone like John Zizioulas, for example, who is an Eastern Orthodox theologian, would hold freedom as being the unique mark of what it is to be made in the image of God. He sees animals as just going around following their own instincts. I think that this distinction is too sharp: there is a gray area where other animals are agents, especially primates.

As I said, the language of freedom or free will is complicated, it is hard to evaluate. It is even harder to get into other animals' minds and work out what they think and whether you can call it freedom or not. Perhaps agency is a bit too demeaning, as well. I think I just have to defer to those who have had years of experience watching and being amongst the bonobos and the chimpanzees. There is clearly something like empathy going on, but is this bad anthropomorphism or a good heuristic tool to work out what is going on in other animals' minds?

Agustín: *That also connects to the next question. That is, following the same narrative thread, what about the sort of role and relationship of morality to human nature? Because in the same context of distinctiveness, uniqueness, free will, morality or a template for ethics is often invoked.*

Celia: Now, this is very interesting. In fact, I have written several papers on animal morality.[15] I got interested in this some years ago, when thinking about the relationship between our creaturely nature and other animals' nature. Again, it was Marc Bekoff's work that alerted me to the fact that other animals have emotions and have capacities for virtue, in a sense, for what you might call wild justice within their own play states.[16]

....
15 See, e.g., Deane-Drummond, Celia. 2014. The Wisdom of the Liminal: Evolution and Other Animals in Human Becoming. Grand Rapids, MI: Eerdmanns.

16 Beckoff, Marc, and Jessica Pierce. 2010. Wild Justice: The Moral Lives of Animals. Chicago: University of Chicgao Press.

It all comes down to how we define morality. If you define it in a very broad sense, as living by the rules, as it were, the rules of a group, then it is very easy to extend the language of morality to other creatures, including dogs, canines, chimpanzees, and so on. If we confine morality to a universalized set of cultural norms that are agreed on by the community and written down in a certain way, then, obviously, you restrict it to the humans. It is down to the definition of what morality means as to whether you can expand it to cover other animals or not.

It is a bit of a catch-22. I know I am not really answering your question. If someone asks me "What about morality?" I would say "What do you mean by morality?" Then, once I would have understood what kind of morality this person is looking for, then I could say whether it does appear in animals or not.

I mentioned earlier that Frans de Waal says there is a tower of morality, that you begin with a basic template and you go up and up and up. Eventually you get to human. I think that is a bit demeaning to other species. I think they have morality within their own worlds that would not necessarily be something we would recognize as being moral in our world.

This is because our moral codes are very different from their moral codes, but this does not mean we do not have a shared evolutionary origin somewhere along the line. We cannot tell whether these codes have any sort of genetic basis, whether they are same as ours, or how far they are genetically connected or not. I remain agnostic because the evidence has not convinced me yet. I find some of the work in evolutionary psychology very flaky. Even though it might look very sophisticated in terms of data, it is often based on correlations only.

As a biologist, I was always taught to be very wary of correlations because correlations do not prove anything. They show matching processes, but they do not show what is in the middle of those. Also, to start speculating about human moral evolution through various happenings in the era of environment of evolutionary adaptedness (EEA) back in the savannah is based on very thin evidence. As Steven Jay Gould rather cynically says, these are simply just-so stories. I tend to be on the cynical side, I'm afraid.

I also find the temptation to modularize mental capacities in humans according to certain characteristics or traits or actions hard to believe. I find it very difficult to be convinced, simply because this modularization takes the shape of computer-type chips. Computerizing mental processes, I would say, is just an outgrowth of our culture, namely, computer culture.[17]

In other words, if someone is growing up in this computer culture, they will start to see computer chips in the brain, and that is a reading into who we are rather than a reading out. John Tooby and Leda Cosmides and some other people there in Santa Barbara, California, suggested some of this.[18] It looks really interesting, and it has a superficial scientific gloss, but when you really start to press it, I do not find the evidence all that convincing.

Agustín: *Would you argue for the antithesis, that plasticity or malleability is a core component of human nature rather than fixed, universal psychology?*

Celia: Yes, exactly. I would say that plasticity is really, really core to human nature. Also, I and you can see evidence of it, the way people change; so human nature is not fixed. It is actually very plastic, very malleable. It goes back to the power of meditation and spirituality and all these other practices which actually can change people's

....

17 One of the most central theses for evolutionary psychology is the massive modularity hypothesis according to which mental processes can be seen as separate, functionally specified programs or mini-computers. Modules take certain input and transfer it to certains outputs and are not sensitive to what happens in other modules. Some evolutionary psychologists have maintained that all human minds consist of hundreds of thousands of modules like this and every single one was favored by natural selection to solve a specific adaptive problem. This would also entail a kind of psychological unity of mankind. Indeed, this is where evolutionary psychologists, like Steven Pinker, place human nature: at the level of universal and innate cognitive mechanisms. See also Chapter 1.

18 The classic is Barkow, Cosmides, and Tooby. See Barkow, Jerome, Leda Cosmides, and John Tooby, eds. 1992. The Adaptive Mind: Evolutionary Psychology and the Generation of Culture. New York: Oxford University Press.

minds and thinking. I am convinced by the power of training, the power of thinking, to train the mind to think in a certain way.

I think back when I was at school, I was not considered particularly bright, but I was very determined and very hard-working. I have always had that sense that I am not all that clever. *[Laughter]* One of my students said to me yesterday, "You know, you're the brightest professor I've ever met in the whole of the university." I was gobsmacked because I thought, "That can't be right. You must have made some sort of error."

He probably had, but what I am saying is that if I have become that, the way he thinks I have, it is because of the training. My mind has changed over time. Something of my nature has changed just through sheer practice. It is like virtues, they come through practice, through repeat, repeat, repeat. Same with any creature, through repeated exposure, repeated rewards, eventually the thinking starts to evolve or change. I think there is a huge amount of plasticity in who we are and who we become. It does mean that people always have the possibility of changing for the better, which is also an optimistic view.

Whereas, if you have this view of the mind as a collection of computerized chip, then once you have inherited it, you are stuck with it. There is no possibility, then, of change, and that, to me, is quite depressing. In that case, why would we teach? If they all had their minds fixed by genes, the students could never grow or change or learn.

Agustín: *Some transhumanists have talked about going beyond our nature by technological means. You must mean something else.*

Celia: Yes. Sometimes this is called the post-human discourse and I find it very interesting. They ask how far technology can take us and whether we are creating our own nature and moving beyond our biological nature.

What I find really problematic is that some scientists involved do not seem to see an ethical problem. They see it as just trying to solve the problems of the present. Yet, there are these other trajectories from philosophers that are all pushing transhumanism further and saying, "Well, maybe it will allow us to increase our longevity," for example, so aging is no longer an issue. There are even some post-human futures, which talk about a type of human perfection.

I actually wrote a book with Peter Scott not so long ago called *Future Perfect?: God, Medicine, and Human Identity*. In that book, we looked at the different kind of trajectories of perfection. The Christian theological tradition is very countercultural nowadays, because it is not about the perfection of the body or the perfection of our age limits or any other sort of limits that most transhumanists seem to be interested in overcoming. The theological tradition is more interested in perfection in the *virtues*, so it is about the perfection of our moral capacities. This point of view is not really coming into the equation when we are talking about these new, post-human futures.

Agustín: *That is very interesting. These new futures are physical ones?*

Celia: Yes, the post-human future is a physical one but not really a spiritual, social or what I would call socially responsible future. This is why many theologians find the transhumanist discourse quite objectionable: it is not getting at the heart of what it is to be human, what it means to be a responsible agent. In fact, one of the chapters of the book I am working on is called "Taking Leave of the Animal" and it is about transhumanism.[19] *[Laughter]*

Agustín: *That is great. That also connects to a certain extent with this idea of human culture, however defined, as a vehicle of interface between human nature as evolutionary processes and other sorts of processes and patterns in becoming human. Do you have a particular way that you integrate theological and evolutionary perspectives as they relate to culture? Do you see this as a potential locus for discussion?*

Celia: I see theology as being, if you like, not beyond culture, but as a type of culture. There is a sense in which, as a theologian, you think that culture can express truths, which are beyond culture.

....

19 Deane-Drummond, Celia. 2012. Trans-human or trans-animal? The theological and ethical implications of transhuman projects. In Transhumanism and Transcendence: Christian Hope in an Age of Technological Enhancement. Ron Cole-Turner, ed. Pp. 115-130. Cambridge, MI: MIT Press; Deane-Drummond, Celia. The technologization of life: Theology and the trans-human and trans-animal narratives of the post-animal. In Technofutures, Nature and the Sacred: Transdisciplinary Perspectives. Celia Deane-Drummond, Sigurd Bergmann, and Bronislaw Szerszynski, eds. Farnham, U.K.: Ashgate.

That is how I would see it. Although from a non-theological point of view, one would probably see theologies and religion as nothing more than parts of culture. From a theologian's point of view, somehow the word of God is beyond all the different cultural variations that you might get. You have a sense of God being there, as it were, in providence over all cultures.

Agustín: *Do you see this maybe as a narrative thread? Do you see faith, both in theology and outside theology, as part of human nature?*

Celia: Yes, I think faith is so much part of who we are as human beings, whether we deny it or not. Just because someone is an atheist, it does not mean they do not have a faith. They have. An agnostic is someone in between, as it were, in a twilight zone. In a sense, it is, I would say, written in our own sense of who we are; faith is ensouled as part of what it is to be human. We have a spiritual dimension as well that is really important.

Now, I am not making judgments on other religious traditions. It may be that they have found their way to God. I am not in a position to judge whether they will be in heaven or not. I grew up as an Anglican and got most of my theological training as a Protestant but I am in the Roman Catholic Church now. *[Laughter]* That gives me a certain skeptical edge, in a way, that maybe I would not have, if I were a cradle Catholic.

So I think that if a culture denies itself a spiritual dimension, it is denying something fundamentally important in the human. In other words, a very secularized culture, a very individualistic culture is denying that spiritual dimension. What is interesting about coming to the United States is that although it is very religious, it is also very individualized and very secularized in some ways, as well. The level to which religion is embedded in the culture is not as deep as in England, where the culture might look very secular, but people still want to be affiliated with the church because of its history and traditions.

What I am saying is there is always a mix between history, culture, religion, and society in a way, which is very interesting; it pans out differently in different places.

Agustín: *In Spain, there is a common phrase. When people ask you, "What religion are you?" You say, "Well, I'm Spanish, so I'm Catholic."*

The one who is asking does not understand that they are the same thing. There are many Spanish atheists but they are Catholic too. [Laughter] In that sense, Catholicism does not come apart from the Spanish culture itself. That is one thing that I have found in the United States is that here people really try to differentiate their cultural and national heritage and tradition from their religious or non-religious beliefs and practices. In most places in the world, I would argue, this would be nonsensical.

Celia: I know. That is what I was trying to say. In England, you have this strong sense of Christianity, even if people do not go to church.

Agustín: *The United States in that sense is different and falls out very much an atypical example of religion in human populations.*

Celia: Yes. Certainly from the outside, the United States looks very religious, but the religion is not as embedded in the culture itself as in other places. It is a bizarre paradox.

Agustín: *Spending lots of time in the United States, you will find many bizarre paradoxes. [Laughter]*

Celia: Yes. I have only been here for six months. I have obviously a lot to learn.

Suggested Readings

Bekoff, Marc. 2014. Rewilding Our Hearts: Building Pathways of Compassion and Coexistence. Novato, CA: New World Library.

Deane-Drummond, Celia, and David Clough. 2009. Creaturely Theology: God, Humans and Other Animals. London: SCM Press.

Deane-Drummond, Celia. 2014. Re-Imaging the Divine Image: Humans and Other Animals. Kitchener, Ontario: Pandora Press.

Deane-Drummond, Celia. 2014. The Wisdom of the Liminal: Evolution and Other Animals in Human Becoming. Grand Rapids. MI: Eerdmans.

Deane-Drummond, Celia. 2012. Trans-human or trans-animal? The Theological and Ethical Implications of Transhuman Projects. *In* Transhumanism and Transcendence: Christian Hope in an Age of Technological Enhancement. Ron Cole-Turner, ed. Pp. 115-130. Cambridge, MA: MIT Press.

Deane-Drummond, Celia. 2014. In God's Image and Likeness: From Reason to Revelation in Humans and Other Animals. *In* Questioning the Human: Perspectives on Theological Anthropology for the 21st Century. Lieven Boeve, Yves De Maeseneer, and Ellen Van Stichel, eds. Pp. 60-75. New York: Fordham University Press.

Deane-Drummond, Celia, and Agustín Fuentes. Human Being and Becoming: Situating Theological Anthropology in Interspecies Relationships in an Evolutionary Context. Philosophy, Theology and the Sciences 1(2):251-275.

Deane-Drummond, Celia. Evolutionary Perspectives on Inter-Morality and Inter-Species Relationships Interrogated in the Light of the Rise and Fall of Homo sapiens. Journal of Moral Theology 3(2):72-92.

Berkman, John, and Celia Deane-Drummond. 2014. Catholic Moral Theology and the Moral Status of Non-Human Animals. Journal of Moral Theology 3(2): 1-10.

Interviewee: Joel Green

Bio. Joel B. Green is dean of the School of Theology at Fuller Theological Seminary, where he has served as professor of New Testament Interpretation since 2007; prior to that, he served for ten years at Asbury Theological Seminary as professor of New Testament Interpretation, as dean of the School of Theology, and as provost. Green has written or edited more than forty books. He is the editor of the New International Commentary on the New Testament and co-editor of both the *Two Horizons New Testament Commentary* and *Studies in Theological Interpretation*. He is editor-in-chief of the *Journal of Theological Interpretation* and serves on the editorial boards of the journals *Theology and Science* and *Science & Christian Belief*. Green has been elected to membership in both Studiorum Novi Testamenti Societas (SNTS) and the International Society for Science and Religion (ISSR).

Slogan. *"If being human means reflecting God's image, then you are reflecting something about God, and so in a sense, we find out who we are in relationship to God."*

Agustín: *The first question is not the easiest or the best but it is the broadest. If you have to present a definition of human nature or natures, what would that be for you? Where would you go with that?*

Joel: I am obviously coming from the perspective of Biblical studies, and so the language that I might use has to do with the image of God. I would define that in terms of vocation, which also means in terms of relationship, and therefore, being human in relation to God, humanity, and to the nonhuman creature. I would talk about what it means to be human in a pretty multifaceted way, but especially in terms of vocation and relatedness. That is to say, if being human means reflecting God's image, then you are reflecting something about God, and so in a sense, we find out who we are in relationship to God.

There is another way to get at that from a specifically New Testament perspective—and that is to say that we see what it means genuinely to be human in Christ. Christ becomes the exemplar, the one who opens the way, who blazes the trail, to show us what it means to be and to live out our vocation as humans.

Agustín: *In your writings, you have really focused a lot on relational views of the imago Dei. How do you see this related to perspectives outside theology, like philosophy and anthropology?*

Joel: I think that is actually a point of tension. There has been a line of neuroscience, for example, and there is certainly a line of philosophy, that treats humans as though they can be looked at one at a time, ever more distinct. Relatedness pushes against both of these lines of thought.

Happily, in certain parts of neuroscience, there has been an increasing awareness of what some people will call nesting relationships. And there has been a turn in some philosophy and theology toward a more relational way of thinking. Insofar as that is the case, there are lots of points of contact, but it seems to me that one of the points of tension has been whether you can talk about humans one at a time or in terms of relationship. I might push that just a little further.

One of the reasons that I think looking at Genesis 1:27 and 28 is so important is that what the text says is that God made "Adam," humanity, in God's own image. It does not say that God made each human person in his image, but that— I am making here a point using Karl Barth—God made the human family, if you will. The notion of relation, relationship within the Godhead, relationships among humans and between humans and the created order, just pushes past the idea that each individual person reflects on his or her own God's image, and that, again, opens up issues of relatedness. It goes right against the grain of the whole history of exegesis that I attribute to Philo of Alexandria that suggests that the soul is the divine image, as though each individual person in his or her soul reflects God's image.

Agustín: *It seems that sometimes there is a bit of a tension between the rationality-based imago Dei and the idea of relationality. In your writings, you weave these narratives together, but I am wondering if you think that that opposition is something that can inhibit theological engagement with other disciplines?*

Joel: One of the places that this presses pretty hard for me is with humans of diminished capacity, among whom you can talk about relatedness, but it is harder to talk about rationality.

If you look at the way rationality was understood in earlier philosophy and theology, it was not simply IQ or knowledge in a sort of turn-of–the-twentieth century way. Instead it had to do with practical wisdom. It has to do with *phronesis*, practical wisdom with embodied knowledge, if you will, and that is the point at which you can begin to talk about links.

As long as you talk about cognition in more or less Cartesian terms, then it becomes more difficult. If you talk about embedded knowledge, if you talk about practical wisdom, then, I think, you are actually talking about humans in relation in certain contexts in particular settings.

Agustín: *How do you think this connects with the role of free will in the extent to which human agency influences human nature?*

Joel: I would see a circularity of human agency and nature. I come from a Wesleyan perspective, which is supposed to be high on free will.[20] Nevertheless, theologian Ted Peters has said to me that free will is "not all it's cracked up to be" and I agree with that. Decisions determine other decisions; relationships shape what is possible for us to even think. Our relatedness actually constrains our free will, not in the sense that it keeps you from making decisions, but in the sense that it shapes the way you even think what decisions are possible.

My covenant relationship with my spouse, my covenant relationship with the seminary, with the community of students and faculty here, constrain what I will see as possible courses of action. If I think about the abused woman, an abused wife, if I think about someone abusing alcohol, I have to think in terms of what choices are even open. That is not only because a series of bad choices has been made; it is because a whole network of decisions and relationships have built a wall around them, concerning what they can see as even possible.

I was talking about this with a woman the other day. She was wondering why her mother, her abused mother, would not just leave her father. I said, can you imagine your mother even thinking in those terms? Is that something that would even occur to her? From a theoretical perspective, of course she has free will, but from the standpoint of her embeddedness in relationship and her formation over a long period of time with respect to her husband, it is hard to imagine that she would even contemplate that—that it would even occur to her. If you suggested it to her, it is hard to imagine she could contemplate what that would even look like.

Agustín: *Do you see this connecting with what Wentzel van Huyssteen says about embodied structures and relationships shaping and reshaping the options in which we actually related to one another?*[21]

....

20 John Wesley was an Anglican theologian who was one of the founders of Methodism and heavily influenced the emergence of Pentecostalism.

21 See van Huyssteen's interview in Chapter 5. See also van Huyssteen, Wentzel. 2006. Alone in the World? Human Uniqueness in Science and Theology. Grand Rapids, MI: Eerdmans.

Joel: Exactly. Structures and relationships open possibilities but they also limit other possibilities.

Agustín: *In this same vein then, how would you see morality as related to all this?*

Joel: I think that is actually one of the biggest problems that we have right now. I just read a little piece on the web this morning about pedophilia as disease. I was thinking, okay, I understand that language, but just because this person is addicted, just because this person has now been formed in a certain way that leads down this road, does that mean, in this case, he cannot control it? Does it mean that he is not responsible for it?

We have tied responsibility to free will to such a degree in terms of morality, and in terms of the legal system, that we will have to re-think all of those things; morality will have to be defined culturally and contextually and not in terms of intent.

It is interesting that you can have, in our tradition, these Ten Commandments that, as it were, fall out of the sky. Never mind how they really came about, evolution or with speaking, but they are presented as falling out of the sky. Here is a community, a new community, that is supposed to base itself in a relationship with these commandments and then spins off a whole series of commandments related to these commandments. It is not tied to free will or intent. It is tied to what it means to be in God's covenant community.

Agustín: *What you have just said and what you have written over the years on this, does resonate very well with anthropology, which sees human behavior always closely related to and shaped by its cultural context. This of course does not mean relativism in which everything goes, but just the fact of diversity of human behavior and culture.*

Joel: It is a distinction I learned first from Francisco Ayala,[22] who urged talk about ethics, and only then talk about particular ethical systems. Do we have a sense of right and wrong versus do we think this is right and this is wrong? This is a useful distinction to make and it is often lost.

....

22   See Francisco Ayala's interview in Chapter 2.

Agustín: *What do you think about the role of plasticity or malleability in this entire discussion?*

Joel: It is basic to the whole thing. In fact, if there was anything in the work I did in neuroscience when I was at the University of Kentucky that surprised me, it was this. It was, first, plasticity, and second, the role of relationships, our relatedness, in literally shaping the morphology of our brain at the sub and larger levels.

I never thought that taking neuroscience classes would teach me the importance of the church, for example, but the importance I gave to ecclesiology was incredibly heightened by what I learned about plasticity.[23] If, in fact, we are always being formed, then how we are being formed becomes critical, and the how is closely tied to the who. Who is helping to form us?

I was just reading this anthropologist who first taught me the word neurohermeneutics, Stephen Reyna.[24] How we see the world, how we interpret the world, shaped by well-formed patterns that are not set in stone, but are constantly being formed in relationships. We tend to see the world in ways that are like the people we are hanging around with. We share with them the way that we see the world and that guides our actions. This ties together the two issues we have been talking about.

Agustín: *The shortcut we use in teaching anthropology at the intro level is "we are who we meet, who we greet, and who we eat with."*

Joel: That is very good. That is very good.

Agustín: *Where do you place biological evolution in your context of imago Dei and relationality?*

Joel: I think that the notion of emergence is helpful there. At what point in the evolution of the human can you say that the kind of relatedness, the capacities for relatedness that Warren Brown talks about, emerged? At that point, I would start talking about humans being the image of God. That is the way that I talk about it.

....

23   Warren Brown and Brad Straw argue along similar lines. See Brown, Warren, and Brad Straw. 2013. The Physical Nature of Christian Life: Neuroscience, Psychology, and the Church. Cambridge: Cambridge University Press.

24   An anthropolgist at the Max Plank Institute.

The pushback I get when I talk about this with my students is this: "So you think that Neanderthals are not saved?" Stuff like that. There is an easy answer to this from a New Testament perspective because Romans 8, for example, talks about the restoration of all things. I have no problem bringing in Neanderthal or whatever else. I just do not want to call them human, or human persons, in the way that I talk about the image of God.

Agustín: *Would you go along with Malcolm Jeeves who says that the capacity for relationships is both essential for humans and uniquely human?*[25]

Joel: Yes, as long as we do not push the word "unique" too far.

Agustín: *We could instead use Warren's word "distinctive."*

Joel: There you go. Yes. There are people I hear saying that we have reached the pinnacle of evolution. I bet people thought like that 50,000 years ago as well. We do not know where it is all going to go, and so we do not know who will ultimately participate in the image of God. We only know where we are right now.

Agustín: *I want to ask you something that relates back to your reference to Genesis 1:2728. You have pointed out that there is a difference between the two versions of Genesis and the translations. On the first account Adam and Eve are created together; on the second account there is all this about Adam's rib.*

We talked about development and formation of perceptions. Such accounts have a huge import for gender roles, the way in which we think about these things. The church plays a big shaping role here.

Joel: Yes, sure. Again, I think that what we are dealing with here is largely an exegesis of Genesis 1-2 that we have inherited from Philo. I would trace a path from Plato past the New Testament—not through the New Testament, but past it—into Philo. Plato wants to talk about the rational nature of the soul, but with Philo, you get the

25 Jeeves, Malcolm A. 2013. Minds, Brains, Souls and Gods: A Conversation on Faith, Psychology and Neuroscience. Downers Grove: IL: InterVarsity Press.

"rational soul," which isn't language Plato actually used. For Philo, this rational soul becomes the image of God in Genesis 1 and then you get this close tie-in between the image of God and soul, and all of that tied into rationality.

The dualism develops from there into the dualism of the Church Fathers, some of whom are themselves card-carrying Neoplatonists, who use Philo's exegesis to help them read Genesis. Given this, it is no wonder that we end up in this situation where we have, for example, Man—this is Plato already, of course—Man identified with rationality, Woman identified with emotionality, body, or lack of control.

This duality-based hierarchy is deeply embedded in our tradition but we can also reread or unread it and dismiss this hierarchy. You dismiss it and you open up possibilities for interrelationality that have been downplayed, I think, because of this dualistic tradition. I think that the way that we approach Genesis 1 and 2 can be huge for the way that we think about gender roles even within a community of faith that holds Genesis 1 and 2 as fictional.

Agustín: *Let me ask you a broader question. How do you see the relationship between culture and faith, as it relates to our human nature?*

Joel: I am struggling a little bit just because you are asking me to separate culture and faith and nature.

Agustín: *This is true. That is a good response.*

Joel: Culture is everything. *[Laughter]* I think it is true to say, for example, in the world in which we live, in North America right now, faith is doing a whole lot of shaping of larger cultural patterns. When it comes to anthropology, I think that the role of faith has been crucial. If you think about the majority—I do not know what the stats would be—but the majority of Western Christians would think in terms of body-soul dualism. The numbers are huge, and that shapes the way that we think about all kinds of things.

For example, when city governments struggle over how to spend money, it is often put in terms of, do we take care of bodies or do we take care of souls? Art is less important than the homeless shelter.

That's because we are not dealing with human beings; we are dealing with bodies or souls. That kind of dichotomy is grounded, I think, in a theological tradition, albeit an implicit one, and a tradition that has not been critically examined very often, that is shaping the way cities see themselves, the way money gets spent. I have suggested to some people who will listen that most arguments that I have seen happen in finance committees in churches are basically anthropological questions.

Agustín: *You called me out on a real error there. I am really interested in faith practices and their influence on culture, so that was what I was thinking when trying to formulate the question. It is interesting that there seems to be almost an unconscious notion of duality in the Western tradition.*

Joel: Yes. I think it is incredibly pervasive. I had someone write a pretty negative review of my *Body, Soul, and Human Life,* and part of what he said was that Green argues that churches struggle over whether they are going to be involved in spiritual activities versus social activities. But, the reviewer wrote, if his students are any indication, then there is no problem with having spiritual activities overwhelm social activities because there is so much social activity going on in churches. From the perspective that I am coming from, however, there is no such thing, no way simply to separate "social" and "spiritual."

There are *human* issues. You can talk about them in aspect-ival terms, but you cannot talk about them in terms of one being this part of a human and that another part of a human, or salvation being related to this or to that part. If you look at the Earth situation that we have right now, I think a case could be made that our theological dualism leads us to our disregarding the importance of ecological ethics. If it is all going to burn anyway, and if what really matters is getting your soul into the ship, crossing the ocean into Heaven, then the cosmos within which we exist is really not a part of what it means to be faithful toward God. It is a matter of the heart. It is not a matter of the body.

Agustín: *What you say about ecology resonates with conservatist thinking, the new wave of conservation biology, anthropology. However, such emphases have hardly been common in theological circles, or at least, only in certain contexts.*

Joel: Nowadays I even find Christians who are involved in ecological ethics, who are doing so from a divine command theory of ethics perspective.[26] They just say "God said to," without taking seriously our organic relationship with the cosmos, and without taking seriously that eschatology is grounded in a renewed cosmos, not in a new cosmos. It is not like God is going to wipe the slate clean and start over!

Agustín: *That is such a great line! Let me ask you another thing. Do you think that these kinds of anthropological issues are discussed in popular culture as well, not just in academic halls?*

Joel: Yes, yes. It is funny that you ask that, because when I do a lecture on this in various places, I start with *Frankenstein* and go to other novels and to movies, and to *Star Trek: The Next Generation*, or *AI*, or *Bicentennial Man*. There is a whole series of these things. The Frankenstein story is interesting because, apparently, humans are just like a car. You can put a bunch of parts together and hit them with a little energy and suddenly, we will have this thing, but what is this thing? Well, it is a thing minus a soul, apparently.

Then, in more modern novels there is this struggle to figure out what it means to say that someone is human. In AI, if you know that movie, the kid not only emotes but attracts an effective response, and at some point you forget that he is a robot and they even save his "life." It's just fascinating.

Then Data in *Star Trek*, who gets an emotion chip, who has a child, creates a child, and maps her with his own neural network, and then gets skin—at what point do you say he is becoming more human? Or not? It is an interesting question. I think, in the end, the question is going to be if humans can create a robot that relates as we relate, would that be human?

....

26 Traditionally theological ethics has been grounded in either divine command ethics or natural law ethics. On natural law views, ethical precepts can be derived from the essential nature of humans and their social life: humans naturally have some forms of behavior and social organizations. Furthermore, these forms of human flourishing are epistemically accessible to theological and secular ethics respectively. On divine command ethics, the moral rightness or wrongness does not ultimately depend on human flourishing but on God's commands.

Agustín: *That's great. We are not dealing with a purely philosophical question here. Robotics make these questions very practical for us. How would you extend this "relationality" to other living forms, primates, dogs, for example?*

Joel: I like the way Warren Brown talks about these things.[27] I do not know what language they use with you. The first time we had long conversations about this was in the book that came out, *Whatever Happened to the Soul?*

Agustín: *Yes. It was in 1998.*

Joel: He was using the word "soulishness" at that point, and I was pushing against that because I urged that if you keep using the word, people will bring the old baggage with them and perhaps say more than you want them to say. If you take out the word, he is still dealing, I think, with the right issues. It is not a matter of this huge gap between primates, for example, or dolphins, and humans. The difference is a matter of degree.

That is why, I think, the notion of emergence is the right way to go. Interestingly, in my tradition, which is the Wesleyan tradition, John Wesley contemplated the end time[28] as humans becoming more than they are and animals becoming more human, so that there would be an ongoing development. He was not thinking of evolution, but he was thinking of nonhuman animals taking on more characteristics of humans than they have already.

Agustín: *I asked Warren specifically about soulishness. It is a fascinating term and it resonates with some folks and not with others for that same reason.*

Joel: I think the instinct is a good one. That is, you want to protect certain aspects of who we are that might get lost in eliminative materialism. I just do not know that the price you pay is worth it.

....

27 See Warren Brown's interview in Chapter 3.

28 The end time is Christian theological language and refers to things that happen before the end of the current world.

Agustín: *Let me ask you about personhood, or more specifically, how personhood is acquired. Many argue that it is in community, that it is in association with other humans and in relation to God that personhood emerges or flowers. Do you ever consider thinking about this in a practical context in the sense of human communities, or church communities?*

Joel: Yes. The position you laid out would be one I would be very much at home with. I would include family in that as well. Let us say that you grow up without proper relationship to your parents, or like teenagers about whom I've heard from Eastern Block countries who have had minimal human contact. What happens is that you develop social handicaps and diminished personality that are almost impossible to overcome.

So, I think that relational community is crucial for the development of personality, but I also think that things have changed pretty radically in the last 300 years. In my tradition, people did not go to church 24/7, but there was a lot of church going on most of the time. You were with the group, whether it was a large group or a small group, repeatedly throughout the week. The church today, if it is a formative influence at all, is not much of a formative influence, in part because one spends so little time there. I travel ten miles to go to church. They really are not my "community." I do not live in La Cañada. I do not network with those people and so on. In some ways, my real church would be my nextdoor neighbors, people here.

Agustín: *Very fascinating. Growing up, I split my time between Spain and the United States. I am Catholic and culturally Catholic. This still means something in Spain even though half of the population never goes to church. We are all still Catholic. There is a strong sense of community: certain ways of behaving and seeing the world are just part of who we are.*

I often take students for projects in Bali and Indonesia and they are always very interested in local religion. The Balinese say there is no such thing as religion. There is the way we live and there is the way you live. Western students have a real problem with that. I think you are right, that more and more of the world is moving away from the cohesive life way to particulate religion or church as a singular entity rather than an existence.

Joel: That is right. Exactly. It is not the way I am. It is a thing I go to. Religious communities do not really have the same influence on people they once had. I wonder what the formative influence of the church was in the eighteenth or nineteenth centuries, or for people like my grandparents. I do not even want to talk about that. It is almost scary when you think about it. *[Laughter]* Are you addicted to Facebook?

Agustín: *Well, I think that is a very good point. There are researchers now looking at such phenomena very closely—not just Facebook but the physiological and neurological outcomes of such activities. I think the earlier emphasis of the formation of the church, too, is ignored by a lot of anthropologists—not as many anthropologists, but biologists for certain. Even philosophers are trying to downplay the fact that they constantly read texts people wrote in the seventeenth, eighteenth and nineteenth centuries that are completely drenched in a very specific image of Christian theology.*

Joel: Exactly. I was just reading an essay written by one of our students talking about St. Paul. They said St. Paul will teach us to think differently about secular practices. I just wrote a little note in the margins: I think St. Paul would call into question whether there is any such thing as a secular practice. The whole category is a problem from an ancient perspective.

Suggested Readings

Berger, Klaus. 2003. Identity and Experience in the New Testament. Minneapolis: Fortress.

Di Vito, Robert A. 1999. Old Testament Anthropology and the Construction of Personal Identity. Catholic Biblical Quarterly 61:217-38.

Green, Joel B. 2008. Body, Soul, and Human Life: The Nature of Humanity in the Bible. Grand Rapids, MI: Baker Academic.

Green, Joel B., ed. 2004. What about the Soul? Neuroscience and Christian Anthropology. Nashville: Abingdon.

Green, Joel B., ed. 2010. In Search of the Soul: Four Views of the Mind-Body Problem. Rev. edition. Eugene, OR: Wipf & Stock.

Middleton, J. Richard. 2005. The Liberating Image: The Imago Dei in Genesis 1. Grand Rapids, MI: Brazos.

Wright, John P., and Paul Potter, eds. 2000. Psyche and Soma: Physicians and Metaphysicians on the Mind-Body Problem from Antiquity to Enlightenment. Oxford: Clarendon.

CHAPTER 6

Parting Thoughts on Human Nature(s)

We are now coming to an end of our conversational foray into human nature. Philosophers, biologists, anthropologists, psychologists, theologians, and people in between these disciplines have said a great number of things about human nature. They have agreed and disagreed, some have expressed skepticism about the various quests for human nature, whereas others have been more optimistic. Although the book is coming to a close, the quest for human nature in the twenty-first century is, we believe, just beginning.

To conclude this book, we will briefly consider a few central themes and future prospects that can help us take the concepts and perspectives that emerged in the course of the interviews and think about moving forward. The first theme has to do with the emerging synthesis of biological and cultural evolution, the Extended Evolutionary Synthesis. The second theme we want to highlight is the ever increasing need for interdisciplinary and transdisciplinary research. The final theme is drawn specifically from the diversity of contents and perspectives in the interviews: variation in what we mean by "human nature" does not imply that there is no benefit in pursuing the topic.

Engaging with the Extended Evolutionary Synthesis

As we have seen in the course of this book, many debates about human nature come down to some invocation of evolution. It is our view of evolutionary forces and the nature of evolutionary explanations that drives our optimism (or pessimism) about getting human nature right. The basic question is what we take "evolution" and "evolutionary" to be. Often when evolution or evolutionary theory is invoked, there is an assumption that it is the traditional Neo-Darwinian toolkit and perspectives that are being utilized. This need not be the case, and increasingly it is not. The Extended Evolutionary Synthesis (EES) is emerging as a central approach in evolutionary biology, and it provides an expansion on the well-established, but limited, toolkit of the traditional Neo-Darwinian perspective.[1] The EES provides a more robust and more dynamic theoretical context for attempts at evolutionarily engaged interdisciplinary, or transdisciplinary, investigations of human nature(s).

Evolution is always a synergy of multiple processes, and natural selection, one of the processes by which biological variants achieve differential representation in subsequent generations, is not the sole architect of function. In our current understandings of evolutionary biology we cannot ignore the other processes (in addition to selection) as salient in any description of evolutionary histories and patterns. The basic idea of extended evolutionary processes is the notion of multiple pathways of inheritance (genetic, epigenetic, symbolic and behavioral). Kevin Laland and others write:

> Evolutionary processes can no longer be reduced to a focus on just genetic material. As the core research group promoting the EES states, "We hold that organisms are constructed in development, not simply 'programmed' to develop by genes. Living things do not evolve to fit into pre-existing environments, but co-construct

1   Fuentes, A. 2009. Evolution of Human Behavior. New York: Oxford University Press; Laland, K., T. Uller, M. Feldman, K. Sterelny, G. B. Müller, A. Moczek, E. Jabonka, and J. Odling-Smee. 2014. Does Evolutionary Theory Need a Rethink?: Yes, Urgently. Nature 514(7521):161-164; Pigliucci, Massimo, and Gerd B. Müller, eds. 2010. Evolution: The Extended Synthesis. Cambridge, MA: MIT Press.

and coevolve with their environments, in the process changing the structure of ecosystems." (Laland et al. 2014, 162)[2]

Other aspects of the EES highlight the interplay of many factors in evolutionary explanations as well. Consider the following:

1. Dynamic organism-environment interaction can result in niche construction (the process by which organisms simultaneously shape and are shaped by their ecologies) which can change/shape the patterns, foci, and intensity of natural selection and create ecological inheritance.

2. Phenotypic plasticity, developmental plasticity/reactivity, and acquisition of non-genetically induced features (via Neo-Lamarckian processes) all can play substantive roles in the patterns and production of variation.

In their classic work on multiple inheritance models, *Evolution in Four Dimensions* (2005),[3] Eva Jablonka and Marion Lamb demonstrate that information, the variation that is the fuel for evolutionary change, is transferred from one generation to the next by many interacting inheritance systems (genetic, epigenetic, behavioral, and symbolic). Epigenetic inheritance, the inheritance of molecular or structural elements outside of the DNA is found in all organisms. This gives rise to phenotypic variations that do not stem from variations in DNA but are transmitted to subsequent generations of cells or organisms.[4] Behavioral inheritance is the transmission, across generations, of behavioral patterns or particulars, and is found in most organisms, and symbolic inheritance, the cross-generational acquisition of symbolic concepts and ideologies, is found only in

....

2   Laland, K., T. Uller, M. Feldman, K. Sterelny, G. B. Müller, A. Moczek, E. Jabonka, and J. Odling-Smee. 2014. Does Evolutionary Theory Need a Rethink?: Yes, Urgently. Nature 514(7521):161-164.

3   Jablonka, E. and M. Lamb. 2005. Evolution in Four Dimensions: Genetic, Epigenetic, Behavioral, and Symbolic Variation in the History of Life. Cambridge, MA : MIT Press.

4   Jablonka, E., and G. Raz. 2009. Transgenerational Epigenetic Inheritance: Prevalence, Mechanisms, and Implications for the Study of Heredity and Evolution. The Quarterly Review of Biology 84(2):131-176.

humans and can have pronounced effects on behavioral patterns. Variation is also constructed, in the sense that, whatever their origin, which variants are inherited and what final forms they assume depend on various filtering and editing processes that occur before and during transmission.

If we adopt this approach to human evolution, we start getting ideas of human nature that are quite far from standard Neo-Darwinian perspectives. Andersson and colleagues[5] note that "Darwinian forces are seen as necessary but not sufficient for explaining observed evolutionary patterns" in humans. They argue that Extended Evolutionary Synthesis is better suited than traditional Neo-Darwinian approaches to encompass aspects of social/cultural systems as central in evolutionary processes.[6]

Consider the following examples. Laland and colleagues[7] illustrate that constructing and inheriting socio-ecological contexts via human material culture (tools, clothes, towns, etc.), and niche construction in general, can occur via cultural means. O'Brien and Laland[8] demonstrate this via reviews of the evolution of dairying by Neolithic groups in Europe and Africa and the rise of the "sickle-cell allele" among certain agricultural groups in West Africa. Fuentes[9] reviews work on early hominin tool making as another example for niche constructive processes in human evolution. In these examples shifting behavioral actions, cultural perceptions, and ecolog-

5   Andersson, Claes, Anton Törnberg, and Petter Törnberg. 2014. An Evolutionary Developmental Approach to Cultural Evolution. Current Anthropology 55(2):154-174.

6   Read, Dwight. 2012. How Culture Makes Us Human: Primate Social Evolution and the Formation of Human Societies. Walnut Creek, CA: Left Coast Press, Inc.

7   Laland, K., J. Kendall, and G. Brown. 2007. The Niche Construction Perspective: Implications for Evolution and Human Behavior. Journal of Evolutionary Psychology 5:51-66.

8   O'Brien, M. and K. N. Laland. 2012. Genes, Culture and Agriculture: An Example of Human Niche Construction. Current Anthropology 53(4):434-470.

9   Fuentes, A. 2015. Integrative Anthropology and the Human Niche: Toward a Contemporary Approach to Human Evolution. American Anthropologist 117(2):302-315.

ical conditions are shown to have mutually interacted to produce genetic and physiological changes which themselves result in further modification to behavior, physiology, and ecologies. Cultural patterns and behavioral actions and perceptions can impact genetic and other biological processes and the functioning of natural selection, which in turn can affect developmental outcomes, which can then feedback into the cultural patterns and behavioral actions continuing the dynamic interface.

In light of contemporary understandings of evolutionary processes, and the advances in human evolutionary studies over the past decade, we can assert a few basic assumptions about evolutionary approaches to understanding humans:

1. Human evolution is a system not best modeled via a focus on individual traits or genic reductionism.
2. Feedback rather than linear models are central in modeling human dynamics, so niche construction is important.
3. Ecological and social inheritance are significant in human systems.
4. Flexibility and plasticity in development, body, and behavior are common.

The EES approach enables a broader template for involving a range of elements (perception, embodiment, history, institutions, etc.) in the conceptualization of how evolutionary processes are at play in the human experience. Therefore the concepts of human becoming and the key dynamics of what it means to have culture become central aspects of the niche construction dynamic.

But does this move us any further in thinking about human nature(s)? Yes it does. It provides us with a non-reductive evolutionary context in which to place the moving target of the human. It enables us to construct meaningful scenarios about human evolutionary histories that include more than genic adaptation as explanatory underpinnings and enables us to identify patterns in the dynamic evolutionary processes of human lives that are shared by members of our species. The EES approach enables us to see how particular evolutionary processes are components of human becoming, of human cultural experience.

The EES perspective also enables non-anthropologists and scholars with no focus on biology or the mechanics of evolutionary processes to participate in a discourse that involves evolutionary theory. If talking about evolution does not automatically limit one to a material reductive explanation and enables a space where human action, histories, institutions, and perceptions can have agency in evolutionary processes, then we can envision that beneficial engagements between different humanistic disciplines, and anthropologists, and even biologists, can occur.

Interdisciplinarity and Transdisciplinarity

The central problem for the research on human nature is its necessarily transdisciplinary nature. Our knowledge about what humans are like is spread across a great many number of approaches, disciplines, and theories. Sometimes we are not even sure what we are looking for, because there are so many different views on the matter. Especially now when it is clear that our knowledge of, for example, human behavior, brains, and cognition is expected to grow significantly in the next decades, we desperately need interdisciplinary and transdisciplinary engagement. Traditionally, it has been the job of the philosopher to synthesize the "big picture" from the results of the individual sciences. However, philosophy is also suffering from fragmentation similar to all other disciplines. Perhaps this synthesizing work is something that we are all, regardless of our respective disciplines, called to do.

In the introduction, we suggested a transdisciplinary approach to human nature. It seems to us that transdisciplinary work on human nature is needed now more than ever, even more so in the future. The goal of transdisciplinarity is to change the disciplines involved by influencing the methods, worldviews, and languages used in each discipline. This change goes deeper than just collaboration over similar subject matter as in interdisciplinarity. In the case of interdisciplinarity, the possibility of actual transformation of disciplinary boundaries or intellectual approaches is unlikely.

With transdisciplinarity there is a goal of developing a relationship that facilitates the possibility of an intellectual transformation that is more thorough, intensive, and generative. This ideal is epitomized by the historian A. J. McMichael when he states "transdisciplinarity is more than the mixing and interbreeding of disciplines. Transdisciplinarity transports us: we then ask different questions, we see further, and we perceive the complex world and its problems with new insights."[10]

A transdisciplinary approach entails the utilization of a suite of factors as central parameters: rigor, openness, and tolerance.[11] *Rigor* implies taking into account as much existing information as is available in order to counteract the tendency for disciplinary biases and distortions to isolate potential explanatory frameworks from one another. This suggests that the disciplinary boundaries should not be the deciding factors in which "data" can be used in the analyses/discussion. *Openness* reflects a process of disciplinary generosity and an acceptance of potential unknowns as a positive context, not necessarily an obstacle. If participants from different disciplines and perspectives relax some of the strict assumptions about what constitutes "valid" approaches it can create a space for emergent and unexpected (even unforeseeable) outcomes between team members. This is not an argument for the conclusion that individuals should reject their own basal philosophical and methodological commitments, rather it is simply the possibility that they should be able to entertain, for the purposes of the project, a (slightly) wider range of data and analytical lenses than is common for their specific disciplinary approach. *Tolerance*, also referred to as intellectual generosity, provides the space for collaborators to hold ideas and truths that may appear opposed to one another and still engage in a mutual process of discovery.

....

10 McMichael, Anthony J. 2002. Assessing the Success or Failure of Transdisciplinarity. *In* Transdisciplinarity: Recreating Integrated Knowledge, Margaret Somerville and David Rapport eds. Pp. 218-222. Montreal, Quebec, and Kinston, Ontario: McGill-Queen's University Press.

11 Kessel, Frank, and Patricia L. Rosenfeld. 2008. Toward Transdisciplinary Research: Historical and Contemporary Perspectives. American Journal of Preventive Medicine 35(2Suppl):S225-S234.

We have suggested above two possible avenues that might help us in our various quests for human nature, namely, applying the EES and practicing transdisciplinarity. Taken together these two minor steps could provide a platform that might enable a more sincere and successful suite of interchanges and analyses about human nature(s). The EES provides a more inclusive, and better supported, theoretical landscape for diverse approaches to seriously engage with evolutionary processes and contexts. The transdisciplinary approach provides a methodological context wherein differences in philosophical and methodological commitments are not de facto lethal blows to collaborative endeavors.

The next steps then are to implement these suggestions. This is best done both in research projects that intentionally bring together two or more potentially divergent disciplines and in the continued practice of holding multidisciplinary conferences and workshops that assume rigor, openness, and tolerance as their basal modes of exchange. That is what we hope the readers of this book will be inspired to do.

Diversity is Good

In the introduction, we described the quite commonly held idea of human nature according to which, there is a causally efficacious species-essence. This essence is something that seeks to express itself regardless of the context, and all of the human traits that are not directly or indirectly caused by it are somehow environmental or cultural. Such a view finds its expression in the popular idea that some traits are "in the genes" or "in the blood" whereas other traits are due to culture, upbringing, or something else like that. Reading through these interviews, we see erosion, across disciplines, of this everyday essentialist notion of human nature: it is not completely absent, but it is a ghost of its former self. Given the discourse laid out in the interviews we suggest that for all practical purposes the idea of robust, essential human nature is neither well supported nor widely held.

This is evident in many ways. As many of our interviewees stated, evolutionary explanations are about much more than simply DNA, genes, or even strict biological function. Genes are not little packets of programs that simply play out all by themselves over the lifespan of an organism. Experience, culture, environment, and community all contribute to the shaping and operating of our genetic inheritance. Second, inheritance mechanisms come in many different forms spanning from the genetic to cultural and symbolic. Genes are now part of a larger system including environments and cultures that humans themselves shape and generate. Instead of a clean and neat metaphor of human nature being "in the genes," we now have a complex mess of interactions that we currently know very little about. In this sense, the quest to expose bare "human nature" as it is "before" culture and experience is a folly: there is no such thing.

Another point we want to highlight here is that when we look at the interviews in this book, we find no evidence that there is one single thread uniting the views or even one single quest for human nature. It is abundantly clear that concepts of what human nature might be or might entail vary from discipline to discipline, from scholar to scholar. For some, the quest for human nature is the quest for human uniqueness; for others it is a quest for innate or universal human traits. Many philosophers and theologians also try to pinpoint what is essential about humans and keep returning to ideas like personhood or selfhood. For some scholars, this diversity suggests that the concept of human nature is too vague or void of content to be scientifically viable or intellectually useful. While most of our interviewees expressed doubts about the existence of a robust, essentialist human nature, they nevertheless continued to use the notion in some engaging, insightful or even minimal, but relevant, way, and that is telling. What we want to point out here is that diversity of viewpoints on the concept itself is not an argument for elimination: the concept of human nature seems to be doing some work in different disciplines, even if it is sometimes difficult to see what that work is. Because of the diversity of human nature concepts, we urge readers to be even more cautious whenever reading a story from the popular press about humans being "essentially" this or that.

Importantly, these interviews testify to how closely worldview assumptions and other normative judgments are linked to our various quests for human nature. If we accept some robust form of naturalism (let's say a purely descriptive account of some properties of the animal), this choice invariably shapes our understanding of human nature and, whether consciously or not, informs our notions of normativity—our ideas of how we should "be" human. But we have seen that naturalism comes in many guises and forms and there are non-naturalists as well. If one believes in the existence of inherent teleology in nature (naturalist or non-naturalist kind), one could have a more robust, normative human nature, for example. If it is indeed the case that there would be some "natural" goals or basic conditions for human flourishing, the study of human nature could yield more than descriptive results. Furthermore, what one believes about, say, the existence of moral facts or other facts that might be difficult to account for scientifically (not to mention supernatural realities) will surely shape one's idea of human nature. Even purely descriptive accounts have often ingested implicit normative or evaluative assumptions. The distinction between fact and value becomes harder and harder to draw in this dialogue.

When we are trying to understand ourselves, what we are, it seems rather difficult to come at the subject neutrally. To study ourselves from "a view from nowhere" seems impossible. In order to get any kind of study of human nature going, we need to make some basic metaphysical and ethical assumptions—assumptions with which not everyone would agree. This is nothing to be feared, but it needs to be remembered when we examine, assess, and participate in our various quests for human nature.

INDEX

 **ABOUT THE AUTHORS**

Agustín Fuentes is a professor and Chair of Anthropology at the University of Notre Dame. His current research focuses on cooperation, community and semiosis in human evolution, ethno-primatology and multispecies anthropology, evolutionary theory, and interdisciplinary approaches to human nature(s). Fuentes's recent books include *Evolution of Human Behavior* (Oxford, 2008), *Biological Anthropology: Concepts and Connections* (McGraw-Hill, 2011), and *Race, Monogamy, and Other Lies They Told You: Busting Myths about Human Nature* (University of California, 2012).

Aku Visala is a senior researcher in the Centre for Excellence in Reason and Religious Recognition at the University of Helsinki. He has previously held research positions in the Department of Anthropology at the University of Notre Dame, the Centre for Anthropology and Mind at the University of Oxford, and the Center for Theological Inquiry at Princeton University. He is the author of *Naturalism, Theism, and the Cognitive Study of Religion: Religion Explained?* (Ashgate, 2011) and a number of other books in the philosophy of religion. His current research interests include the cognitive and biological bases of recognition and theological and philosophical anthropologies as they relate to the cognitive sciences and evolutionary psychology.